Short Story Workshop

Key Stage 4

Jeffrey and Lynn Wood

CAMBRIDGE
UNIVERSITY PRESS

To Emile Couturier

Published by the Press Syndicate of the University of Cambridge
The Pitt Building, Trumpington Street, Cambridge CB2 1RP
40 West 20th Street, New York, NY 10011–4211, USA
10 Stamford Road, Oakleigh, Melbourne 3166, Australia

First published 1990
Third printing 1995

Printed in Great Britain by Scotprint Ltd, Musselburgh, Scotland

British Library cataloguing in publication data

Wood, Lynn
Short story workshop
1. Short stories in English. Critical studies
I. Titles. II. Wood, Jeffrey

823-0109

ISBN 0 521 378060

GO

CONTENTS

THE PLUMBER

Assignment

○   This activity can be done in small groups.
Here is a story narrated entirely in pictures. Take it in turns to tell the story,
frame by frame.

The Plumber

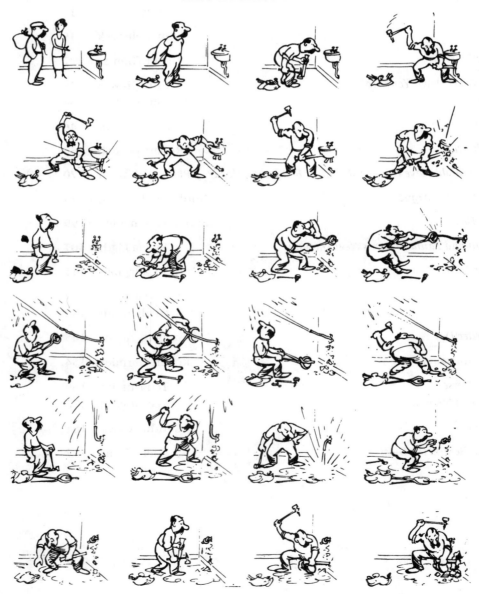

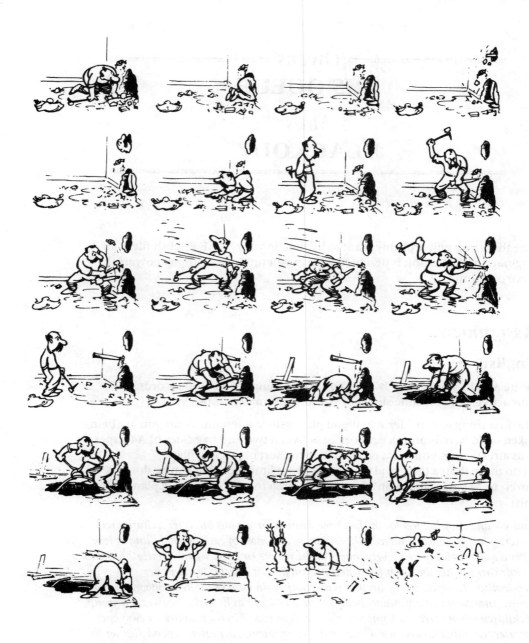

What can you add to what H.M. Bateman has 'told' us?
What is the plumber thinking to himself?
What noises does the water make?
What does he find when he investigates that hole in the wall?
What does the woman hear before she reappears on the scene? . . .

When you've run through the story a few times, you might like to make a tape
of your version of it and compare it with what other groups have done.

★

BUS QUEUE

Mais

BLACKOUT

One thing you will probably want to include in your GCSE English file is an original story. This unit is designed to help you produce a simple, powerful piece of writing.

Assignment

English

○ Write a short story called *Waiting for the Bus*. Length 250–1000 words.
This activity can be done singly or working in small groups.

The first thing to consider when you plan a story is length. What you are being asked to do here is produce a story of between two and five sides of A4 paper. This already tells you what is possible, what sort of piece to plan.
In no more than a thousand words, there are limits to what can be done. A dozen or so paragraphs don't give you enough room to develop a plan such as this:

Andrew and Angela meet for the first time waiting for the last bus after a charity rock concert. Over the next six months they see more and more of each other, falling in love. After a quiet wedding in a lovely chapel in the remote Orkneys where Angela's father is a vicar (her mother died in infancy and Angela finds it difficult to accept her step-mother, Lavinia, whose brother is a vet), they have an exotic honeymoon during which Andrew narrowly escapes being crushed to death as he saves the lives of a group of children when there is a bomb scare at the Olympics. Angela becomes a newspaper reporter travelling all over the world on her assignments (she covers a flood disaster in Argentina, earthquakes in Los Angeles and a civil war in South Africa) whilst Andrew sets up a photographic studio in London and almost has an affair with a lovely model called Sabrina whose cousin, Vince, is involved in an international drugs ring . . .

A short story which tries to be a novel will have problems!

Most of the best short stories include very little 'action': they concentrate upon what happens in a few days, hours, minutes even, and focus upon the experience of just one or two people.

In this story, we suggest you remain at the bus stop and write about what happens over a period of about twenty minutes.

Powerful writing is truthful. The reader must believe what you're telling him/her. You will convince a reader if you are convinced yourself.

The easiest way to write 'the truth' is to recall something which happened to you. As well as needing space, *The Rise and Fall of a Drugs Baron* needs more knowledge of the drugs racket than most people possess. But we are *experts* about what lies in our own experience.

To turn experiences into excellent stories requires time and care, but the stories are already there in your head, waiting to be written. There's nothing to 'imagine'. If an experience meant so much to you that you still remember it, it will interest your readers.

Most storytellers invent very little. They change details, rearrange them, put together things that happened at different times, improve a bit on what they remember . . . just as most people do when they tell friends about something which really happened. What gives their writing strength is that it is dramatic but believable. It is true to the world we all live in.

If we read:
And he took the chopper and hit open the driver's head and brains were everywhere. He got the magic gun and shot the rest of the gang . . .
we know it's just a silly story; life isn't like that.

But when we read something like this:
I was holding the ladder but it was very bendy and there was a blustery wind. Grandfather was a heavy man and as he scrubbed at the wall to get the muck off, the ladder pushed frighteningly in my hands, as if it wanted to walk away. I decided to climb up the ladder a bit to see if that would steady it but as I started to climb, Grandad shouted out something and before I knew what was happening, something hard and silver shoved against my shoulder, the sky turned over and I was punched on the nose. I found myself face down among the brambles. I couldn't turn my head, there was what felt like a sack of cement digging into my back, I could hardly breathe. I knew there was a ton of pain coming, my legs felt as if they were burning . . .
we can't tell if it is a real memory or a 'story': the way things are described makes us live them. Perhaps you've stood on a ladder and felt it wanting to walk away; remember that sometimes when you fall over, you feel it's the world turning, not yourself. We all know that pain is sometimes most awful when it's delayed.

This piece rings true.

Dramatic, powerful writing doesn't need to be about emergencies. What makes us enjoy reading something is vividness, sharpness of detail, the feeling of things recorded well. The difference between good and bad writing is the difference between a photograph and a snapshot. We want to look at the photograph again and again because it's well composed, focused and contains nothing to distract the eye from the subject.

Waiting for the Bus may be an unexciting title, but it suggests a framework within which some very exciting writing can be produced.

If you have ever waited in the cold, wondering if you would have to wait all night; ever stood at a bus stop anxious or curious about the other people in the queue; ever felt the temperature slowly fall and the drizzle turn to something decidedly hostile, then you should be able to write a convincing, dramatic piece without needing to include anything sensational.

Here is a simple plan for a story in six paragraphs.

Paragraph one	: You stayed too long at the party. Promised you'd be in by twelve. No-one to give you a lift. Last bus may have gone. Approach bus stop. Deserted. Watch stopped. What to do?
Paragraph two	: Somebody else turns up to wait. Describe him/her. Girl? Old man? Someone you half know? Do you/ don't you talk?
Paragraph three	: Chilly night, suddenly gets colder. Drizzle turning to rain. Smells, sounds, feel of a dark, wet night. No sign of the bus. Time seems to be standing still.
Paragraph four	: In the distance, sound of an approaching group of people. Drunks? A gang? Rivals from school? Describe your growing edginess.
Paragraph five	: Group arrives at bus stop. Describe them. At first they ignore you, then start to taunt. Remarks get gradually more threatening. Sense of panic.
Paragraph six	: Bus comes around the corner: light, warmth and safety.

This plan is designed to let you show in a short space that you can do different kinds of dramatic writing. Of course, there is no need to stick to it rigidly. Here are some suggestions for how you might develop it:

Paragraph one sets the scene, the situation, gives the reader some idea of the mood of the person who is telling the story.
Think of a particular bus stop you know. Jot down five things which make it that particular bus stop and no other, e.g. the bright yellow plastic seats which squeak as you push them down; a particular bit of graffiti; the smells which come from the chip shop close by; the great oak tree which overshadows it . . .
Use the best detail, save the rest for later in the story.

Paragraph two is a chance to do some vivid description of a person.
Begin by picturing the person in your head as she/he comes towards you. What is striking about the way that person moves, dresses? e.g. an old woman in a long green coat, wearing a pair of bright white trainers; a man in a smart navy pin-striped suit carrying a Tesco bag; someone wearing a knitted woolly hat and sucking Polos.
Think about the way different people behave whilst they're waiting, e.g. fidgeting; striding up and down; in a trance, listening to a Walkman; continually looking up the road to see if the bus is coming; humming contentedly . . .
If you decide to talk to the person, think about how he/she will speak, e.g. with an accent perhaps, either in very abrupt or very full sentences . . .
If you decide against talking to him/her, explain why.

In *paragraph three* is a chance to share a strong sense of time and place. Decide on the time of year, the state of the weather. Think about how a place looks different in June, in September, in January . . .
Colours and shapes aren't the same at midnight as they are at midday.
You may be aware of even very quiet sounds and subtle smells when there is no hustle and bustle to distract you, e.g. the singing of street lamps; the tap-tapping of a twig against the bus shelter.

Paragraph four should create a sense of menace, of danger approaching. Think how varying the length of sentences will help to suggest growing anxiety. How do your hands, back, feet feel when you are nervous? Do you hear the group before you see it? What does it look like as it approaches?

Paragraph five introduces dialogue. Can you give the reader a strong sense of people just from what they say and how they say it?
Perhaps you try to ignore what's said to/about you? What sorts of remark make you feel really uncomfortable? For example,
   "What do you think his Mum's going to say about the holes in his jacket?"
   "Do you think her nose is going to get any bigger?"
   "He/she looks like he/she needs some exercise . . ."

Paragraph six should be a short, sharp, tidy ending. Don't spoil a careful, convincing piece of work with a cliché or anything 'sensational'.

If you work on this story as a group, you can work in two ways.
Either
Each person writes a complete story, using the plan printed here or using one you have written together. The different versions are read out, and discussed, the best details are selected and put together to make a joint story.
Or
Each person is responsible for one stage of the story. Begin by agreeing on the details: where it's set; time, place, season; what characters will be involved; how the story will end . . .
When you have each written out your instalment, read them to each other and discuss any changes which need to be made before the final version of the story is presented to the class.

☆

Here are two stories which might have been written to the title *The Last Bus*. Read through each of them carefully and then consider the Talking/Thinking Points.

Bus Queue

The boy was out of breath. He had been running hard. He reached the bus stop with a sinking heart. There was only a solitary woman waiting – the bus must have gone.

"Is the bus away missus?" he gasped out. The woman regarded him coldly. "I really couldn't say," then drew the collar of her

regarded *looked at.*

7

well-cut coat up round her face to protect herself against the cold wind blowing through the broken panes of the bus shelter. The boy rested against the wire fence of the adjacent garden taking in long gulps of air to ease the harshness in his lungs. Anxiously he glanced around when two middle-aged females approached and stood within the shelter.

adjacent *next to.*

"My it's awfy cauld the night," said one. The well-dressed woman nodded slightly, then turned her head away.

awfy cauld *awfully cold.*

"Ah hope that bus comes soon," said the other woman to her companion, who replied, "The time you have to wait would sicken ye if you've jist missed one."

"I wonder something is not done about it," said the well-dressed woman sharply, turning back to them.

"Foks hiv been complainin' for years," was the cheerful reply, "but naebody cares. Sometimes they don't come this way at all, but go straight through by the main road. It's always the same for folk like us. If it was wan o' these high-class districts like Milngavie or Bearsden they wid soon smarten their ideas."

Milngavie, Bearsden *suburbs of Glasgow.*

At this point a shivering middle-aged man joined them. He stamped about impatiently with hands in pockets. "Bus no' due yet Maggie?" he asked one of the women.

"Probably overdue."

Her friend chipped in, "These buses would ruin your life. We very near missed the snowball in the bingo last week through the bloody bus no' comin'." The man nodded with sympathy.

snowball *big prize.*

"Gaun to the bingo yersel' Wullie?"

"Naw. Ah'm away to meet ma son. He's comin' hame on leave and is due in at the Central Station. Ah hope this bus comes on time or Ah might miss him."

"Oh aye – young Spud's in the army ower in Belfast. It must be terrible there."

"Better that than bein' on the dole."

"Still Ah widny like bein' in Belfast wi' all that bombin' and murder."

widny *wouldn't.*

"Oor Spud's got guts," said the man proudly.

The boy leaning on the fence began to sway back and forth as if he was in some private agony.

The well-dressed woman said loudly, "I shouldn't wonder if that fence collapses."

The other three looked over at the boy. The man said, "Here son, you'll loosen that fence if you don't stop yer swingin'."

The boy looked back in surprise at being addressed. He gradually stopped swaying, but after a short time he began to kick the fence with the backs of his heels as if he was obliged to keep moving in some way.

addressed *spoken to.*

"You wid think the young wans nooadays all had St Vitus dance," remarked the man.

St Vitus dance *a childhood disease characterised by fidgeting.*

The well-dressed woman muttered, "Hooligans."

It was now becoming dark and two or three more people emerged

9

from the shadows to join the queue. The general question was asked if the bus was away, and answered with various pessimistic speculations.

"Hi son," someone called, "you'd better join the queue." The boy shook his head in the negative, and a moody silence enveloped the gathering. Finally it was broken by a raucous female voice saying, "Did you hear aboot Bella's man? Wan night he nivver came hame. When he got in at eight in the morning she asked him where hud he been. 'Waitin' for a bus', said he."

Everyone laughed except the well-dressed woman and the boy, who had not been listening.

"Look, there's a bus comin' up," spoke a hopeful voice. "Maybe there will be wan doon soon."

"Don't believe it," said another, "Ah've seen five buses go up at times and nothin' come doon. In this place they vanish into thin air."

"Bring back the Pakkies," someone shouted.

"They're all away hame. They couldny staun the pace."

"Don't believe it. They're all licensed grocers noo."

"You didny get ony cheap fares aff the Pakkies, but at least their buses were regular."

Conversation faded away as despondency set in. The boy's neck was painful from looking up the street. Suddenly he stiffened and drew himself off the fence when two youths came into view. They walked straight towards him and stood close, one at each side.

"You're no' feart," said one with long hair held in place with a bandeau.

"How?" the boy answered hoarsely.

"The Rock mob know whit to expect if they come oot here."

"Ah wis just visitin' ma bird."

"Wan of oor team is in hospital because of the Rock. Twenty-four stitches he's got in his face – hit wi' a bottle."

"Ah had nothin' to dae wi' that."

"You were there, weren't ye?"

"Ah didny know big Jake wis gaun tae put a bottle on him."

"Neither did oor mate."

All this was said in whispers.

"Hey yous," said an irate woman, "Ah hope you don't think you're gaun tae jump the queue when the bus comes."

"That's all right," said the one with the bandeau. "We're jist talkin' tae oor mate. We'll get to the end when the bus comes."

The crowd regarded them with disapproval. On the other side of the fence where the youths were leaning, a dog which was running about the garden began to bark frantically at the bus queue.

"Shut yer noise," someone shouted, which incensed the dog further. One of the youths aimed a stone at its back. The bark changed to a pained howl and the dog retreated to a doorstep to whimper pitifully for some minutes.

"Nae need for that," said the man, as murmurs of sympathy were

pessimistic speculations *gloomy predictions.*

enveloped *gathered around.*
raucous *rough, harsh.*

despondency *hopelessness.*

feart *afraid.*
bandeau *headband.*

irate *angry.*

incensed *angered.*

10

taken up for the dog.

"Don't believe it," said another, "Ah've seen five buses go up at times and nothin' come doon. In this place they vanish into thin air."

"This generation has nae consideration for anyone nooadays," a voice declared boldly.

"Aye, they wid belt you as soon as look at you."

Everyone stared hard at the youths as if daring them to start belting, but the youths looked back with blank expressions.

"They want to join the army like ma son," the man said in a loud voice. "He disny have it easy. Discipline is what he gets and it's done him the world of good."

"Ower in Ireland, that's where Wullie's son is," declared one of the women who had joined the queue early.

"Poor lad," said the woman with the raucous voice, "havin' to deal wi' the murderin' swine in that place. They should send some o' these young thugs here tae Ireland. They'd soon change their tune."

"They wid be too feart to go," the man replied. "They've nae guts for that sort of thing."

At this point the youth in the middle of the trio on the fence was reflecting the possibility of asking the people in the queue for help. He considered that he was safe for the moment but when the bus came he would be forced to enter and from then on he would be trapped with his escorts. But he didn't know how to ask for help. He suspected they wouldn't listen to him, judging by their comments. Even if the bizzies were to pass by at this moment, what could he say? Unless he got the boot or the knife they would only laugh.

bizzies *police.*

Then someone shouted, "Here's the bus," and the queue cheered. The blood drained from the youth's face.

"Mind yous two," said a warning voice as the bus moved up to the stop, "the end of the queue."

"That lad in the middle can get to the front. He was wan o' the first here," a kindly voice spoke. The well-dressed woman was the first to climb aboard, saying, "Thank goodness."

"That's OK," said the youth with the bandeau, "we're all gettin' on together," as both he and his mate moved in front of the other youth to prevent any attempt on his part to break into the queue.

"Help me mister!" he shouted, now desperate. "These guys will not let me on." But even as he said this he knew it sounded feeble. The man glanced over but only momentarily. He had waited too long for the bus to be interested. "Away and fight like ma son," was his response. In a hopeless attempt, the youth began punching and kicking at his guards when everyone was on. The faces of those who were seated peered out at the commotion. The driver started up the engine in an effort to get away quickly. One of the youths shouted to his mate as he tried to ward off the blows. "Quick, get on. We're no' hingin aboot here all night." He had already received a painful kick which took the breath from him. The one with the bandeau had a split second to make up his mind, but he was reluctant to let his victim go without some kind of vengeance for his mate in hospital. Whilst dodging wild punches from the enemy, he managed to get his hand into his pocket. It fastened on a knife. In a flash he had it out and open. He stuck it straight into the stomach of the youth. His companion who had not noticed this action pulled him onto the platform of the bus just as it was moving away.

"Get aff," shouted the driver, angry but unable to do anything about it. The other youth, bleeding, staggered against the fence, immersed in a sea of pain. The last words he heard when the bus moved away were, "Ah wis jist waitin' on wan number . . .". Then he heard no more.

immersed *deep.*

Someone peering out of the back window said, "There's a boy hingin ower the fence. Looks as if he's hurt bad."

"Och they canny fight for nuts nooadays. They should be in Belfast wi' ma son."

"True enough." The boy was dismissed from their thoughts. They were glad to be out of the cold and on their way.

Thinking/Talking Points

▷ Which details in the first two paragraphs hint that the boy is afraid of something?
See if you can find a detail from later in the story which suggests he's feeling uneasy.

▷ What is your impression of 'the well-dressed woman'? Which words suggest her personality?

▷ There is very little scene-setting, yet we get a strong sense of the place where the story happens. Which descriptive details do you find effective?

▷ How would you describe the outlook of the man whose son is in the army? What does he think of the boy by the fence?

▷ What is the mood at the bus shelter immediately before the two youths appear?

▷ How does the writer signal to us that they mean trouble before they start to speak?

▷ Notice how the writer builds up the tension after the youths appear by focusing first on the dog and then on the conversation of the older people at the bus shelter.

▷ 'The driver started up the engine in an effort to get away quickly.' What do you think the driver of the bus would say he saw?

▷ What do you think *Bus Queue* gains/loses from being written mostly in conversation which has a strong Glaswegian flavour?

Blackout

The city was in partial blackout; the street lights had not been turned on, because of the wartime policy of conserving electricity; and the houses behind their discreet aurelia hedges were wrapped in an atmosphere of exclusive respectability.

aurelia *shrub with golden flowers.*

exclusive respectability *wealthy superiority.*

The young woman waiting at the bus stop was not in the least nervous, in spite of the wave of panic that had been sweeping the city about bands of hooligans roaming the streets after dark and assaulting unprotected women. She was a sensible young woman to begin with, who realised that one good scream would be sufficient to bring a score of respectable suburban householders running to her assistance. On the other hand she was an American, and fully conscious of the tradition of American young women that they don't scare easily.

Even that slinking black shadow that seemed to be materializing out of the darkness at the other side of the street did not disconcert her. She was only slightly curious now that she observed that the shadow was approaching her, slowly.

materializing *turning into a person.*

disconcert *worry.*

It was a young man dressed in conventional shirt and pants, and wearing a pair of canvas shoes. That was what lent the suggestion of slinking to his movements, because he went along noiselessly – that, and the mere suggestion of a stoop. He was very tall. There was a curious look of hunger and unrest about his eyes. But the thing that struck her immediately was the fact that he was Black; the other particulars scarcely made any impression at all in comparison. In her country, not every night a white woman could be nonchalantly approached by a Black man. There was enough novelty in all this to intrigue her. She seemed to remember that any sort of adventure might be experienced in one of these tropical islands of the West Indies.

pants *trousers.*

nonchalantly *casually, coolly.*

"Could you give me a light, lady?" the man said.

It is true she was smoking, but she had only just lit this one from the stub of the cigarette she had thrown away. The fact was she had no matches. Would he believe her, she wondered? "I am sorry. I haven't got a match."

The young man looked into her face, seemed to hesitate an instant and said, his brow slightly wrinkled in perplexity: "But you are smoking."

perplexity *confusion*

There was no argument against that. Still, she was not particular about giving him a light from the cigarette she was smoking. It may be stupid, but there was a suggestion of intimacy about such an act, simple as it was, that, call it what you may, she could not accept just like that.

a suggestion of intimacy *it might suggest she was being more friendly than she should be.*

There was a moment's hesitation on her part now, during which time the man's steady gaze never left her face. There was pride and challenge in his look, curiously mingled with quiet amusement.

mingled *mixed.*

She held out her cigarette towards him between two fingers.

"Here," she said, "you can light from that."

13

In the act of bending his head to accept the proffered light, he came quite close to her. He did not seem to understand that she meant him to take the lighted cigarette from her hand. He just bent over her hand to light his.

Presently he straightened up, inhaled a deep lungful of soothing smoke and exhaled again with satisfaction. She saw then that he was smoking the half of a cigarette, which had been clinched and saved for future consumption.

"Thank you," said the man, politely; and was in the act of moving off when he noticed that instead of returning her cigarette to her lips she had casually, unthinkingly flicked it away. He observed this in the split part of a second that it took him to say those two words. It was almost a whole cigarette she had thrown away. She had been smoking it with evident enjoyment a moment before.

He stood there looking at her, with cold speculation.

In a way it unnerved her. Not that she was frightened. He seemed quite decent in his own way, and harmless; but he made her feel uncomfortable. If he had said something rude she would have preferred it. It would have been no more than she would have expected of him. But instead, this quiet contemptuous look. Yes, that was it. The thing began to take on definition in her mind. How dare he; the insolence!

"Well, what are you waiting for?" she said, because she felt she had to break the tension somehow.

"I am sorry I made you waste a whole cigarette," he said.

She laughed a little nervously. "It's nothing," she said, feeling a fool.

"There's plenty more where that came from, eh?" he asked.

"I suppose so."

"This won't do," she thought, quickly. She had no intention of standing at a street corner jawing with – well, with a Black man. There was something indecent about it. Why doesn't he move on? As though he had read her thoughts he said: "This is the street, lady. It's public."

Well, anyway, she didn't have to answer him. She could snub him quietly, the way she should have properly done from the start.

"It's a good thing you're a woman," he said.

"And if I were a man?"

"As man to man, maybe I'd give you something to think about," he said, still in that quiet, even voice.

"In America they lynch them for less than this," she thought.

"This isn't America," he said. "I can see you are an American. In this country there are only men and women. You'll learn about it." She could only humour him. Find out what his ideas were about this question, anyway. It would be something to talk about back home. Suddenly she was intrigued.

"So in this country there are only men and women, eh?"

"That's right. So to speak there is only you an' me, only there are hundreds and thousands of us. We seem to get along somehow

proffered *offered.*

clinched *nipped, extinguished.*

speculation *wondering.*

contemptuous *disapproving.*

lynch *hang without trial.*

14

without lynchings and burnings and all that."

"Do you really think that all men are created equal?"

"It don't seem to me there is any sense in that. The facts show it ain't so. Look at you an' me, for instance. But that isn't to say you're not a woman, the same way as I am a man. You see what I mean?"

"I can't say I do."

"You will, though, if you stop here long enough."

She threw a quick glance in his direction.

The man laughed.

"I don't mean what you're thinking," he said. "You're not my type of woman. You don't have anything to fear under that heading."

"Oh!"

"You're waiting for the bus, I take it. Well, that's it coming now. Thanks for the light."

"Don't mention it," she said, with a nervous sort of giggle.

He made no attempt to move along as the bus came up. He stood there quietly **aloof**, as though in the consciousness of a male strength and pride that was justly his. There was something about him that was at once challenging and disturbing. He had shaken her supreme confidence in some important sense.

> **aloof** *apart, detached, feeling superior.*

As the bus moved off she was conscious of his eyes' quiet **scrutiny**, without the interruption of artificial barriers, in the sense of **dispassionate appraisement**, as between man and woman, any man, any woman.

> **scrutiny** *inspection.*
>
> **dispassionate appraisement** *coolly weighing up.*

She fought resolutely against the very natural desire to turn her head and take a last look at him. Perhaps she was thinking about what the people on the bus might think. And perhaps it was just as well that she did not see him bend forward with swift hungry movements, retrieving from the gutter the half-smoked cigarette she had thrown away.

Thinking/Talking Points

▷ Suggest an alternative title for this story.

▷ Which details give you an impression of the woman's personality?
If she had been asked before this incident what she thought about black people, how do you think she would have replied?

▷ What is your impression of the man?
Choose some words from this list to describe him:
strong; weak; rich; poor; dignified; humble; confident; shy; aggressive; hostile; shrewd; perceptive; rough; poised; clever; forceful; inadequate; rude; polite; disturbing; angry.
Add some words of your own to those you have selected.

▷ 'Still, she was not particular about giving him a light from the cigarette she was smoking. It may be stupid, but there was a suggestion of intimacy about such

an act, simple as it was, call it what you may, she could not accept just like that."
See if you can explain in your own way how the woman is feeling here.

▷ 'There was pride and challenge in his look, curiously mingled with quiet amusement."
What thoughts do you think are running through the man's head here?

▷ 'She had casually, unthinkingly flicked it away."
Why do you think she did this?
How do you think the man felt about it?

▷ 'He seemed quite decent in his own way, and harmless; but he made her feel uncomfortable. If he had said something rude she would have preferred it."
How would you explain the discomfort she is feeling?

▷ 'As man to man, maybe I'd give you something to think about."
What do you think he means?

▷ 'In this country there are only men and women."
Explain in your own words what the man feels is different about America and the West Indies.

▷ 'He had shaken her supreme confidence in some important sense."
See if you can describe the way the woman is feeling as she gets onto the bus.
How has the man managed to shake her confidence?

▷ What is the effect of the final sentence?

How do these two stories compare with the ones you wrote?
What, if anything, would you change to make the stories more effective?

Assignments

○ *Constable Gilroy's Report on the Incident at Park Street Bus Stop* (after Agnes Owens's short story *Bus Queue*)

You are the police officer who discovered the boy bleeding badly and sent for the ambulance. Your job is to discover whether the boy was criminally wounded or got hurt in a brawl.

Following an appeal for witnesses, two of the people who were at the bus stop and the bus driver have come forward and made statements about what they thought they saw on the night of the stabbing. You have to decide whether there is enough evidence to identify, arrest and charge the two youths who boarded the bus. Or was the boy who was hurt as much to blame?

Prepare your report by making a summary of what you have been able to find out from questioning the witnesses and, perhaps, from the victim himself. Quote from their statements. You may find that what one witness says contradicts what another witness says. People often 'improve' on what they remember or see what they want to see!

Then write your report. This is how it might begin:

> On the evening of Saturday 11th March I was proceeding down Park Street when I observed a youth slumped over a wire fence which adjoins the bus shelter. Upon investigation, I discovered the youth to be bleeding from a wound to the stomach . . .

End your report with a recommendation either to pursue the investigation or to abandon it for lack of hard evidence.

o *Blackout: His Version* (after the short story by Roger Mais)

This story is told very much from the woman's point of view. We share her impressions of the man and see how she is feeling. We have to guess what thoughts are running through the man's head from what he says and the way his expression is described.

Imagine you are the man writing about this incident. See if you can show how the woman appeared to him and what he felt about the way she behaved.

You could begin your story like this:

> The city was dark and I was on my way home from work. It had been a long hard day. I felt like a cigarette but although I had a stub in my pocket, I was out of matches. Then as I turned up King Street, on the other side of the road, I noticed a young white woman waiting for the bus . . .

★

Do certain moments linger in your memory, even though they were not
particularly important?
See if you can recall a place you visited (or a person you met) just once but can
still picture vividly.
Jot down as many details as you can recall.

In this piece, John Steinbeck paints a sharp picture of what he remembers of a very simple but intensely pleasant event.

Breakfast

This thing fills me with pleasure. I don't know why, I can see it in the smallest detail. I find myself recalling it again and again, each time bringing more detail out of a sunken memory, remembering brings the curious warm pleasure.

It was very early in the morning. The eastern mountains were black-blue, but behind them the light stood up faintly coloured at the mountain rims with a washed red, growing colder, greyer and darker as it went up and overhead until, at a place near the west, it merged with pure night.

And it was cold, not painfully so, but cold enough so that I rubbed my hands and shoved them deep into my pockets and I hunched my shoulders up and scuffled my feet on the ground. Down in the valley where I was, the earth was that lavender grey of dawn. I walked along a country road and ahead of me I saw a tent that was only a little lighter grey than the ground. Beside the tent there was a flash of orange fire seeping out of the cracks of an old rusty iron stove. Grey smoke spurted up out of the stubby stovepipe, spurted up a long way before it spread out and dissipated.

scuffled *shuffled.*

dissipated *dispersed.*

I saw a young woman beside the stove, really a girl. She was dressed in a faded cotton skirt and waist. As I came close I saw that she carried a baby in a crooked arm and the baby was nursing, its head under her waist out of the cold. The mother moved about, poking the fire, shifting the rusty lids of the stove to make a greater draught, opening the oven door; and all the time the baby was nursing, but that didn't interfere with the mother's work, nor with the light quick gracefulness of her movements. There was something very precise and practised in her movements. The orange fire flicked out of the cracks in the stove and threw dancing reflections on the tent.

waist *blouse.*
nursing *feeding from its mother.*

I was close now and I could smell frying bacon and baking bread, the warmest, pleasantest odours I know. From the east, the light grew swiftly. I came near to the stove and stretched my hands out to it and shivered all over when the warmth struck me. Then the tent-flap jerked up and a young man came out and an older man followed him. They were dressed in new blue dungarees and in new dungaree coats with the brass buttons shining. They were sharp-faced men, and they looked much alike.

odours *smells.*

The younger had a dark stubble beard and the older had a grey stubble beard. Their heads and faces were wet, their hair dripped with water, and water stood out on their stiff beards and their cheeks shone with water. Together they stood looking quietly at the lightening east; they yawned together and looked at the light on the hill rims. They turned and saw me.

19

"'Morning," said the older man. His face was neither friendly nor unfriendly.

"'Morning, sir," I said.

"'Morning," said the young man.

The water was slowly drying on their faces. They came to the stove and warmed their hands at it.

The girl kept to her work, her face averted and her eyes on what she was doing. Her hair was tied back out of her eyes with a string and it hung down her back and swayed as she worked. She set tin cups on a big packing-box, set tin plates and knives and forks out too. Then she scooped fried bacon out of the deep grease and laid it on a big tin platter, and the bacon cricked and rustled as it grew crisp. She opened the rusty oven door and took out a square pan full of high big biscuits.

When the smell of that hot bread came out, both of the men inhaled deeply. The young man said softly: "Keerist!"

The elder man turned to me: "Had your breakfast?"

"No."

"Well, sit down with us, then."

That was the signal. We went to the packing-case and squatted on the ground about it. The young man asked: "Picking cotton?"

"No."

"We had twelve days' work so far," the young man said.

The girl spoke from the stove. "They even got new clothes."

The two men looked down at their new dungarees and they both smiled a little.

The girl set out the platter of bacon, the brown high biscuits, a bowl of bacon gravy and a pot of coffee, and then she squatted down by the box too. The baby was still nursing, its head up under her waist out of the cold. I could hear the sucking noises it made.

We filled our plates, poured bacon gravy over our biscuits and sugared our coffee. The older man filled his mouth full and he chewed and chewed and swallowed. Then he said: "God Almighty, it's good," and he filled his mouth again.

The young man said: "We been eating good for twelve days."

We all ate quickly, frantically, and refilled our plates and ate quickly again until we were full and warm. The hot bitter coffee scalded our throats. We threw the last little bit with the grounds in it on the earth and refilled our cups.

There was colour in the light now, a reddish gleam that made the air seem colder. The two men faced the east and their faces were lighted by the dawn, and I looked up for a moment and saw the image of the mountain and the light coming over it reflected in the older man's eyes.

Then the two men threw the grounds from their cups on the earth and they stood up together. "Got to get going," the older man said.

The younger turned to me. "'F you want to pick cotton, we could maybe get you on."

"No. I got to go along. Thanks for breakfast."

averted *turned away.*

cricked *crackled.*

biscuits *savoury scones.*

Picking cotton *the story is set in the long valley of California, USA.*

20

The older man waved his hand in a negative. "OK. Glad to have you." They walked away together. The air was blazing with light at the eastern skyline. And I walked away down the country road.

That's all. I know, of course, some of the reasons why it was pleasant. But there was some element of great beauty there that makes the rush of warmth when I think of it.

Thinking/Talking Points

▷ Notice how many different bits of information we are given in the first two paragraphs. Imagine a painting of the scene.

▷ Which descriptive details give you a vivid sense of:
(a) the place (b) the time of day (c) the young woman (d) the younger man (e) the older man.

▷ Pick out four quotations from the story which give you a strong sense of how the writer was feeling.

Assignment

English

○ *A Particular Place at a Particular Time*
Write a similar piece of your own – perhaps about a special moment on holiday somewhere or when you were out walking early one morning or late at night.

Nothing needs to happen: do not worry if the piece does not seem to have any direction to it. You are trying to share with the reader your own powerful memory of one particular place at a particular time. Nothing more.

Before you start to draft your piece, close your eyes and try to recall as many distinct details as you can about the experience you are going to write about.

Think about the time of day, the season, the weather.
Think about colours, textures, smells and noises.
Think about exactly what feelings are tied to that experience. See if you can locate in your memory exactly what prompted those feelings.

Some further reading

Dylan Thomas   *A Child's Christmas in Wales*
                Holiday Memory

<h1>── *Thomas* ──
AFTER THE FAIR</h1>

A girl has run away.
She takes shelter in a fairground caravan.

Think about how you would make a story out of those two ideas.

Imagine a fairground at night, when all the visitors have left.
Jot down some descriptive details : sights, sounds, atmosphere.
Picture one caravan, standing apart from the rest.
Who might be living there?
Describe him/her/them.

Now picture the girl : her clothes, the expression in her eyes, her movements.
What is she doing at the fairground, on her own, so late at night?
Why does she decide to approach the caravan?
How is she received?

Assignment

English

o   Write a story about a boy or girl who has run away from something or someone
and who hides in a travelling circus, theatre company or a fair. Let some of the
reasons why he/she ran away come out slowly but don't give away everything.
Concentrate on giving the reader:
(a) a strong sense of the place where the story happens
(b) vivid pictures of the people involved.

Here is Dylan Thomas's version of the story.

After the Fair

The fair was over, the lights in the coconut stalls were put out, and
the wooden horses stood still in the darkness, waiting for the music
and the hum of the machines that would set them trotting forward.
One by one, in every booth, the naphtha jets were turned down and   **naphtha jets** *gas lamps.*
the canvases pulled over the little gaming tables. The crowd went
home, and there were lights in the windows of the caravans.

Nobody had noticed the girl. In her black clothes she stood against
the side of the roundabouts, hearing the last feet tread upon the
sawdust and the last voices die in the distance. Then, all alone on

the deserted ground, surrounded by the shapes of wooden horses and cheap fairy boats, she looked for a place to sleep. Now here and now there, she raised the canvas that shrouded the coconut stalls and peered into the warm darkness. She was frightened to step inside, and as a mouse scampered across the littered shavings on the floor, or as the canvas creaked and a rush of wind set it dancing, she ran away and hid again near the roundabouts. Once she stepped on the boards; the bells round a horse's throat jingled and were still; she did not dare breathe again until all was quiet and the darkness had forgotten the noise of the bells. Then here and there she went peeping for a bed, into each gondola, under each tent. But there was nowhere, nowhere in all the fair for her to sleep. One place was too silent, and in another was the noise of mice. There was straw in the corner of the Astrologer's tent, but it moved as she touched it; she knelt by its side and put out her hand; she felt a baby's hand upon her own.

shrouded *covered.*

gondola *swing boat.*

Astrologer *fortune-teller.*

Now there was nowhere, so, slowly, she turned towards the caravans on the outskirts of the field, and found all but two to be unlit. She waited, clutching her empty bag, and wondering which caravan she should disturb. At last she decided to knock upon the window of the little, shabby one near her, and, standing on tiptoes, she looked in. The fattest man she had ever seen was sitting in front of the stove, toasting a piece of bread. She tapped three times on the glass, then hid in the shadows. She heard him come to the top of the steps and call out, "Who? Who?" but she dare not answer. "Who? Who?" he called again.

She laughed at his voice which was as thin as he was fat.

He heard her laughter and turned to where the darkness concealed her. "First you tap," he said, "then you hide, then you laugh."

She stepped into the circle of light, knowing she need no longer hide herself.

"A girl," he said. "Come in, and wipe your feet." He did not wait but retreated into his caravan, and she could do nothing but follow him up the steps and into the crowded room. He was seated again, and toasting the same piece of bread. "Have you come in?" he said, for his back was towards her.

"Shall I close the door?" she asked, and closed it before he replied.

She sat on the bed and watched him toast the bread until it burnt.

"I can toast better than you," she said.

"I don't doubt it," said the Fat Man.

She watched him put the charred toast upon a plate by his side, take another round of bread and hold that, too, in front of the stove. It burnt very quickly.

charred *burnt.*

"Let me toast it for you," she said. Ungraciously he handed her the fork and the loaf.

ungraciously *not gently.*

"Cut it," he said, "toast it, and eat it."

She sat on the chair.

"See the dent you've made on my bed," said the Fat Man. "Who are you to come in and dent my bed?"

"My name is Annie," she told him.

Soon all the bread was toasted and buttered, so she put it in the centre of the table and arranged two chairs.

"I'll have mine on the bed," said the Fat Man. "You'll have it here."

When they had finished their supper, he pushed back his chair and stared at her across the table.

"I am the Fat Man," he said. "My home is Treorchy; the Fortune-Teller next door is Aberdare."

Treorchy, Aberdare, Cardiff *towns in South Wales.*

"I am nothing to do with the fair," she said, "I am Cardiff."

"There's a town," agreed the Fat Man. He asked her why she had come away.

"Money," said Annie.

Then he told her about the fair and the places he had been to and the people he had met. He told her his age and his weight and the names of his brothers and what he would call his son. He showed her a picture of Boston Harbour and the photograph of his mother who lifted weights. He told her how summer looked in Ireland.

"I've always been a fat man," he said, "and now I'm the Fat Man; there's nobody to touch me for fatness." He told her of a heat-wave in Sicily and the Mediterranean Sea. She told him of the baby in the Astrologer's tent.

"That's the stars again," he said.

"The baby'll die," said Annie.

He opened the door and walked out into the darkness. She looked about her but did not move, wondering if he had gone to fetch a policeman. It would never do to be caught by the policeman again. She stared through the open door into the inhospitable night and drew her chair closer to the stove.

inhospitable *unwelcoming.*

"Better to be caught in the warmth," she said. But she trembled at the sound of the Fat Man approaching, and pressed her hands upon her thin breast as he climbed up the steps like a walking mountain. She could see him smile through the darkness.

"See what the stars have done," he said, and brought in the Astrologer's baby in his arms.

After she had nursed it against her and it had cried on the bosom of her dress, she told him how she had feared his going.

"What should I be doing with a policeman?"

She told him that the policeman wanted her. "What have you done for a policeman to be wanting you?"

She did not answer but took the child nearer to her wasted breast. He saw her thinness.

wasted *thin and unhealthy.*

"You must eat, Cardiff," he said.

Then the child began to cry. From a little wail its voice rose into a tempest of despair. The girl rocked it to and fro on her lap, but nothing soothed it.

"Stop it! Stop it!" said the Fat Man, and the tears increased. Annie smothered it in kisses, but it howled again.

"We must do something," she said.

"Sing it a lullaby."

She sang, but the child did not like her singing.

"There's only one thing," said Annie, "we must take it on the roundabouts." With the child's arm around her neck she stumbled down the steps and ran towards the deserted fair, the Fat Man panting behind her.

She found her way through the tents and stalls into the centre of the ground where the wooden horses stood waiting, and clambered up onto a saddle. "Start the engine," she called out. In the distance the Fat Man could be heard cranking up the antique machine that drove the horses all the day into a wooden gallop. She heard the spasmodic humming of the engines; the boards rattled under the horses' feet. She saw the Fat Man get up by her side, pull the central lever, and climb on to the saddle of the smallest horse of all. As the roundabout started, slowly at first and slowly gaining speed, the child at the girl's breast stopped crying and clapped its hands. The night wind tore through its hair, the music jangled in its ears. Round and round the wooden horses sped, drowning the cries of the wind with the beating of their hooves.

spasmodic *irregular.*

And so the men from the caravans found them, the Fat Man and the girl in black with a baby in her arms, racing round and round on their mechanical steeds to the ever-increasing music of the organ.

Thinking/Talking Points

▷ How was Dylan Thomas's piece most/least like your own?
What do you like/dislike about his story?
Think about ways in which your own piece can be improved.

▷ Pick out half a dozen details from *After the Fair* which give you a strong picture of the fairground, a sense of atmosphere.

▷ What clues are we given about why Annie is there?

▷ How would you describe the personality of the Fat Man?
Which of these words best fit him:
  tender; gruff; jolly; kind; nosy; respectful; greedy; stubborn;
  strong; hospitable; rude; mysterious; proud; docile; intelligent.
Add some words of your own to those you select.
Which details give you that impression of him?

▷ What might happen next?

Read *After the Fair* again before attempting the next assignment.
Notice how much information Dylan Thomas packs into each paragraph.

Assignment

○ *After the Fair* continued.

Write two or three more pages, continuing Dylan Thomas's story. Try to write in a similar style.

Do not 'finish' the story. Don't explain too much.
Concentrate on telling the reader more about the fairground and its atmosphere. Think about colours, shapes, textures, smells and noises.
Develop the personalities of the people in the story : the Fat Man, Annie and one or two more of the fairground people. Describe them but let them tell us most about themselves from the way they talk.

Perhaps we meet the Astrologer. What does he/she look like?
How does he/she speak? Do we learn any more about the baby?
Does the Astrologer offer Annie shelter?

Does someone offer Annie a job on the coconut stall?
Maybe someone else turns up who knows her . . .

Some further reading

Vernon Scannell   *The Fair*
Elizabeth Mann   *Spring Fair*
Dylan Thomas   *A Prospect of the Sea*
Film
Louis Malle   *Viva Maria!*

★

RAPUNZEL, LET DOWN YOUR HAIR

Storr
NEW GIRL

Mills and Boon, the international publishers of romantic fiction (nine new titles each month) sell about fifteen million volumes every year. They reckon to have five million regular readers in the UK.
Why do you think their publications are so popular?
What do you think the ingredients of a successful love-story are?

In their advice to would-be authors, Mills and Boon stress the following points:
'. . . there is no truth in the rumour that they're all written to a rigid formula. Otherwise they'd all be the same, and our readers would soon lose interest. The story must be presented in a believable way . . .
Most of all we're looking for novels which communicate the magic of falling in love and the tension that comes from identifying with the characters and wondering whether they will be able to settle their differences by the end of the book.
The important thing is that the characters should come alive as sympathetic, plausible individuals . . .
Quite simply, if you're not involved with the story, the reader won't be.'
(from *And Then He Kissed Her . . . A Mills and Boon Guide to Writing Romantic Fiction.*)

Whether the stories Mills and Boon publish exemplify these qualities is a matter you will have to decide for yourself after reading a few of their novels. But it's good advice to anyone who wants to write convincingly.

Here we print two teenage love stories.

Before you read them, think about what the writers must include/avoid if you are to enjoy their stories.

Rapunzel, Let Down Your Hair

I was so much in love with you that I spent all that day standing outside your house, just standing there, with the rain pouring into my hair, into my collar, through the lace-holes in my shoes, but I couldn't feel it any more, couldn't feel anything but the ache, the

actual physical ache, I hadn't known it was *physical* like that, a real pain like the one you get from a bad tooth or your appendix, somewhere just under the edge of my ribs, nagging away at me whether I just sat and brooded about you or tried to distract myself with the words on the sides of cereal packets or the news on telly or my mum's conversation, one-sided as usual, more of a monologue really, or whether I tried to do something decisive and concrete about you like walking to the call-box and phoning your house, and being told that you weren't in, though of course I knew you were, that you'd told your mum to say that, but I thought you see that if I stood there for long enough you would take pity on me, or that you'd be moved and impressed by the vigil I was keeping, by my clear devotion to the cause of my love for you, that you'd understand that I meant the things I said to you on the phone the first time I telephoned and you *did* answer, the things that caused you to tell me I was mad and that I should stop bothering you or you would tell your dad to come out and *do* me, as you put it, so I rang off, and there then seemed to be nothing else for me to do but walk the mile or so to your house and just stand there in the street while the rain poured into my hair and down my face and, as I said into my collar too, but as I also said, I didn't notice it because I was . . .

I felt a bit silly, too, especially when your mum came out with a cup of tea, as if I was trying to do something that might get me into the *Guinness Book of Records*, like pole-squatting, I drank the tea, though, thanks to your mum, although she couldn't ask me in because of your instructions . . .

And your dad was looking at me very suspiciously from the upstairs front room where he was wallpapering, I waved once and a sort of smile played round his lips for a few seconds and then vanished, and was replaced by a thin nasty line when he turned his head from time to time and saw that I was still there, hardly able to believe my nerve at still being there, but how could he understand what was going on under my ribs, that pain like a sort of heartburn, that's not a bad name for it, and once . . .

And once you came to the window of the *downstairs* front room, remember, and sort of looked out at me, your arms folded, head sort of on one side, then putting your head on the other side as if considering the problem from another angle, your expression quite blank, we stood there for some time looking at each other separated by that window and the road and by the rain but looking actually looking into each other's eyes, I can't pretend it was a look of love from your side, far from it really, sort of anger and bewilderment and worst of all a kind of embarrassment, while I tried to battle back with as much *love* from behind my eyes, as much intensity as I could manage, putting as much feeling as I could into a supercharged look that would zap you from across the street, evaporate the rain, turn the glass to steam . . .

Remember how we stood like that for a long time, what semed to be a long time, though I couldn't now say how long, a minute, an hour, holding that look like a thread between us, and how I suddenly became aware that something had changed, that you were saying something with your mouth, your beautiful mouth that I dreamed about even when I was awake, that you were *mouthing* some kind of a message to me through the glass and the rain, a message like to the deaf, lip-language, what was it, I couldn't quite . . .

Make out what it was, and then suddenly I could, it was nastily clear to me all of a sudden that what you were mouthing was, "Go Away" . . .

But I wasn't one to take "Go Away" for an answer, was I? You must have known that I wouldn't just go as easily as that, so I just shook my head and made a round "No" with my lips, shaking my head and going "*No* . . ." and there it was, it seemed, a stalemate, your dad looking down again from his wallpapering and catching me in mid-shake, with my mouth in an O from the "*No* . . .", his hand with the wallpaper brush halfway to the wall and the paste running down his sleeve . . .

How much longer did it go on after that? At what point did you finally take pity? Though I must admit you held out well, you didn't give in easily, but in time you had to admit that I had held out better, that the knight who's made up his mind to vigil will go ahead and vigil and won't let a bit of rain . . .

How did you feel on your side of the door when you inched it open? What did you think you were letting in. What kind of lunatic mad with love, to drip on to your hall carpet and then your kitchen lino, to stand there suddenly speechless having achieved that bit of kitchen lino and your presence, thinking of the fairy story I read when I was a kid about the knight and the vigil outside the golden tower and Rapunzel letting down her hair from her high window and the prince climbing up? And how did you know what to say to me when you did speak, which was after an awkward silence when neither of us knew what to . . .?

"I suppose this is supposed to impress me, is it? I suppose this is supposed to make me fall madly in love with you and want to go out with you?" you said.

"Not in that order," I said. "You could go out with me first and maybe falling in love would happen later."

"It wouldn't happen later. It wouldn't happen ever. It couldn't be like that, that would be too usual for you. You never can do things in the usual way. You just think you're so different."

"I am. I am different."

"You certainly are."

"I love you."

"You say you love me. It's not love. It's just . . . an infatuation. You don't know me."

"I *do* know you. I've known you for years. I've watched you walking down that corridor at school. I've watched you cycling past my house. I know how your face goes when you feel things. I've seen every mood."

"That's not knowing."

"It's a sort of knowing."

"You can't just suddenly decide that you're in love with someone."

"I didn't just suddenly. I knew it the first time . . ."

"You knew it the first time you saw me! You sound like a silly film."

At least your face stopped being stern, then. At least you didn't look at me like a teacher, telling me off.

"Those films aren't what it's like. It's like a pain. It doesn't get any better, looking at you. It doesn't get any better being here, talking to you."

"If it's like a pain, go and see a doctor."

"A lot of good, he'd do. It's not being ill. It's happened to lots of people. People like poets. Poets write poems about it."

"You and your poetry."

"Songwriters write songs about it. Quite modern ones do. Who's your favourite singer?"

"What's that got to do . . ."

"No, go on, tell me, who's your favourite? I'm proving a point."

"Dunno," you went, "I like Blondie."

"There you are," I said, "she's on about love all the time, it's all she sings about. If so many people are writing songs and singing them and writing poems, are you telling me that it doesn't exist? They make those silly films about it an' all."

"That's not life. People see those silly films and try to make it happen that way to them. It's never really like that."

"It *is*."

"Not in real life it isn't."

"It *is*. I'm here proving it is, now."

"You're not proving anything."

"I *am*."

"Not to me, you're not," you said.

"I suppose you wouldn't make me a cup of tea?" I said.

I held out the empty mug that had held the tea that your mum had brought out to me an hour before, not empty now, it had rain water in it, which you tipped into the sink and switched on the kettle with a sort of a sigh, a sort of defeated sound, giving in to the extent of a cup of tea at least . . .

"Is this the way you usually get what you want?" you said, "by standing there all pathetic until people get all sorry for you and let you have things?"

"I've never behaved like this before," I said. "About anything."

You gave me a sort of look that didn't believe me.

When your father came in you were giving me that look, across the room.

"I've just come in to wash my hands," he said.

"Wallpaper paste," he explained.

We didn't say anything to him, didn't even hardly notice he was there . . .

The look was the same sort of look you'd given me through that front-room window, when I was out there in the rain, only this time I could see it properly, look *into* it properly, and when you'd done it before, it had given me a bit more of a reason for being there, and now that I could see it properly all the more reason . . .

"Making some tea, are you?" asked your dad. "'Cause if you are, you can make me one an' all . . ."

You turned then, and switched the look away and went on with making tea at the kettle, while your dad washed the wallpaper paste from his hands and then turned and sort of smiled at me, though he looked doubtfully at the puddle I was making on his lino . . .

I was still sort of shaking from the look you'd given me, just from the effect of having eye contact with you for as long as I had, you trying I think to see into me and puzzle me out a bit, just as I tried to see into you . . .

So it was as if your dad wasn't there at all hardly . . .

You turned round again and gave him his tea and then brought me mine, this time not looking at me, sort of keeping your eyes to the side and not looking, deliberately, and the three of us supped our tea, your dad leaning against the sink looking embarrassed and me hardly noticing he was there, I don't think I could even give a description to the police, isn't that strange . . .?

That cup of tea, that moment seemed suspended, in a time-warp, like in a sci-fi thingy. I was shivering slightly and the rain on the windows was ever so clear, like I could see every tiny drop, and as you turned again and with both hands clasped round your mug of tea, keeping them warm, you bent your head to take a sip of tea and then at that moment your hair seemed to gleam golden, a bit of sun came in through the window at that moment and just caught at the filaments and sort of lit them up, I wouldn't have missed that bit, that was worth all the waiting out in the rain that I'd done, that was a bit of magic . . .

filaments *fine strands of hair.*

And when your dad had gone, something had changed in the room, hadn't it? Something was different, it was like the sun coming out, how strange, it was enough, then, I felt foolish all of a sudden stood there in my sodden clothes, not like a knight in a story at all, just a bit daft, a bit mad I suppose, wondering what happens to you when you do daft things like that, go without food, sleep, think about somebody every second every micro-second of the day and night, what do you say to them when you're there?

Remember how you put down your mug of tea and sort of moved towards me? Then I felt a bit panicky all of a sudden, you actually moving across the room towards me, fixing me with one of those

33

looks you do, with your eyes all wide and looking into me, I couldn't believe your hand actually reaching up and pushing the wet hair out of my eyes . . .

"Nobody ever stood out in the rain for me before," you said.
    "Oh," I said.

You being nice to me . . .
You stroking the hair out of my eyes . . .
    I thought:

"What on earth am I going to do now?"

New Girl

There was only one new pupil at the beginning of the school term in January. She was the prettiest girl Nicko had ever seen.

The other boys thought so too. In the first morning break, he saw John Ellerman and Jimmy Tindall crowding up to her. He wished he had their nerve. How often he'd seen them and the other boys walk in that cocky, self-assured way up to a girl they fancied. He knew it was that air of confidence which was half the battle, which accounted for their success if you could believe their stories. In bed at night, he imagined himself dating a girl like Stephie Green, in the class above, who was known to be ready to go out with anyone. Nicko didn't want to go with Stephie. He just wanted to know that if he had wanted to, he could.

How did you get started? If he could only get started, he thought, he'd be able to go on. Once he'd tried walking home after school with Diana O'Malley, who looked like a rabbit, with a soft white nose that twitched when she talked, and below the nose big rabbit teeth with a wire round them as if they had to be caged in or they'd jump out of her wet pink mouth.

He'd asked her, "What are you doing tomorrow, then?", it being a Friday.

She'd said, "Going shopping for Mum like always."

He'd said, "That take all day?"

"Evening I have to go to confession. Sunday, I'm free after Mass," she said, looking at him hopefully out of her pink-rimmed eyes, waiting for him to suggest they should go out together. But when he saw that she was more than willing, he was overcome by horror of her peeled look, as if she had one skin or one coat of paint too few. Not just a rabbit, a skinned rabbit. He'd invented a forgotten errand and left her. For days afterwards Diana's soft nose twitched at him reproachfully whenever he came near her in school.

He noticed with interest that being quick off the mark didn't seem to have done John or Jimmy any good with the new girl. She was in

a group of other girls at the dinner break, and after school he saw that John was with Margaret Brady and Jimmy whizzing off on his bike. He didn't see the new girl. She must have gone off like a streak of lightning.

For two weeks he did no more than look at her. He wanted to know her by heart. At any minute, if he shut his eyes, he could see her face in front of him. She was dark-rosy, with well-opened hazel eyes. Her cheekbones were a fraction higher than those of other girls, her mouth a little larger. Not a big mouth, but one with an infinity of changes. It could stretch into a grimace — sometimes at her own mistakes. Sometimes, with the effort over some difficulty, it was pursed up into a delicious pout. Sometimes it flew open in a great laugh that rocked her whole body; sometimes it drooped at the corners as if she was sad. It was a wonderful, expressive, give-away mouth. Nicko loved it.

The only thing about her that he loved even more was the little fringe of newly growing hairs that sprang over her forehead, growing from the hairline downwards. Tiny soft hairs, not long enough to be brushed back, curling, baby hairs. They seemed to Nicko the tenderest thing he'd ever seen. He wanted to touch them. The most intimate thing he could imagine would be to smooth those hairs on the forehead of Estanella. Estanella! Extraordinary name! But her second name was Smith.

Coming back from school on a Friday, a bitter January evening, when the rain had frozen on the pavements, he saw a woman slip, fall, and stay fallen, her full shopping basket discharging most of its contents around her. No one else seemed to be around, and Nicko reluctantly went to her rescue. She was sitting up by the time he reached her, and was rubbing her wrist.

"You hurt badly?" he asked.

"Don't think so. It's a shock, though."

"Your coat's all muddy," said a voice from the other side of the woman. Nicko saw Estanella.

"These came out of your basket." She held out two blue-green mackerel, escaping from a damp paper wrapping.

"I'd some eggs as well," the woman said.

"They're all gone," Estanella said, looking at a slimy trail of yellow and white, trickling towards the frozen gutter.

"You had them all in one basket," Nicko said, and was astonished when Estanella giggled.

"Lucky I didn't break my arm," the woman said. She got up clumsily, turning first on to her hands and knees, then hoisting herself upright. Her coat was soaked from seat to hem, her hands and elbows black with mud.

"You all right?" Estanella asked.

"Bit shaken, but I'll do."

"Your purse must've come open. There's a fifty p. piece," Nicko said, picking it up.

"You'd better keep it for your trouble. You and your girlfriend go

discharging *spilling.*

36

and get yourselves a coffee or something. I'll be all right now."

Nicko froze. He waited to hear Estanella deny knowing him. He doubted if she even knew him by sight. He heard her say, "Thanks. If you're sure you're all right."

As the woman went carefully off, Nicko said, "You'll have a coffee?"

"Why not?"

"Where?"

"You know this place. I don't. You say."

Delicious dependence. Feeling taller than ever in his life before, Nicko led her to the Witches' Cauldron, a place with a reputation in the school for unmentionable vice. This evening, however, it looked disappointingly ordinary. It was also nearly empty. They chose a table as far from the door as possible, and were visited by a sleepy-looking girl who asked them what they wanted with an air that implied that whatever they said would be an affront.

"Two coffees. Pastries?" Nicko asked Estanella.

"Fifty p. won't run to pastries as well."

"I'll stand you them."

"No pastries," said the affronted one.

"Hamburgers, then?"

"No hamburgers."

Nicko looked at the spotted menu. "We'll have hot buttered toast."

"No toast." She sounded pleased about it.

"You've got biscuits in that glass case. We'll have them."

"They're cheese biscuits. We haven't got any cheese."

"We'll have them, anyway." He wasn't going to be cheated of giving Estanella something, even if it were no better than biscuits without cheese.

"She'd have said they were cardboard dummies if she could," Estanella said.

Sitting opposite to her, nearer than he'd ever been before, Nicko went over his inventory of her face. Taken separately her features weren't anything special. Put together, in just this way, they added up to a miracle.

"'ve I got a smut?" Estenella asked.

"Pardon?"

"I said, have I got a smut? You keep looking as if something was wrong."

Without knowing he was going to, Nicko surprised himself by saying, "It's just, you're so pretty."

"Why didn't you ever speak to me in school?"

He said, "I wanted to."

"Why ever didn't you, then?"

Instead of trying to explain, he said, "I've never known anyone called Estanella before."

"My grandma's name."

"It's just right for you."

---

delicious dependence *it was lovely to have her depending upon me.*

vice *wickedness.*

affront *insult.*

inventory *checklist.*

smut *dirty mark.*

"You can call me Stella if you like."

He considered this, but decided against it. "Estanella just suits you. It's different."

She drank the insipid coffee and bit delicately into one of the dry, stale biscuits.

"Do you live round here?" Nicko asked.

"No." But she didn't say where she was living.

"I live in the next street. Almost."

"Handy for getting to school, then."

It was a failure. He could feel that she was bored, wanted to get away from him. It didn't surprise him when, five minutes later, she said she'd got to be getting back. Nor that she refused his offer to walk her home. It was only an excuse, he was sure, that she still had her shopping to do. When they were out in the street again, he waited for her to leave him. Probably she wouldn't even pretend to go shopping. He was not worth deceiving. But then, seeing her again in the light of the street lamps, he had to make a last desperate plea.

"Come out with me again?"

"Ask me." She was smiling at him.

Stars flashed from the sky and burst into music round his feet. He had to collect his thoughts quickly. "There's a spy picture on at the Gaumont tomorrow. I could come and fetch you."

"I'll be in here anyway. I'll meet you. Where? When?"

"Picture starts half three. Three o'clock, here? They might have got in some cheese, seeing it'll be Saturday."

She laughed. Said, "I'll be here. Super. 'Bye, Nicko" and was gone.

Astonishingly Nicko found himself established as Estanella's boyfriend. Had it really taken no time at all? Or was it that time now had a scale quite different from any he'd known before? The only hours that dragged came when he had to force his mind away from her in order to concentrate on school work. Even the days in class were tinged with the gold of her presence, and the hours out of school, when they could be together, always seemed to be coming to an end before he had properly realised them. The whole thing was unbelievable. He didn't understand his luck. "Why me? Don't you ever want someone like Bob Reynolds? Or Steenie?" mentioning two of the school's heroes.

"Why should I? I like being with you. You're nice."

Disappointing. Who wanted just to be nice? Hoping for something more positive, he pursued it. "Steenie and Bob have been around a lot."

"They're show-offs. They're stupid. I like you." It was marvellous the way she always knew what she wanted and what she didn't. No doubts. He kissed her. Her firm cool cheek turned, and his mouth met soft, parted lips. He drew back in surprise and something like consternation. But she didn't let him pull away. "Kiss me, Nicko. Kiss me again."

He surprised himself by what he found he knew without being taught. How did he know to create a sort of vacuum between Estanella's mouth and his own, so that they seemed to grow into each other like one person? Her mouth tasted sweet, slightly pepperminty. Toothpaste? Her hair smelled appley, felt like silk, just as he'd imagined. His hands explored her shoulders, her delicately boned spine, her delicious waist. He put both arms around her and held her close, right up against him. She was warm and supple. Lovely!

She pulled away, but so gently there was no reproach.

"Estanella. Why . . .?"

"Not now, Nicko. I've got to run. My mum'll think I've got lost." She kissed him lightly on the lips and left him, taut, unsatisfied, but loving.

He took her home. His father, of course, fell for her and made shambling advances – a paw on her arm when he spoke to her, a touch on her thigh as she went past his chair. Nicko's mum, that tormented woman, told her, "You're Nicko's friend. I've heard a lot about you," and put on the table the over-grand shop cake she'd bought to impress. She tried. She didn't put newspaper down over the lino in the kitchen as she did for Nicko and his dad. She'd made a trifle for supper. But she couldn't – and Nicko didn't expect it – take Estanella calmly.

"Your mother hates me," Estanella said to Nicko when they were alone.

"She doesn't. It's just her way."

"Has she always been miserable?" Estanella asked.

Nicko was surprised and a little angry. "She's not miserable!"

"She's a lot more miserable than my mum. Even if . . ."

"Even if what?"

"Nothing. But it isn't just me. She hates everyone. You're the only one she loves."

Nicko couldn't get over the way she could use that difficult word love as if it were the natural thing between parents and children. He said, "What's your mum like? Does she . . ." but he couldn't bring himself to ask, "Does she love you?"

"She's all right."

"You don't talk about her. Or your dad. Hardly ever."

"Nothing to talk about. Never mind about them. Think about us."

Too easy, with that generous mouth searching for his, and that soft hand caressing the back of his neck and only now and then checking his fingers when they became too bold.

It worried him, all the same, that Estanella didn't tell him anything about her home and never asked him back there. His mother, of course, was on to this in no time.

"She's been here often enough. Why doesn't she take you to meet her mum and dad?"

"They're busy. They both work." That much he had gathered.

"Sometimes they must be home. She's ashamed to take you there, that's what. May be living in a slum. Or thinks you're not good enough. One or the other."

"She's not like that. That's stupid."

"Don't you dare say that to me! Do you know what her father's job is? Do you?"

He couldn't say he did. Something to do with the entertainment business, he'd understood. That could mean anything from being a TV personality to the chorus line. He wasn't going to tell his mother that, nor that Estanella had been at more schools than she could count. Fourteen she could remember the names of. His mum wouldn't like that. She didn't approve of changing jobs.

"Smith!" His mum made it sound like Mud. "What's his first name?"

Nicko said reluctantly, "Edward." He'd tried to get more out of Estanella. He'd asked, "Is your dad famous? What does he do exactly?" But she didn't answer, and when he had her in his arms in the breathless darkness of the park, he didn't care. What her dad did didn't matter beside the all-important fact that she was there with him. "Estanella" he sighed, and she softly but urgently cried back, "Nicko! Oh, Nicko!"

She was easy to please. She didn't want the bright lights, nor the deafening music of the disco. She was uneasy, more so than Nicko had ever seen her, when they bluffed their way into a pub.

"Afraid someone'll see you and tell your mum?" he teased her, and though she said, with conviction, "Mum wouldn't mind," he could tell that she wasn't her usual relaxed self.

She was happier in the cheap seats at the pictures, sharing a bench in a dark coffee bar, happiest of all alone with him outside under the trees, when the weather permitted. She wouldn't even go with him to the circus. He was astounded. He'd already bought the tickets – good ones. He'd been sure she'd love it, he could hear her great laugh at the clowns, her indrawn breath when the high-wire act was at its most terrifying.

astounded *amazed.*

"I'm sorry, Nicko, I really am."

"I thought you'd like it."

"Take someone else."

"Now you're being really stupid."

They made it up deliciously. He threw the tickets down the toilet to demonstrate how little they mattered. His mother, who nagged the story out of him, was outraged.

"You could have given them to Jack. Selfish. That's what you've been, ever since you started going with that girl."

Selfish? Was he? Yes, probably. He couldn't think about anything or anyone else. Only Estanella. She was the only person who mattered in the whole world.

It irked him, though, that he didn't know more about her parents, her background. Trying a new approach, he said to her one day, "Does your mum mind you going out with me?"

irked *bothered.*

40

"Why should she?"

"Seems funny she doesn't want to see me." Subtle this.

"I told her you were all right."

" Suppose I did something terrible?"

"Like what? You never would. Stupid." Very lovingly.

"Suppose you got pregnant?"

She was suddenly fierce. "I'm not ever going to have babies."

"Why ever not?" It seemed unlike her. He could have seen her as a mother. Lovely, she'd be.

"I shan't have any. People shouldn't have babies, who . . ."

"Who what?"

"Nothing. I don't know. Kiss me, Nicko. Don't talk."

He was happy to obey. But in spite of the excitement, he remained puzzled. "Who what? Who shouldn't have babies?"

"Forget it. I just think some people have babies who shouldn't."

"When they're not married, you mean?"

"That. Kiss me again."

"You're in a hurry," he teased.

"We haven't got long."

"What d'you mean?"

"I won't be here much longer."

Fear bit his vitals. "What d'you mean?"   **vitals** *insides*.

"We're moving on. I told you. We don't ever stay anywhere long."

"*When*?"

She said, "Tomorrow." He was thunderstruck.

"You never said."

"I didn't know how to."

Holding her tighter, he cried, "We could get married." and heard her sigh, "Don't be stupid, Nicko."

"You want to go!"

"You're being horrible to me." He had never seen her cry before.

"You'll have other boys."

"I won't! I won't!"

"Those other places you've been in. Did you have boys in all of them?"

"Not like you."

"Promise! Not like me? Not like this?"

"Promise."

"You won't. Will you? You won't have other boys?"

"I won't, Nicko. Promise."

He dared, at last, to say it. "I love you."

"I love you, Nicko."

"When I've got out of school we'll get married. I'll come and find you. You'll see."

He couldn't get her to share his castle-building. She grew more   **castle-building** *fantasies*.
and more silent. She had to catch the last bus back. He didn't know how to let her go.

"Let's say good-bye now, Nicko."

41

"I want to see you tomorrow. I'll come and see you off."

"You can't. I'll write."

"Why can't I?" But she wouldn't explain. The bus came lumbering up, heartlessly bright. She tore herself out of his arms and leapt for the step. She looked back, a dark small shape, outlined against the illuminated interior, waving. He couldn't hear what she was calling. He walked home, hurting all over. Any physical pain would have seemed a relief. He didn't know how to contain what he was feeling.

lumbering moving slowly.

He knew which suburb she'd been living in. He went early and hung around the exit roads, bicycling madly from one point to another. She'd said they were going north. That meant they weren't going by train. He was in an agony in case he missed her. Cycling dangerously, swooping among vans and cars gave him a sort of angry relief.

suburb part of the town.

Something like a crowd was collecting at a road junction. For want of something to distract him, he joined it.

"What's going on?" he asked a bystander.

"Circus people leaving town."

The Christmas season had lasted till the middle of March, and he'd never persuaded Estanella to come with him. His chest burned. Did everything have to remind him of her? He watched the great vans lumber past, brightly coloured, with names on their sides. A vast lorry load of metal poles and canvas rattled past; then came a van marked *Selina and her Astounding Seals.* Followed by horses looking sheepishly out of tall horse-boxes and a long trailer containing the big cats. Nicko imagined he could smell the sawdust and the acrid smell of wild animal. Then caravans. *Joey the Clown, Marietta, Gypsy Beatrice.*

acrid sharp.

Between the caravans and the cars were groups of the circus performers, some of them in ordinary clothes, and somehow smaller than they'd appeared in the ring. Some of them were in their professional costumes, the ring-master, superb in blue tailcoat and grey top hat, the clowns in their bright, baggy trousers, grotesquely made up, leaping around, ragging the crowd, falling over their own feet in those enormous boots, peeping up the skirts of the women onlookers, getting a lot of laughs. Among them were the little people, the midgets, with their huge heads and long bodies, with their absurd stumpy little arms and legs. A whole troupe of them were scurrying around, getting in the clowns' way; one of them was carrying a suitcase larger than himself, playing the fool, apparently enjoying the effect he was having. It had become a royal entertainment.

Nicko himself couldn't help laughing, for a moment forgetting his restless misery. He pushed forward in the growing crowd till he was in front, able to see everything. One of the little people, the last to go by, was a tiny woman, smaller than any of the others, wearing rakishly a huge scarlet wide-brimmed hat with a feather in it. Just as

42

she was level with Nicko she made a run and a jump up to the open doorway of the caravan passing her at walking pace. She stood on the caravan step, snatched off her hat and waved it at the crowd. "'Bye, all you big people! See you next year!" she called, in a hoarse, cheerful voice, and the crowd, loving her, called back, "'Bye, Nellie! Be seeing you!"

Nicko didn't yell. He had seen the names painted on the side of the caravan. *The Smallest Show on Earth. Tom and Thumbelina. (Eddie and Eleanor Smith)*. And now he saw in that grotesque, grinning face, the clear, dark colouring, the wide mobile mouth, even the fringe of baby hairs, which in Estanella had been translated into beauty. The little woman disappeared into the caravan after a final flourish of the hat. She shut the door. Somewhere inside that gaudy house-on-wheels Estanella must be hiding. In case she might look surreptitiously out of a window, Nicko fought his way back into the safety of the crowd. She must not see him. It was the last service he could render her.

"What happened to that girl?" his mother asked, days later.

His eyes burned in his head, and he had to swallow the lump in his throat before he could answer, "She's gone."

"Gone where?"

"Somewhere north."

He wouldn't look up to see the satisfaction on his mother's face.

"Treated you badly, didn't she?"

"No."

"What? Leaving you like that? Leading you on like she did?"

"She couldn't help it." He could hardly bring himself to add, "Her dad had a job. They all had to go." He didn't want to have to speak of the relationship aloud. That made it come alive in his imagination.

"She upset you, properly. It'd have been better if you'd never set eyes on her."

Nicko cried out, "No!" And realised as he spoke, that it was true. In spite of the misery, the pain which seemed never quite to let go of him, in spite of the blackness of repulsion and despair, he found he wouldn't be without it. Not to be suffering like this would have meant not having known Estanella, that lovely, generous girl. Not to have known what it was like to love and be loved by her. For the first time since she'd left, he stopped fighting against the misery of feeling. He let it possess him.

" . . .well rid of her," he heard his mother finish.

Estanella had been right about her. His mother hated everyone, she didn't know what it was to want to give and to be given. Some of Nicko's sorrow flowed towards her. He'd had something she had never had.

He said, "In a year or two I'll find her."

But he didn't know if he ever would.

☆

Thinking/Talking Points

▷ Have these writers created (a) convincing situations (b) characters you can identify with (c) stories you enjoyed?
Pick out and discuss a dozen or so details from each story which you found funny/moving/convincing/unlikely.
Is there anything you would alter to improve either story?

Assignments

English

○ *Rapunzel's Version/Rapunzel's Father's Version*
Rewrite the first part of *Rapunzel, Let Down Your Hair* (up to the point where the two finally speak, face to face) as if *either* the girl *or* her father were telling it.
Write in a style which you think suits the person telling the story.
Use details from the original version but add lots of ideas of your own — especially about what the writer feels about the boy and his 'vigil'.

○ Write two or three more pages of the story. Try to maintain Chris Hawes's style.

○ *New Girl : the sequel.*
Does Nicko follow Estanella north? What happens when they meet again? Is there any basis for a long-term relationship? What problems do they face?

Or does Nicko notice another new girl . . .?

Tell the story *either* in the third person (as in Catherine Storr's story) — as if you are watching what happens *or* in the first person — as if you are Nicko.

○ Write a love-story of your own. You may like to use one of these titles: *First Date; Once Bitten, Twice Shy; Jealous Guy; Valentine's Day Blues.*

English Literature

This is an activity which could be done individually or by a small group.

○ Read three or four novels from one of the popular series of romantic fiction, and then see if you can draw up a list of any ingredients which you feel the stories have in common.

For example, are the heroes drawn from certain social backgrounds? What sorts of jobs do they do? Do they have any physical similarities? Do they tend to have similar personalities? What are their attitudes to money, to women, to family life, to people from different backgrounds? What kind of behaviour do you think the reader is expected to admire? Do many of the heroes have characteristics which you dislike?

What about the women in the stories? Do they fall into certain types? Do they tend to come from a particular social background? Do they have physical similarities? What are their attitudes to themselves, to their careers, to men in general, to families, to money, to other people? What kinds of behaviour is the reader expected to approve/disapprove of? Do you find the women characters generally convincing? Likeable? Is there any thing about them which you don't like?

What sort of places are the stories set in?
What sort of places do not figure in the stories?

Are there any similarities between the plots of the novels you have studied? How do they begin? How does the story develop? Are there certain kinds of complications/crises/periods of suspense? How do the stories end?

When you have drawn up some notes about what you have found, write an essay entitled: *Written to a Formula?*
Advising would-be authors, Mills and Boon say :
' . . .there is no truth in the rumour that they're all written to a rigid formula. Otherwise they'd all be the same, and our readers would soon lose interest.'

Does your own research tend to confirm or qualify this statement?
Discuss what you have found in your studies of the men and women, locations, situations and plots to be found in popular romantic fiction.
How convincing a picture of relationships do you think the novels you have studied paint? What does reading the novels suggest to you about the expectations of the people who buy them?
Quote particular details from the novels you have studied to support your case.

Some further reading

Miriam Hodgson	*The Teens Book of Love Stories*
Lynn Reid Banks	*The L Shaped Room*
Alan Garner	*Red Shift*
Ursula Le Guin	*A Very Long Way from Anywhere Else*
D.H. Lawrence	*The Virgin and the Gipsy*
E.M. Forster	*A Room with a View*

★

Khan
SEEING ME

In what ways do you think being a teenager is (a) more like being a child (b) more like being an adult?

How are you more independent of adults than you were five years ago?
What do you still rely on them for?
What responsibilities do you have which you didn't have five years ago?
How do these responsibilities make you feel?

How do your parents limit your freedom? Do you think that's sensible?
Which house rules would you like changed?
If you have a teenage son/daughter, what rules will you lay down about going out, doing homework, manners, boy/girlfriends etc.?

Which school rules do you feel unreasonably limit your freedom?
Are there any you would change? Are there any that you think are missing?
In what ways do you think school could prepare teenagers better for the adult world?
What aspects of school life will you be pleased to leave behind?
Is there anything that you think you might miss about school?

What conflicts have you experienced between what your parents tell you is right and wrong, and what school says about things?

In this story, Rahila Khan explores what can happen when what school and what home think is right for a teenage girl come into conflict . . .

Seeing Me

The classroom was filled with a low, persistent buzz of voices; not the studious hum of a group of people working in unison, but the constant, troublesome distraction of bored teenagers filling the gaps between bells. Above the noise, the teacher tried to keep some sort of continuity of instruction, but with little success. The average age of the group of girls was fifteen years and three months; soon they would be released into a wider world of boredom and neglect, and other authorities would try to occupy them between giros. Soon their days would be measured out by the regular visits to the Job Centre and the corner cafés. Perhaps they would even look back on the classrooms as places of relative happiness and occupation, places of companionship in lassitude.

In the midst of this education, a few girls still tried to keep involved, tried to prolong their learning to the last minute. They allowed the teacher to believe that the anarchic hum of the majority

persistent *unending*.
studious *hard-working*.
in unison *together*.

continuity of instruction *shape to the lesson*.

giros *social security payments*.

lassitude *tiredness*.

anarchic *disruptive*.

was a diversion from his real achievement. He ignored the chattering groups scattered through the room and concentrated on the faces which did turn in his direction, hoping for contact.

The greater noise never threatened to become overwhelming. There was an unspoken agreement that if the small knots of young women would limit themselves to intimate conversation rather than loud protestations or revolt, then nothing would be done. To an inspector, pausing outside the door to listen, the lesson would seem to be a well-disciplined, free discussion period. Alongside the tolerated digressions about boyfriends and dates, new hair-does and make-up, about the latest film or televison heroes, and fantasies about jobs, alongside these, the teacher kept his little group entertained with expeditions into short stories, novels and plays. As an English lesson went, it was not unsuccessful. For one of the girls, it was the most important part of her day.

Amina was a lonely girl, and she had found more friends and companions in the books described in her English lessons than she had in the corridors and playgrounds of the school. It was not that she didn't fit into the school because of her colour – nearly half of the girls were Asian or Afro-Caribbean. She didn't fit because she was too English, not because she wasn't English enough.

By the time Amina was born, her brothers and sisters were nearly old enough to leave home. Kept in at home in the afternoons and evenings, she never had the opportunity to meet other children her own age. The little corner shop where she lived made overwhelming demands on her parents; it was open until nine o'clock every evening, including Sundays, so until quite recently she was already in bed by the time her parents were free. Her evenings were not spent in the quiet enclosed Urdu world of other girls, or in the lively chattering groups of teenagers on the streets. Alone, she would sit watching television programmes, or she would wander in her mind through the dirty streets of the London of Dickens, or the hot, inexorable country lanes of Thomas Hardy. Amina's view of providence and circumstance had a pessimistic nineteenth-century colour. The Yorkshire moors of the Brontës had more life and dramatic conviction for her than the drab Midlands streets outside the shop, with its vandal-proof grill, its sturdy bolts and shabby, mismatched displays of sweets, cleaning materials and magazines.

And the people: Amina recognised the people from the television programmes when she saw them in the street. There was no doubt they were of the same type. But she never met the people from the books. She hoped one day to go to London, so that she could see people like Mr Jaggers and Mr Jarndyce. She had never been to the country, so she didn't expect to meet the rough, strangely courteous people of Hardy books, but she never doubted they were there.

It was in the English lessons that she was able to ask about the people in the books. The teacher was always ready to spend time answering her endless questions. Sometimes he hadn't read a book she would ask about, especially some of the ones by Dickens, and

protestations *calling out.*

tolerated *put up with.*
digressions *private conversations.*

Urdu *principal language of Moslem Pakistanis.*

Dickens, Hardy *nineteenth-century English novelists.*
inexorable *never-ending.*
providence *fate.*
pessimistic *gloomy.*
Brontës *family of nineteenth-century English novelists.*
dramatic conviction *reality.*

Mr Jaggers and Mr Jarndyce *characters in Dickens's novels.*
courteous *polite.*

this surprised her. But he knew so many other books and stories that he was able to keep her moving all the time to new people. He seemed to know all there was to know about life and about the people in it. Often he gave her his own books to take home. Once he had caused her to be beaten by her father.

He gave her a book by a man called Lawrence, telling her that Lawrence was a great writer who understood all about people. And so, because she trusted the teacher, and because he knew so much, she took the book home. It was called *Sons and Lovers*. She knew she would have to keep it hidden.

As she read the book, Amina felt herself growing in understanding. Her mind became clear for the first time. The people in the other books she had admired seemed to distort as she read until she saw them as grotesque parodies of living people. For the first time, she felt distant from them and, although this was only the beginning of an historical sense, at the time it was like a realisation of the absolute. At home, religion had been part of the atmosphere she had breathed, but it had never entered into her heart. This book was like an ecstasy of insight. It was a revelation. No longer would she look in the streets for people who could not exist, people who moved through a photograph of the past, slipping through the pages of books into the everyday life of a Pakistani girl isolated from both her family and those of her own age and experience. From now she would see real people and it was her teacher she must thank. It was the teacher who had understood first and then shown her.

But the book was first to break into the intimate stability of her family. She had taken every care to conceal it, with its suggestive title. When the book was out of her schoolbag she never put it down. She would read it in the bathroom or at night when all the family was in bed and she was safe from disturbance. The violence that followed its discovery was like the arrest of a prisoner in a reign of terror.

Her bedroom door was pushed open, slamming against the wall with the force of the entrant. Before she could turn, half-awake, Amina was grabbed by the arm and pulled up in bed. Losing her balance, she nearly slipped over the edge onto the floor. Her father caught her and held her in a rigid embrace, slightly away from him.

There was anger in the man's face, and surprise and fear in the girl's. The sudden shock from sleep left a sensuous and yielding mark on her features. Her hair was in wild disorder and she fought to pull the bedclothes up to her chin.

"Yes. Look." Her father saw the direction of Amina's stare as her eyes focused after the jolt from sleep. "Look. Such a book. In your bag."

Amina was frightened, but she made no response to her father. Rather than causing his anger to abate, this silence seemed to increase it.

"You must answer," he demanded.

grotesque parodies *ugly distorted versions.*

an historical sense *an understanding of how the present has been shaped by the past.*

realisation of the absolute *discovering the whole truth about life.*

it was a revelation *it opened her eyes.*

intimate stability *closed security.*

suggestive *improper.*

sensuous *appealing.*

abate *die down.*

48

"You have not asked me anything," Amina replied in a steady voice.

Her father's hand rose to strike her, but he hit her only with more shrill words, not with any blow.

"Why do you read this? Where is it from? Who gives you such a book?"

The questions showered down and Amina made no attempt to answer any of them. At last the questions stopped and blows showered down in their place. Amina's mother tried to put herself between her husband and her daughter, but she was pushed away.

Through it all, Amina stayed silent. At last, it was over. The man left the room and the two women, one old and experienced in the brutality of life, the other young and fresh to its hurtful inequalities, stared after him. Amina's mother gathered the girl into her arms and rocked back and forth, crooning tunelessly.

brutality *cruelty.*

crooning *singing to herself.*

There was no hiding the truth. Amina's father eventually discovered the owner of the book. He complained to the school, and threatened to take his daughter away for the few months that remained to her before the law said that she could leave.

A smooth and carefully worded letter from the headmistress poured wine and oil on his wounded pride. Amina would certainly not be allowed to borrow any books of which her father might disapprove and her reading would all be checked by the headmistress herself. Proper respect would be given to the religious and cultural standards of such a caring home.

Amina's father felt able to allow her back to school. Amina was at first ashamed at the incident and she was afraid that the teacher would punish her in subtle and furtive ways. But nothing seemed altered. The life of the class went on as before. She still joined the small group of girls who paid attention while the others went their own ways. Slowly, she recovered her own pride and even grew to respect her teacher more. After all, he understood. He did not embarrass her with reference to the difficulty and he did not ask for the return of the damaged book. Within herself she held inviolate the insight she had gained from reading the book and the relationship with the one man who could teach her something about insight into other people and herself. At least there was one person who knew how she felt and who respected her.

subtle *clever, not easily noticed.*

furtive *sly, indirect.*

inviolate *unspoiled.*

She decided that although it would cause her great shame and would be difficult to express, somehow she would thank him. A few days before the end of term, when she would leave the school for ever, she lingered after lessons had finished to catch him alone in his classroom and to thank him, both for his teaching and for his discretion over the matter of the book.

When the noise of pupils banging down desk lids and shouting their goodbyes had died down, she made her way softly to his room to look in and see if there was a moment when he would be alone for her to speak. She made no sound as she drew near to the door. She didn't want to invent a lie if he wasn't alone.

discretion *keeping quiet.*

A few minutes later, she sped back along the corridor, paying no need to the slamming of her feet against the dusty floor or the shattered silence as the door swung shut after her.

That evening, she announced that things were still bad at school and that they expected her to read more bad books. She had learned her lesson she said, she did not want to be exposed any more to their dangerous teaching. Her father nodded agreement and asked no questions. The days remaining were few. By the time the school organised itself to object to her absence, term would be over and she would be free. He did not expect there would be any problem.

The next day Amina started work in the shop. For several nights she lay awake, tired from the day behind the counter, running over in her mind the conversation she had overheard as she had silently approached the classroom. Her teacher was speaking in a low voice, and she had strained to catch his words.

"Only a few days, thank God. What a hellish term."

"Glad it's over?" his colleague had asked, with little real interest.

"Fifth form lessons are always a pain. Most of them never want to learn. D'you know, this year I nearly got the sack." And he began the tale of Amina and the book. As he told it, the colleague's interest became genuine.

"Why did you do it?" the other teacher asked at last. "These Paki girls never come to anything. It's a waste of time sticking your neck out."

Her own teacher's face was hidden from Amina as she listened through the open door. She did not see the slight flinch he gave as the question was asked, almost as though a fist had been raised to strike him. There was a long pause before he answered.

flinch *quick movement, as if hurt.*

"You're probably right. Strange though. I used to think . . ."

But Amina's footsteps beating through the corridor meant that the sentence hung unfinished between them.

Thinking/Talking Points

▷ 'the wider world of boredom and neglect'
What do you think the writer means here?
What sort of lives does she think the girls will lead a year or so after leaving school?
What do you think they might remember with pleasure about their school years?

▷ Why do you think Amina spends so much time reading?
How do you think books help her?
In what ways do they distance her from her family?

▷ Just from what we are told in the story, see if you can explain why reading *Sons and Lovers* has such a different effect upon Amina from the books she has read before.
Which books/films have made a strong impression on you?

▷ How do you explain Amina's father's reaction to *Sons and Lovers*?
How do you think he would justify his behaviour? Do you think he had read the book?

▷ What impression are we given of the headmistress of Amina's school?

Assignments

Role-play (working in pairs)

○ Try putting yourself in Amina's father's position.
Imagine he goes up to Amina's school to see the English teacher to complain about the book she's been given.
What would his objections be? How do you think he would feel about the teacher? What views might he have about education? What sort of girl do you think he would want Amina to grow up into?
What other aspects of the school might he criticise?

How might the teacher react to such a visit?
How might he justify giving the book to Amina?
How might his idea of education be different from that of Amina's father?
How do you think the teacher would like Amina to grow up?
What do you think he might feel about Amina's upbringing?
How much of that would he feel able to talk about?

Improvise their conversation. If you have time to swap roles, you may like to try the conversation with two types of teacher : one who is defensive and rude, another who is understanding and caring.

○ The headmistress calls the young English teacher to her room.
Do you think her views about *Sons and Lovers* will be more like the English teacher's or more like those of Amina's father?
How will she react to Amina's father's complaints?
Will she be critical of the teacher or supportive?

Will the teacher be angry about the headmistress's decision to control the books Amina is allowed to read?
What will he want the headmistress to put in the letter?
Will the incident bring other issues to the surface?

Improvise their conversation. Experiment with different types of teacher/headmistress.

○ What do you think Amina would have said to her teacher if she had found him alone in his classroom? How do you think he would have responded?

51

English Literature

○ Write a series of diary entries made by Amina over the period of this story. Include details from the text but add plenty of ideas of your own: other things that happened; some of Amina's hopes and fears about the future; more of her feelings about her family, her religion and the school.

○ 'A smooth and carefully worded letter from the headmistress poured wine and oil on his wounded pride.'
Write the sort of letter you think Amina's father received.

English

○ *Dear Sir,*
Imagine you are one of the students who used to chat in Amina's class. Write a letter to your old English teacher telling him about your life a year on and your memories of life at school.

○ *All I Want Is the Truth!*
Write a story of your own in which there is a conflict between what school and what home say is right and in which a student is put into the difficult position where satisfying one will upset the other.

Some possible themes :
Mum/Dad says homework is a waste of time . . . you should be working in the shop/enjoying yourself/babysitting . . . *or* Mum/Dad complains that the school doesn't set enough homework so she/he sets extra;

School encourages you to stay on, parents think it's time you got a job;

What you're taught in English/History/RE/Sex Education lessons at school leads to arguments/confusion at home.

You may like to write from your own experience.

Some further reading

D.H. Lawrence   *Fanny and Annie*
Tickets Please
The Prussian Officer
Sons and Lovers
Women in Love

★

THE NIGHT OUT

You are having a snack in a motorway restaurant when through the window you see a group of motorcyclists pull in.
Write down half a dozen words or phrases to describe them.

How do you think bikers are thought of :
(a) by themselves (b) by people of your age (c) by their parents (d) by elderly people?

If you were writing a story in which a gang of bikers figured, how would you go about making the scenes on the road feel 'real'?

The Night Out

Me and Carpet were just finishing a game of pool, working out how to pinch another game before the kids who'd booked next, when Maniac comes across.

Maniac was playing at Hell's Angels again. Home-made swastikas all over his leathers and beer mats sewn all over his jeans. Maniac plays at everything, even biking. Don't know how we put up with him, but he hangs on. Bike Club's a tolerant lot.

tolerant *easy-going.*

"Geronimo says do you want go camping tonight?" chirps Maniac.

"Pull the other one," says Carpet. 'Cos the last we seen of Geronimo, he was pinching forks and spoons out of the Club canteen to stuff up Maniac's exhaust. So that when Maniac revved up, he'd think his big end had gone. Maniac always worries about his big end; always worries about everything. Some biker.

big end had gone *part of the engine had a fault.*

I'd better explain all these nicknames, before you think I'm potty. Geronimo's name is really Weston; which becomes Western; which becomes Indian chief; which becomes Geronimo. Carpet's real name is Matt; but he says when he was called Matt everybody trampled on him. Some chance. Carpet's a big hard kid; but he'd always help out a mate in trouble. Maniac's really called Casey equals crazy equals Maniac. Got it?

Anyway, Geronimo himself comes over laughing, having just fastened the club secretary to his chair by the back buckles of his leathers, and everyone's pissing themselves laughing, except the secretary who hasn't noticed yet . . .

"You game?" asks Geronimo.

game *willing.*

I was game. There was nowt else going on, except ten kids doing an all-male tribal dance right in front of the main amplifier of the disco. The rest had reached the stage where the big joke was to pour

somebody's pint into somebody else's crash helmet. Besides, it was a privilege to go anywhere with Geronimo; he could pull laughs out of the air.

"Half an hour; Sparwick chippie," said Geronimo, and we all made tracks for home. I managed seventy up the main street, watching for fuzz having a crafty fag in shop doorways. But there was nobody about except middle-aged guys in dirty raincoats staring in the windows of telly shops. What's middle age a punishment for? Is there no cure?

fuzz *police.*

At home, I went straight to my room and got my tent and sleeping bag. Don't know why I bothered. As far as Geronimo was concerned, a tent was just for letting down the guy ropes of, on wet nights. And a sleeping bag was for jumping on, once somebody got into it. I raided the larder and found the usual baked beans and hot dogs. My parents didn't eat either. They bought them for me camping, on condition that I didn't nick tomorrow's lunch.

Stuck me head in the lounge. Dad had his head stuck in the telly, worrying about the plight of the Vietnamese boat refugees. Some treat, after a hard week's work!

"Going camping. Seeya in morning."

"Don't forget your key. I'm not getting up for you in the middle of the night if it starts raining."

Which really meant, "I love you and take care not to break your silly neck 'cos I know what you're going to get up to." But he'd never say it, 'cos I've got him well trained. Me Mum made a worried kind of grab at the air, so I slammed down the visor of me helmet and went, yelling "Seeya in morning" again to drown her protests before she made them.

Moon was up, all the way to Sparwick chippie. Making the trees all silver down one side. Felt great, 'cos we were *going* somewhere. Didn't know where, but *somewhere*. Astronaut to Saturn, with Carpet and Geronimo . . . and Maniac? Well, nobody expected life to be perfect . . .

Carpet was there already. "What you got?" he said, slapping my top-box.

"Beans an' hot dogs. What you got?"

"Hot dogs an' beans."

"Crap!"

"Even that would make a change."

"No it wouldn't. We have that all week at the works canteen."

We sat side by side, revving up, watching the old grannies in their curlers and carpet-slippers coming out of the chippie, clutching their hot greasy packets to their boobs like they were babies, and yakking on about who's got cancer now.

"If I reach fifty, I'm goin' to commit suicide," said Carpet.

"Forty'll do me."

"Way you ride, you won't reach twenty."

Maniac rode up, sounding like a trade-in sewing machine. He immediately got off and started revving his bike, with his helmet shoved against his rear forks.

"What's up?"

"Funny noise."

"No funnier than usual," said Carpet. But he took his helmet off and got Maniac to rev her again, and immediately spotted it was the tins in Maniac's top-box that were making the rattling. "Bad case of Heinz," he muttered to me, but he said to Maniac, "Sounds like piston-slap. We'd better get the cylinder head off . . ."

Maniac turned as white as a sheet in the light from the chippie, but he started getting his toolkit out, 'cos he knew Carpet knew bikes.

Just as well Geronimo turned up then. Carpet's crazy; he'd sooner strip a bike than a bird . . .

"Where to then?" said Geronimo.

Nobody had a clue. Everybody had the same old ideas and got howled down. It's like that sometimes. We get stuck for a place to go. Then Maniac and Carpet started arguing about Jap bikes versus British, and you can't sink lower than that. In a minute they'd start eating their beans straight from the tins, tipping them up like cans of lager. Once the grub was gone, there'd be no point to going anywhere, and I'd be home before midnight and Dad would say was it morning already how time flies and all that middle-aged smarty-crap.

And Geronimo had lost interest in us and was watching the cars going past down the main road. If something interesting came past worth burning off, like a Lamborghini or even a Jag XJ12, we wouldn't see him again for the rest of the night.

burning off *race against.*

So I said I knew where there was a haunted abbey. I felt a bit of a rat, 'cos that abbey was a big thing with Dad. He was a mate of the guy who owned it and he'd taken me all over it and it was a fascinating place and God knew what Geronimo would do to it . . . but we'd got to go somewhere.

"What's it haunted by?" Geronimo put his helmet against mine, so his voice boomed. But he was interested.

"A nun. There was a kid riding past one night, and this tart all clad in white steps out right under his front wheel and he claps his anchors on but he goes straight into her and arse over tip. Ruins his enamel. But when he went back there was nothing there."

claps his anchors on *brakes hard.*

enamel *paintwork.*

"Bollocks," said Geronimo. "But I'll go for the sex interest. What's a nun doing in an *abbey*? He was no fool, Geronimo. He could tell a Carmelite from a camshaft when he had to.

abbey *religious house (Geronimo mistakenly thinks only for monks).*

Carmelite *a reclusive order of nuns.*

camshaft *part of an engine.*

"Ride along," he said, and took off with me on his shoulder, which is great, like fighter pilots in the war. And I watched the street lights sliding curved across his black helmet, and the way he changed gear smart as a whip. He got his acceleration with a long hard burst in second.

I found them the abbey gate and opened it and left it for Maniac to close. "Quiet – there's people living here."

"Throttle-down," said Geronimo.

throttle-down *reduce speed.*

56

But Maniac started going on about the abbey being private property and trespass; a real hero.

"Have a good trip home," said Geronimo. "Please drive carefully."

Maniac flinched like Geronimo'd hit him. Then mumbled "OK. Hang on a minute, then."

Everybody groaned. Maniac was a big drinker, you see. Shandy-bitter. Lemonade. He'd never breathalyse in a million years. But it made him burp all the time, like a clapped-out Norton Commando. And he was always having to stop and go behind hedges. Only he was scared to stop, in case we shot off without him. That time, we let him get started, and *went*. Laughing so we could hardly ride, 'cos he'd be pissing all over his bulled-up boots in a panic.

It was a hell of a ride, 'cos the guy who owned the abbey kept his drive all rutted, to discourage people like us. Geronimo went up on his foot rests like a jockey, back straight as a ruler. Nobody could ride like Geronimo; even my Dad said he rode like an Apache.

It was like scrambling; just Geronimo's straight back and the tunnel of trees ahead, white in the light of Geronimo's quartz-halogen, and the shining red eyes of rabbits and foxes staring out at us, then shooting off. And our three engines so quiet, and Maniac far behind, revving up like mad, trying to catch up. I wished it could go on forever till a sheet of water shot up inside my leathers so cold I forgot if I was male or female . . .

Geronimo had found a rut full of water, and soaked me beautifully. He was staring back at me, laughing through his visor. And here was another rut coming up. Oh, hell – it was lucky I always cleaned my bike on Saturday mornings. Anyway, he soaked me five times, but I soaked him once, and I got Carpet twice. And Maniac caught up; and then fell off when Carpet got *him*. And then we were at the abbey.

A great stretch of moonlit grass, sweeping down to the river. And the part the monks used to live in, which was now a stately home, away on the right all massive and black, except where our lights shone on hundreds and hundreds of windows. And the part that used to be the abbey church was on the left. Henry the Eighth made them pull that all down, so there was nothing left but low walls, and the bases of columns sticking out of the turf about as high as park benches, like black rotten teeth. And at the far end of that was a tall stone cross.

"That's the Nun's Grave," I said. "But it's not really. Just some old bits and pieces of the abbey that they found in the eighteenth century and put together to make a good story . . ."

"Big 'ead," said Geronimo. "Let's have a look." He climbed onto the base of the first column; and, waving his arms about, leapt for the base of the second column. Screaming like a banshee. "I AAAAAMM the Flying Nun." It was a fantastic leap; about twelve feet. He made it, though his boots scrawped heavily on the sandstone blocks. I shuddered, and looked towards the house. Luckily, there wasn't a light showing. Country people went to bed early. I hoped.

breathalyse *have one's breath tested for traces of alcohol by the police.*

Norton Commando *old make of motorcycle.*

rutted *full of ridges and dips.*

Apache *tribe of North American Indians famous for skilled horsemanship.*

scrambling *riding over rough terrain.*

quartz-halogen *bright headlamp.*

rut *hollow.*

banshee *ominously wailing Irish female spirit.*

57

"I AAAAAAAMMM the Flying Nun," wailed Geronimo, "and I'm in LOOOOOOVE with the Flying Abbot. But I'm cheating on him with the Flying Doctor."

He attempted another death-defying leap, missed his footing, and nearly ruined his married future.

"Amendment," said Carpet. "He *was* the Flying Nun."

amendment correction.

"Never fear. The Flying Nun will fly again," croaked Geronimo from the grass. His helmet appeared to have turned back to front, and he was holding his crotch painfully.

"Amendment," said Carpet. "The Flying Soprano will fly again."

soprano singer with a high voice.

We were all so busy falling about (even Maniac had stopped worrying about trespass) that we didn't see the bloke at first. But there he was, standing in the shadow of his great house, screaming like a nut-case.

"Hooligans! Vandals!" Sounded like he was having a real fit.

"Is that that mate of yours?" Carpet asked me.

"Mate of my Dad's," I said.

"Your Dad knows some funny people. Is he an outpatient, or has he climbed over the wall?" Carpet turned to the distant raging figure and amiably pointed the two fingers of scorn.

He shouldn't have done that. Next second, a huge four-legged shape came tearing towards us over the grass. Doing a ton with its jaws wide open and its rotten great fangs shining in the moonlight. It didn't make a sound; not like any ordinary dog. And the little figure by the house was shouting things like, "Kill, kill, kill!" He didn't seem at all like the guy I met when Dad took me round the house . . .

doing a ton at a hundred miles an hour.

Maniac turned and scarpered. Geronimo was still lying on the grass trying to get his helmet straight. And the rotten great dog was making straight at him. I couldn't move.

scarpered ran off.

But Carpet did. He ran and straddled over Geronimo. Braced himself, and he was a big lad; there was thirteen stone of him.

straddled stood with his legs apart.

The dog leapt, like they do in the movies. Carpet thrust his gauntleted fist right up its throat. Carpet rocked, but he didn't fall. The dog was chewing on his glove like mad, studs and all.

gauntleted wearing a heavy glove.

"Naughty doggy," said Carpet reprovingly, and gave it a terrific clout over the ear with his other hand.

reprovingly telling him off.

Two more clouts and the dog stopped chewing. Three, and it let go. Then Carpet kicked it in the ribs. Sounded like the big bass drum.

"Heel, Fido!" said Carpet.

The dog went for Geronimo, who was staggering to his feet; and got Carpet's boot again. It fell back, whimpering.

The next second, a tiny figure was flailing at Carpet. "Leave my dog *alone*. How *dare* you hit my dog. I'll have the RSPCA on you — that's all you hooligans are good for, mistreating dogs." He was literally foaming at the mouth. "I don't know what this country's coming to . . ."

flailing striking out.

"It's going to the dogs," said Carpet. He pushed the man gently away with one great hand, and held him at arm's length. "Look,

58

mate," he said sadly, wagging one finger of a well-chewed gauntlet, "take the Hound of the Baskervilles home. It's time for his Meaty Chunks . . ."

Hound of the Baskervilles *gigantic ghostly dog in a story by Conan Doyle.*

"I am going," spluttered the little guy, "to call the police."

"I would, mate," said Carpet. "There's a highly dangerous dog loose round here somewhere . . ."

The pair of them slunk off. Maniac returned from the nearest bushes, to the sound of cheers. Geronimo slapped Carpet on the shoulder and said "Thanks, mate," in a voice that had me green with envy. And we all buggered off. After we had ridden three times round the house for luck. Including the steps in the formal garden.

"There's another way out," I said, "at the far end."

The far drive seemed to go on forever. Or was it that we were riding slowly, because Carpet was having trouble changing gear with his right hand. I think the dog had hurt him right through the glove; but that was not something Carpet would ever admit.

Just before we went out through the great gates, with stone eagles on their gateposts, we passed a white Hillman Imp, parked on the right well off the road, under the big horse-chestnut trees of the avenue. It seemed empty as we passed, though, oddly enough, it had its sunshields down, which was a funny thing to happen at midnight.

Hillman Imp *make of small car.*

Outside, Geronimo held up his right hand, US Cavalry-fashion, and we all stopped.

"Back," said Geronimo. "Lights out. Throttle down. Quiet."

"What?"

But he was gone back inside. All we could do was follow. It was lucky the moon was out when he stopped. Or we'd all have driven over him and flattened him.

"*What?*" we all said again.

But he just said, "Push your bikes."

We all pushed our bikes, swearing at him.

"Quiet!"

The white Hillman glimmered up in the moonlight.

"Thought so," said Geronimo. A white arm appeared for a moment, behind the steering wheel and vanished again.

Maniac sniggered.

"You can't *do* it," said Carpet. "Not in a Hillman Imp!"

"You have a wide experience of Hillman Imps?" asked Geronimo.

"Let's stay and watch," said Maniac.

Carpet and I looked at Geronimo uneasily.

"What do you think *I* am?" said Geronimo, crushing Maniac like he was a beetle. "Mount up, lads. Right. Lights, sound, music, enter the villain."

Four headlamps, three of them quartz-halogen, coned in on the Imp. I noticed it was L-reg. It shone like day, but for a long moment nothing else happened.

coned in *focused on.*

Then a head appeared; a bald head, with beady eyes and a rat-trap mouth. Followed by a naked chest, hairy as a chimpanzee. The eyes glared; a large fist was raised and shaken.

"Switch off," said Geronimo. "And *quiet.*"

We sat and listened. There was the mother and father of a row going on inside the Imp.

"Drive me *home!*"

"It was nothing. Just a car passing. They've gone now."

We waited; the voices got lower and lower. Silence.

"Start your engines," said Geronimo. *"Quietly."*

"What for?" asked Maniac plaintively.

"You'll see," said Geronimo, and laughed with pure delight.

He and Carpet and me had electric starter motors; which of course started us quietly, first press of the button. Good old Jap-crap. Maniac, buying British and best, had to kick his over and over again.

"I'm going to buy you a new flint for that thing," said Carpet.

Maniac's bike started at last.

"Lights," said Geronimo.

There was a wild scream; then an even wilder burst of swearing. The bald head reappeared. The car-lights came on; its engine started and revved.

"Move!" shouted Geronimo, curving his bike away between the tree-trunks.

"Why?" yelled Maniac.

"He'll never live to see twenty," said Carpet, as we turned together through the branches, neat as a pair of performing dolphins.

Then the Imp was after us, screeching and roaring in second gear fit to blow a gasket.

blow a gasket *damage the engine.*

We went out of those gates like Agostini, down through the slumbering hamlet of Blackdore and up towards the moors. We were all riding four-hundreds, and we could have lost the Imp in ten seconds. But it was more fun to dawdle at seventy, watching the Imp trying to catch up. God, it was cornering like a lunatic, right over on the wrong side of the road. Another outpatient got over the wall. Even more than most motorists, that is.

Agostini *fifteen times world motorcycle racing champion.*

hamlet *tiny village.*

four-hundreds *400cc : bikes with powerful engines.*

dawdle *ride along slowly.*

And old Maniac was not keeping up. That bloody British bike of his; that clapped-out old Tiger was missing on one rotten cylinder.

missing *not firing.*

He was lagging further and further behind. The Imp's lights seemed to be drawing alongside his. He was riding badly, cowering against the hedge, not leaving himself enough room to get a good line into his corners. I knew how he'd be feeling; mouth dry as brickdust; knees and hands shaking almost beyond control.

cowering *hiding away.*

Then the Imp did draw alongside, and made a tremendous side-swipe at him, trying to knock him off into the hedge at seventy. The guy in the Imp was trying to kill Maniac. And there was nothing we could do. I pulled alongside Carpet and pointed behind. But Carpet had seen already and didn't know what to do either.

Then Geronimo noticed. Throttled back, waved us through. In my rear-view mirror I watched him drop further and further back, until he seemed just in front of the Imp's bumper. Up went two fingers. Again and again. He put his thumb to his nose and waggled his fingers. I swear he did – I saw them in silhouette against the Imp's lights; though afterwards Carpet made out I couldn't have done and that it was something I made up.

At last, the Imp took notice; forgot Maniac cowering and limping beside the hedge, and came after Geronimo.

"Out to the left," gestured Carpet, and we shot off down a side road, turned and came back behind the lunatic's car.

So we saw it all in comfort. Oh, Geronimo could have walked away from him; Geronimo could do a hundred and ten if he liked. But just as he was going to, he saw this riding school in a field on the left, on the outskirts of the next village, Chelbury. You know the kind of place – all white-painted oildrums and red-and-white striped poles where little female toffs try to learn to show-jump.

toffs *rich people.*

In went Geronimo. Round and round went Geronimo. Round the barrels, under the poles. And round and round went the Imp. Into the barrels and smashing the poles to smithereens. He couldn't drive for toffee – like a mad bull in a china-shop and Geronimo the bull-fighter. *Boing, boing, boing* went the drums. Splinter, splinter, splinter in the moonlight went the poles.

smithereens *tiny fragments.*

Geronimo could have gone on forever. But lights were coming on in the houses; curtains being pulled back on the finest display of trick-riding the villagers of Chelbury will ever see – not that they'd have the sense to appreciate it.

Just as Maniac turned up, minus a bit of paint, we heard the siren of the cop car. Some toffee-nosed gent had been on the phone.

Of course the cop car, bumping across the grass through the shambles, made straight for Geronimo; the fuzz always blame the motorcyclist and the Imp had stopped its murder-attempts by that time.

toffee-nosed *upper-class, snooty.*

shambles *wreckage.*

"You young lunatic," said the fuzz getting out, "You've caused damage worth thousands . . ."

Geronimo gestured at his bike, which hadn't a scratch on it in the cop car's headlights. Then he nodded at the Imp, which had four feet of striped pole stuck inside its front bumper.

Then the fuzz noticed that the guy at the wheel was completely starkers. And that there was a long-haired blonde on the back seat trying to put her jumper on inside out and back to front. The fuzz kept losing his grip on the situation every time the blonde wriggled. Well, they're human too. All very enjoyable . . .

starkers *naked.*

We got back to Carpet's place about seven, still laughing so much we were wobbling all over the road. We always end up at Carpet's place after a night out. It's a nice little detached bungalow on top of a hill. And we always weave round and round Carpet's Dad's crazy paving, revving like mad. And Carpet's Mum always throws open the one upstairs window and leans out in her blue dressing-gown, and asks what the hell we want. And Geronimo always asks, innocent-like, "This is the motorway café, isn't it?" And Carpet's

Mum always calls him a cheeky young tyke, and comes down and lets us in and gives us cans of lager and meat pies while she does a great big fry-up for breakfast. And we lie about till lunchtime with our boots on the furniture, giving her cheek, and she's loving it and laughing. I used to wonder why she put up with us, till I realized she was just that glad to have Carpet back alive.

And that was our night out.

On Monday night, when I got home from work, Dad took me in the front room alone. I knew something was up. Had the guy from the abbey rumbled us? But Dad gave me a whisky, and I knew it was worse.

He told me Geronimo was dead; killed on his bike. I wouldn't believe it. No bastard motorist could ever get Geronimo.

Then he told me how it happened. On a bend, with six-foot stone walls either side. Geronimo was coming home from work in the dark. He'd have been tired. He was only doing fifty; on his right side, two feet out from the kerb. The police could tell from the skid marks.

The car was only a lousy Morris Marina. Overtaking on a blind corner. The driver didn't stop; but the other driver got his number. When the police breathalysed him, he was pissed to the eyeballs.

I believed it then; and I cried.

We gave him a real biker's funeral. A hundred and seventy bikes followed him through town, at ten miles an hour, two by two. I've never seen such disciplined riding. Nobody fell off; though a few of the lads burned their clutches out. We really pinned this town's ears back. They know what bikers are now; bikers are *together*.

The Pope died about that time. The Pope only had twelve motorbike outriders; Geronimo had a hundred and seventy. If he met the Pope, in some waiting room or other, Geronimo would have pointed that out. But laughing, mind. He was always laughing, Geronimo.

Afterwards, we all went back to the Club and got the drinks in. Then there was a bloody horrible silence; the lads were really down, like I've never seen them. It was terrible.

Then Fred, the Club secretary, gets to his feet, and points at the pool table, where Geronimo used to sit, putting the players off their stroke by wriggling his backside.

"If he was standing there," said Fred, "if he could see you now, d'you know what he'd say? He'd say, 'What you being so piss-faced for, you stupid nerks?'" And suddenly, though nobody saw or heard anything, he *was* there, and it was all right. And everybody was falling over themselves to tell Geronimo-stories and laughing.

We all went to the court case too, all in our gear. The Clerk to the Court tried to have us thrown out; but one or two of us have got a few O Levels, and enough sense to hire our own lawyer. Who told the Clerk to the Court where he got off. We were all British citizens, of voting age, as good as anybody else. Har-har.

tyke *riff-raff.*

rumbled us *found out who we were.*

pissed to the eyeballs *very drunk.*

pinned this town's ears back *made everyone take notice.*

piss-faced *sombre.*
nerks *fools.*

And the police proved everything against the driver of the Marina. He lost his licence, of course. Then the judge said six months' imprisonment.

Then he said sentence suspended for two years . . .

suspended *to be enforced only if there is another offence.*

Why? 'Cos he was middle-aged and big and fat with an expensive overcoat and a posh lawyer? 'Cos he belonged to the same golf-club as the judge?

The lads gave a kind of growl. The Clerk was shaking so much he couldn't hold his papers. So was the Marina-driver, who'd been whispering and grinning at his lawyer till then.

The Clerk began shouting for silence; going on about contempt of court. Fred got up. He's sixteen stone of pure muscle, and he's about forty-five with a grown-up son in the Club.

"Not contempt, your honour. More disgust, like."

I think the lads might have gone too far then. But Geronimo's Mum (she looked very like him) put her hand on Fred's arm and asked him to take her home. And when Fred went we all followed; though a few fingers went up in the air behind backs.

Maniac and Carpet and me tried going on riding together. But it didn't work out. Whenever we rode together, there was a sort of terrible hole formed, where Geronimo should be. Maniac went off and joined the Merchant Navy, 'cos he couldn't stand this town any more. He still sends Carpet and me postcards from Bahrein and Abu Dhabi (clean ones too!). And we put them on the mantlepiece and forget them.

Carpet and I went on riding; even bought bigger bikes. I still see him sometimes, but we never stop for more than two minutes' chat.

But when I ride alone, that's different. You see you can't hear very much inside your helmet, when your engine's running. And the helmet cuts down your view to the side as well. So when we need to talk to each other on the move, we have to pull alongside and yell and yell. And when you first notice a guy doing that, it oftens comes over funny. Well, I keep thinking I hear him; that he's just lurking out of the corner of my eye. I just know he's somewhere about; you *can't* kill someone like Geronimo.

I got engaged last week. Jane's a good lass, but she made one condition. That I sell my bike and buy a car. She says she wants me to live to be a grandfather. And when my Mum heard her say it, she suddenly looked ten years younger.

So I'm taking this last ride to the abbey in the moonlight, and I've just passed Sparwick chippie. And the moon is making one side of the trees silver, and I'm *going* somewhere. Only I'm not going with Geronimo; I'm getting further away from Geronimo all the time. Nearer to the old grannies with their hair in curlers coming out of the chippie, clutching their hot greasy bundles. The middle-aged guys staring in the telly-shop windows.

And I'm not sure I like it.

☆

Thinking/Talking Points : looking closely at the text

▷ What is unusual about the style in which *The Night Out* is written?
What do you think a story gains/loses from being written like that?

▷ Pick out three examples of *technical* detail from the story.
See how precisely you can explain in simple English what they mean.
Why do you think Robert Westall uses such details?

▷ 'Maniac plays at everything, even biking.'
What do you think this means?
From what we are told about Maniac in the story, how would you describe
him? Why do you think the others put up with him?

▷ Pick out half a dozen things we are told about Carpet (Matt).
At what point in the story do we learn most about him?
What do you like/dislike about him?

▷ '. . . it was a privilege to go anywhere with Geronimo; he could pull laughs out
of the air.'
What are some examples of Geronimo's sense of fun?
Which details give you the strongest impression of him?
Do you like him? Give your reasons.

▷ 'What's middle age a punishment for? Is there no cure?'
How does the story-teller feel about getting old?
See if you can put this bit into your own words.

▷ Look again at the passage which begins
'Going camping. Seeya in morning.'
and ends
'. . . to drown her protests before she made them.' (page 55)
What is your impression of the story-teller's relationship with his parents?

▷ 'We sat side by side, revving-up, watching the old grannies in their curlers and
carpet-slippers coming out of the chippie, clutching their hot greasy packets to
their boobs like they were babies, and yakking on about who's got cancer now.'
Imagine that, as the boys sat there, a bunch of schoolgirls *or* a middle-aged
businessman in a smart suit *or* an old man came out of the chippie.
Write a description of one of them in a similar style.

▷ 'I felt a bit of a rat, 'cos that abbey was a big thing with Dad.'
Can you remember a situation in which you felt you'd let down your parents
by giving something away to your friends?

▷ 'Maniac was a big drinker, you see. Shandy-bitter. Lemonade.'
What tone of voice would you read this sentence in?

▷ Look at the paragraph which begins
'A great stretch of moonlit grass, sweeping down to the river . . .' (page 57)
How many different bits of information are we given in this paragraph?
What impression does it give you of the abbey?

▷ 'Geronimo slapped Carpet on the shoulder and said, "Thanks, mate," in a voice
that had me green with envy.'
Why do you think the narrator feels envious?

▷ '. . . we passed a white Hillman Imp . . . oddly enough it had its sunshields down, which was a funny thing to happen at midnight.'
What is your explanation of this odd fact?

▷ See if you can describe in your own words exactly what Geronimo did after he noticed the driver of the Imp trying to force Maniac off the road up to the point where the policeman arrived (page 60).

▷ How would you describe Carpet's Mum?

▷ Imagine you were the motorist who saw the accident in which Geronimo died. Describe what you saw.

▷ What impression are we given of the driver of the Morris Marina?

▷ 'Not contempt, your honour. More disgust, like.'
See if you can explain what Fred meant when he said this to the judge.

▷ How would you describe the story-teller's feelings at the end of the story?

Assignments

English

○ *The Night Out*
Write a story about a group of friends enjoying themselves on a Saturday night. Decide on three or four strong, very different personalities.
Think about their appearance, their behaviour, the way they talk. Try to make each one an individual.
Think about how they will/will not get on with each other. What will they argue about? How will they deal with 'outsiders'?
Decide on two or three 'settings' : perhaps a friend's house, the town centre, a deserted factory. Think about how you will create a strong sense of the atmosphere of each place.
Do not include so much 'action' that it becomes unbelievable. Try to use some technical detail to make the story sound authentic. For example, the friends might be discussing a match or a gig or a place they have visited. Make your characters sound as if they know what they are talking about – as the bikers here clearly do about their machines.
You may like to write (as Robert Westall did) as if you were one of the group.

English Literature

○ *A Biker's Farewell*
Write and illustrate a newspaper story about Geronimo's funeral.
In your report, describe the funeral procession. Discuss the way the residents of the town reacted to it. Quote from your interviews with some of Geronimo's friends. Refer to the coming court case. Does the boy come across as a local hero or as a local hooligan?

○ Essay : What impression does Robert Westall's story *The Night Out* give you of Geronimo?
Were you moved by the ending of the story? Why?

(Look at what Geronimo does and says in the story. Look at the way other people, especially the story-teller, feel about him. Use half a dozen brief quotations from the story to give your essay a shape.)

○ Talking about this story, Robert Westall said :
'Motorcyclists fascinate me. I'm very proud to be President of the Cheshire Albion Motorcycle Club. They're very generous with their technical chat – I couldn't have written the story without them . . .'
Pick out two or three passages from the story which you found exciting. Write about the way Robert Westall has used technical knowledge to make these bits convincing.

○ Using the characters in *A Night Out*, invent your own *Geronimo Story*.

○ Write or improvise the conversation in which the police interview the driver (and/or the passenger) of the Hillman Imp.

Some further reading

Robert Westall	*The Haunting of Chas McGill and Other Stories*
S.E. Hinton	*Rumble Fish*
Poems	
Thom Gunn	*The Unsettled Motorcyclist's Vision of His Death*
	On The Move
	Black Jackets
	Blackie, The Electric Rembrandt
David Holbrook	*Unholy Marriage*

★

Dickinson

WHAT ELSE MIGHT HAVE HAPPENED TO LITTLE RED RIDING HOOD?

Most of the stories in this collection explore human relationships : people the reader can identify with, involved in situations which are true to life.

But sometimes it can be fun to push reality aside, to simplify characters and relationships and invent complicated, fantastic, sometimes ridiculous plots just to engage what Agatha Christie's Inspector Poirot calls 'the little grey cells'.

Our advice in the first unit was to write a story in which there were very few events so that the personalities and situations you wrote about could develop convincingly. In the next three parts, we will see what can be done just with a plot.

Here's a story you may have heard before :

The Three Little Pigs

Once upon a time, there were three little pigs. They lived happily at home with their mother and father until one day the van from the bacon factory called and the three little pigs found themselves all alone in the world.

"If they think I'm sticking around here, waiting to be eaten, they must have swallowed too many pot noodles," said the eldest little pig, whose name was Fatty. "Fatty's got brains," said Rasher, his hare-brained younger brother. "I reckon we'd better go and live with Aunt Porker."

"She's probably next on the hit list," mumbled the darkest, slyest, youngest, little pig, Smoky. "The only sensible thing to do is split up and keep our heads down. These supermarkets are pretty ruthless. One glimpse of a curly pink tail and 'Vroom!' you're in little plastic envelopes on special offer.

So the three little pigs disguised themselves as first time buyers and went off to find somewhere to live.

Soon they met a man with a dilapidated Ford Transit full of straw. "So what are you asking for the straw?" asked Fatty, waving his credit card in the air, "I want to build me a house."

"To you, for the smartest little house in Purly, five quid," said the van driver, who couldn't believe his luck. He'd been taking the straw to be burnt when the van got a puncture.

So Fatty quickly built himself a house of straw.

"Eat your heart out, Mr Tesco," said Fatty and shut the door.

Rasher and Smoky carried on their way. "I liked the utility room but it didn't look very substantial, did it?" said Rasher.

"Could be a bit whiffy if it rains," commented Smoky.

Then they met a man who was carrying some sticks.

"Carry your sticks for you, if you like," said Rasher, winking significantly at Smoky.

"Whatever turns you on," said the man, who was sweating buckets.

But as soon as the man's back was turned, Rasher and Smoky charged off with the sticks and lost the man in the underpass.

Smoky helped Rasher build a house of sticks. "Sure you wouldn't like to rent the attic?" asked Rasher as they finished fitting the bidet.

"I've never told you this before," said Smoky. "But you really could use a deodorant. And you snore fit to wake Mum and Dad. Reckon I'll find a place of my own."

So Smoky strolled along until he saw a huge Jones and Finch lorry unloading bricks at a building site.

"You the blokes from Jones and Finch?" asked Smoky. "Got the wrong site again, haven't we?" he continued before the men had time to think.

"Bovary Road South, two miles beyond the Raskolnikov Estate. Big field with grass and stuff in it. You can't miss it. On second thoughts, give me a lift and I'll show you the way."

So, to cut a long story short, Smoky built himself a smart bungalow of bricks.

Six months later, the man from Sainsbury's consulted his schedule.

"Fatty, Rasher and Smoky are due for the chop, fillet, slice and the left overs can go into the dog food," he said to Mr Leer, the butcher. "Send out Nasty and Face in the van."

Now although the three little pigs were resourceful, they were also dumb. They should never have sent Change of Address cards to Aunt Porker. Especially as they knew she was due for a visit from the van which never smiled. So it didn't take Nasty and Face long before they discovered where each of them lived.

Assignment

○   Individually, or in small groups, write the rest of the story.
To remind you, these are the traditional ingredients :
> The Big Bad Wolf says "Little pig, little pig, let me come in."
>
> "No, no," says the little pig. "By the hair of my chinny chin chin, I will not let you in."
>
> "Then I'll huff and I'll puff and I'll blow your house in," says the Wolf.
>
> And he huffs and he puffs, and he huffs and he puffs and the house of straw (and then the house of sticks) collapses and the Wolf eats the pig.
>
> But when the Wolf repeats the performance with the house of bricks, he just gets out of breath. Realising that this is a clever little pig, he pretends to be friendly. He tries to trap the little pig in various ways but each time he is outwitted.
>
> Finally, in desperation, the Wolf clambers onto the roof and starts to climb down the chimney. The pig realises what the Wolf is up to and puts a huge pan of boiling water on the fire. The Wolf tumbles in.

Some further reading

Jan Mark   *William's Version*

As you can see, concentrating on plot can lead to endless complications; from a small seed, a giant tree of a saga can develop. Just doodling with a plan suggests dozens of possible developments when the personalities involved are simple and the situation fantastic.

Here's what Peter Dickinson came up with as he wondered how else that popular story of *Little Red Riding Hood* could have turned out.
Here is a summary of one familiar version:
> Little Red Riding Hood is asked by her mother to take some cakes to her grandmother who is ill. She sets off through the forest, remembering her mother's warning to beware of the Big Bad Wolf.
>
> Red Riding Hood meets the Wolf who asks her where she is going.
>
> "To visit my sick grandmother," she replies.
>
> The Wolf runs ahead of Little Red Riding Hood, eats her Grandmother and climbs into Grandmother's bed, disguised in the old Lady's clothes.
>
> Little Red Riding Hood sees through the disguise and runs into the forest, pursued by the Wolf. A Huntsman hears her screams, comes to the rescue, kills the Wolf.
>
> They all live happily ever after.

Peter Dickinson's chart follows on the next page.

69

What Else Might Have Happened to Little Red Riding Hood?

R = Red Riding Hood, W = Wolf, G = Grandmother, H = Huntsman,
P = Prince, T = Toad. (There is more than one W in the forest.)

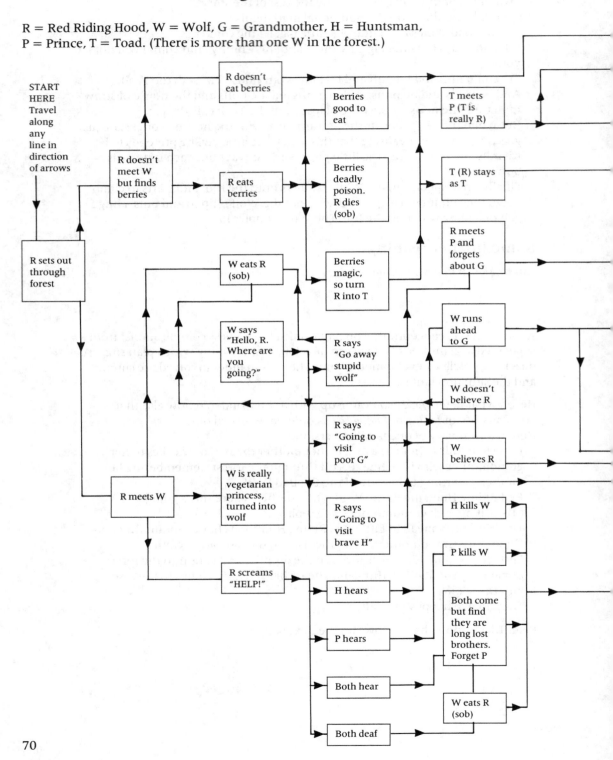

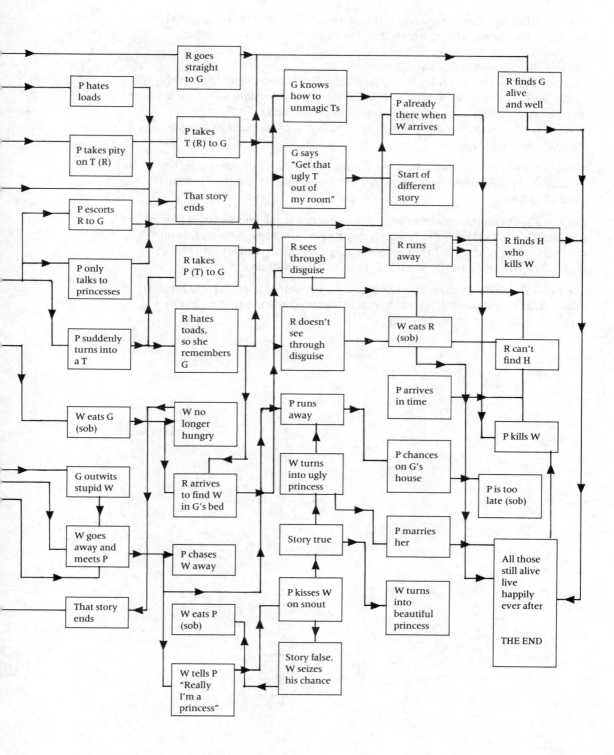

Assignments

○ Take another familiar story, reduce it to a plot outline and then make a chart like Peter Dickinson's from which could develop dozens of alternative storylines.

Some plots you might like to experiment with :

Jack and Jill Went up The Hill; Three Blind Mice; Doctor Foster Went to Gloucester; O Soldier Soldier, Will You Marry Me?; Hansel and Gretel; Dick Wittington; Snow White and the Seven Dwarfs; Jack and the Beanstalk; Goldilocks and the Three Bears; Cinderella; The Gingerbread Boy; The Ugly Duckling; Charlie and the Chocolate Factory; The Wizard of Oz . . .

If you need to remind yourself of the details of a story, The *Ladybird* series includes very simple versions of most traditional children's tales. They are in most libraries.

○ Choose a set of characters from one of the popular children's series of stories (e.g. *Postman Pat; Thomas the Tank Engine and Friends; Paddington Bear*) and write *either* a 'straight' children's story, using the setting and style of the original stories *or* a parody, intended for a teenage audience.

○ Use Peter Dickinson's chart to write a revised version of the story of *Little Red Riding Hood* in a style which you think a modern young reader would enjoy. You may like to illustrate the story.

COMPUTERS DON'T ARGUE

Assignment

This activity can be done singly or working in pairs.

○   Here is a story written in an unusual way.
You work for Pick, Sift and Scrutin, a firm of private detectives. The firm has been hired by a Mrs W. Childs to investigate what has happened to her husband. She has returned to her home in Illinois, USA, after a long holiday with her sister in India to discover the house empty, her husband nowhere. Two days ago, she received this extraordinary letter :

ILLINOIS STATE PENITENTIARY
Joliet
Illinois

August 4th, 1995

Dear Mrs Children,

Following the execution of <u>your husband</u> on <u>July 1st, 1995</u> please find enclosed account in the sum of <u>$4000</u> in respect of <u>funeral and other expenses</u>. Your cheque for the full amount should reach us within <u>fourteen days</u> to avoid penalty.

Yours respectfully and with condolence,

E.E. Smith.

E.E. Smith (Ms), Mortuary Clerk

Mrs Childs is utterly confused. She had no idea her husband had done anything to land himself in prison; indeed he was such a law-abiding and timid man that she naturally assumes there has been some mistake. Yet no-one seems to know where he is and none of the departments she has contacted has been able to give her any information.

What she has found is this bundle of documents.
See if by sorting through them you are able to come up with an explanation of what happened to Mr Walter Childs.

Exhibit 1

I, HUBERT DANIEL WILLIKENS *, Governor of the State of Illinois, and invested with the authority and powers appertaining thereto, including the power to pardon those in my judgement wrongfully convicted or otherwise deserving of executive mercy, do this day of* 1 JULY 1995 *announce and proclaim that* WALTER A. CHILD (A. WALTER) *now in custody as a consequence of erroneous conviction upon a crime of which he is entirely innocent, is fully and freely pardoned of said crime. And I do direct the necessary authorities having custody of the said* WALTER A. CHILD (A. WALTER) *in whatever place or places he may be held, to immediately free, release, and allow unhindered departure to him . . .*

Interdepartmental Routing Service

Exhibit 2

CRIMINAL RECORDS DIVISION
POLICE DEPARTMENT
CHICAGO, ILLINOIS

June 6 1995

To: United States Statistics Office
Attn: Information Division
Subject: RE. File no. 189623

NO FURTHER INFORMATION REQUIRED

thank you.

Records Search Unit

Exhibit 3

NOTES

TO POLICE DEPARTMENT, PANDUCK, MICHIGAN

REFERENCE YOUR REQUEST TO PICK UP AND HOLD A. (COMPLETE FIRST NAME UNKNOWN) WALTER WANTED IN PANTUCK STATUTE 1567, CRIME OF KIDNAPPING.

SUBJECT ARRESTED AT OFFICES OF TREASURE BOOK CLUB, OPERATING THERE UNDER ALIAS WALTER ANTHONY CHILD AND ATTEMPTING TO COLLECT $4.98 FROM ONE SAMUEL P. GRIMES, EMPLOYEE OF THAT COMPANY.

DISPOSAL: HOLDING FOR YOUR ADVICE.

Exhibit 4

CRIMINAL RECORDS DIVISION
POLICE DEPARTMENT
CHICAGO, ILLINOIS

June 7 1995

To: Tonio Malagasi, Records Division
Re: Ref: judgement No. 456789—victim is dead.

Records Search Unit

Exhibit 5

PLEASE DO NOT FOLD, SPINDLE OR MUTILATE THIS CARD

Failure to route Document properly

To: GOVERNOR HUBERT DANIEL WILLIKENS

Re: Pardon issued to Walter A. Child, 1 July, 1995

Dear State Employee;
You have failed to attach your Routing Number

PLEASE: Resubmit document with this card and form 876, explaining your authority for placing a TOP RUSH category on this document. Form 876 must be signed by your Departmental Superior.

RESUBMIT ON: Earliest possible date
ROUTING SERVICE office is open. In this case, Tuesday 5 July, 1995

WARNING: Failure to submit form 876 WITH THE SIGNATURE OF YOUR SUPERIOR may make you liable to prosecution for misusing a Service of State Government. A warrant may be issued for your arrest.

There are NO exceptions. YOU have been WARNED.

1994 507936

66 - 13758

Exhibit 6

OFFICE OF THE GOVERNOR OF ILLINOIS

17 June 1995
Mr Michael R. Reynolds
49 Water Street
Chicago, Illinois

Dear Mr Reynolds,

In reply to your query about the request for pardon for Walter A. Child (A. Walter); may I inform you that the Governor is still on his trip with the Midwest Governors Committee. He should be back next Friday.

I will bring your request and letters to his attention the minute he returns.

Very truly yours,

Clara B. Jilks

Clara B. Jilks
Secretary to the Governor

Exhibit 7

```
437 Woodlawn Drive
Panduk, Michigan
31 May 1995

Samuel P. Grimes
Vice President, Treasure Book Club
1823 Mandy Street
Chicago, Illinois

Grimes,
This business has gone far enough. I've got to come
down to Chicago on business of my own tomorrow. I'll
see you then and we'll get this straightened out once
and for all, about who owes what to whom, and how
much!

Yours,
```

Walter A. Child

```
Walter A. Child
```

Exhibit 8

27 June 1995
Michael Reynolds
49 Water Street
Chicago, Illinois

Dear Mike,
   Where is that Pardon?
My execution date is only
five days from now!

Walter.

78

Exhibit 9

```
           437 Woodlawn Drive
           Panduk, Michigan
           21 January 1995

           Treasure Book Club
           1823 Mandy Street,
           Chicago, Illinois

           Dear Sirs,

           May I direct your attention to my letter of 16
           November 1994? You are still continuing to dun me
           with computer punch cards for a book I did not order.
           Whereas, actually, it is your company that owes me
           money.

           Sincerely yours,
```

Walter A. Child

```
           Walter. A. Child.
```

Exhibit 10

PICAYUNE COURT

From the desk of the clerk

Harry   The attached computer card from Chicago's Minor Claims Court against A. Walter has a 1500 series statute number on it. That puts it over in criminal with you, rather than in civil, with me. So I herewith submit it for your computer instead of mine. How's business?   Joe.

Exhibit 11

REQUEST
RECORDS SEARCH UNIT

June 3 1995

Re: Ref. Judgement No. 456789
was victim harmed?
Tonio Malagasi
Records Division

Exhibit 12

MICHAEL R. REYNOLDS
49 Water Street, Chicago, Illinois

Attorney-at-law

29 June 1995
Walter A. Child (A. Walter)
Cell Block E
Illinois State Penitentiary
Joliet, Illinois

Dear Walt,

The Governor returned, but was called away immediately to the White House in Washington to give his views on inter-state sewage.

I am camping on his doorstep and will be on him the moment he arrives here.

Meanwhile, I agree with you about the seriousness of the situation. The warden at the prison there, Mr Allen Magruder will bring this letter to you and have a private talk to you. I urge you to listen to what he has to say.

Yours,

Mike

Exhibit 13

7 June 1995

To: Judge Alexander J. McDivot's Chamber

Dear Jack: <u>Ref: Judgement No. 456789.</u>

The victim in this kidnap case was apparently slain. From the strange lack of background information on the killer and his victim, as well as the victim's age, this smells to me like a gangland killing. This for your information. Don't quote me. It seems to me, though, that Stevenson — the victim — has a name that rings a faint bell with me. Possibly, one of the East Coast Mob, since the association comes back to me as something about pirates — possibly New York dockage hijackers — and something about buried loot.

As I say, above is only speculation for your private guidance.

Any time I can help . . .

Best

Tony Malagasi

Tony Malagasi
Records Division

Exhibit 14

June 30 1990

Michael R Reynolds
49 Water Street
Chicago, Illinois

Dear Mike,
(This letter is being smuggled out by Warden Magruder)
As I was talking to Warden Magruder in my cell here, news was brought to him that the Governor has at last returned for a while to Illinois, and will be in his office early tomorrow morning, Friday. So you will have time to stop my execution on Saturday.

Accordingly, I have turned down the warden's kind offer of a chance to escape: since he told me that he could by no means guarentee to have all the guards out of the way when I tried it; and there was a chance of my being killed escaping. But now everything will straighten itself out. Actually an experience as fantastic as this had to break down sometime under its own weight.

Best, <u>Walt</u>

81

Exhibit 15

MICHAEL R. REYNOLDS
49 Water Street, Chicago, Illinois

Attorney-at-law

8 June 1995

Dear Tim,

Regret — I can't make the fishing trip. I've been court-appointed here to represent a man about to be sentenced tomorrow on a kidnapping charge.

Ordinarily, I might have tried to beg off, and McDivot, who is doing the sentencing, would probably have turned me loose. But this is the damndest thing you ever heard of. The man being sentenced has apparently been not only charged, but adjudged guilty as a result of a comedy of errors too long to go into here. He not only isn't guilty — he's got the best case I ever heard of for damages against one of the larger Book Clubs head-quartered here in Chicago. And that's a case I wouldn't mind taking on.

It's inconceivable — but damnably possible, once you stop to think of it in this day and age of machine-made records — that a completely innocent man could be put in this position.

There shouldn't be much to it. I've asked to see McDivot tomorrow before the time for sentencing, and it'll just be a matter of explaining to him. Then I can discuss the damage suit with my freed client at his leisure. Fishing next weekend?

Yours,

Mike

Exhibit 16

437 Woodlawn Drive
Panduk, Michigan
5 February 1995

Dear Mr Grimes

Will you stop sending me punch cards and form letters and make me some kind of a direct answer from a human being?
   I don't owe you money. You owe me money. Maybe I should turn your company over to a collection agency.

Walter A. Child

Walter A. Child

Exhibit 17

Court of Minor Claims

CHICAGO, ILLINOIS

Judgement was passed this day of ..27 May 1995.. under Statute $15.66 Against...Child,..Walter A.................................. of ..347 Woodlawn.......... Drive,.Panduk,............ Michigan.........................

Pray to enter a duplicate claim for judgement.

For amount: Statute 941

PHYSICAL INVENTORY

DO NOT FOLD OR BEND THIS CARD
ALL CARDS MUST BE ACCOUNTED FOR

TAG No.

QUANTITY	UNIT OF MEASURE	UNIT PRICE	TOTAL VALUE	TAG NUMBER	DEPT No.	PART NUMBER	CLASS

83

Exhibit 18

MICHAEL R. REYNOLDS
49 Water Street, Chicago, Illinois

Attorney-at-law

10 June

Dear Tim,

In haste —

No fishing this coming week either. Sorry.

You won't believe it. My innocent-as-a-lamb-and-I'm-not-kidding client has just been sentenced to death for first-degree murder in connection with the death of his kidnap victim.

Yes. I explained the whole thing to McDivot. And when he explained his situation to me, I nearly fell out of my chair.

It wasn't a matter of my not convincing him. It took less than three minutes to show him that my client should never have been within the walls of the County Jail for a second. But — get this — McDivot couldn't do a thing about it.

The point is, my man has already been judged guilty according to the computerized records. In the absence of a trial record — of course there never was one (but that's something I'm not free to explain to you now) — the judge has to go by what records are available. And in the case of an adjudged prisoner, McDivot's only legal choice was whether to sentence to life imprisonment, or execution. The death of the kidnap victim, according to the statute, made the death penalty mandatory. Under the new laws governing length of time for appeal, which has been shortened because of the new system of computerizing records, to force an elimination of unfair delay and mental anguish to those condemned, I have five days in which to file an appeal, and ten to have it acted on.

Needless to say, I am not going to monkey with an appeal. I'm going directly to the Governor for a pardon — after which we will get this farce reversed. McDivot has already written the governor also, explaining that his sentence was ridiculous, but that he had no choice. Between the two of us, we ought to have a pardon in short order.

Then, I'll make the fur fly. . .

And we'll get in some fishing.

Best

Mike

Exhibit 19

From the Desk of Judge Alexander J. McDivot

2 June 1995

Dear Tony,

I've got an adjudged criminal coming up before me for sentencing Thursday morning - but the trial transcript is apparently misfiled.

I need some kind of information (Ref. A. Walter-Judgement No. 456789, Criminal). For example, what about the victim of the kidnapping. Was victim harmed?

Jack McDivot

Jack McDivot

Exhibit 20

POLICE DEPARTMENT. PANDUK, MICHIGAN

TO POLICE DEPARTMENT, CHICAGO, ILLINOIS

CONVICTED SUBJECT: A. (Complete first name unknown) Walter, sought here in connection ref. your notification of judgement for kidnap of child named Robert Louis Stevenson, on 16 November 1994 Information here indicates subject fled his residence, at 437 Woodlawn Drive, Panduk, and may be again in your area.

Possible contact in your area:

The Treasure Book Club, 1823 Mandy Street, Chicago, Illinois. Subject not known to be dangerous. Pick up and hold, advising us of capture . . .

Exhibit 21

RECORDS SEARCH UNIT/CRIMINAL RECORDS DIVISION
POLICE DEPARTMENT
CHICAGO, ILLINOIS

June 3 1995

To: United States Statistics Office

Attn: Information Section

Subject: Robert Louis Stevenson

Query: Information concerning

Exhibit 22

5 June 1995

To: Records Search Unit
      Criminal Records Division
      Police Department
      Chicago, Illinois

Subject: Your query re Robert Louis Stevenson
          (File no. 189623)

Action: Subject deceased. Age at death, 44
         yrs.
         Further information requested?

A.K.
Information Section
US Statistics Office

Exhibit 23

POLICE DEPARTMENT. PANDUK, MICHIGAN

TO POLICE DEPARTMENT, CHICAGO, ILLINOIS

Ref: A. Walter (Alias Walter Anthony Child)
subject wanted for crime of kidnap, your ref:
your computer punch card notification of
judgement, dated 27 May 1995. Copy our
criminal records punch card herewith forwarded
to your computer section.

Exhibit 24

CRIMINAL RECORDS PANDUK MICHIGAN

PLEASE DO NOT FOLD, SPINDLE OR MUTILATE THIS CARD

Convicted:(Child) A. Walter

On: 26 May 1995

Address:
437 Woodlawn Drive,
Panduk, Michigan

Crim: Statute: 1566
(Corrected) 1567

Crime: Kidnap

Date: 16 November 1994

Notes:
At large. To be
picked up at once.

PHYSICAL INVENTORY

DO NOT FOLD OR BEND THIS CARD
ALL CARDS MUST BE ACCOUNTED FOR

TAG No.

QUANTITY · UNIT OF MEASURE · UNIT PRICE · TOTAL VALUE · TAG NUMBER · DEPT No. · PART NUMBER · CLASS

Exhibit 25

Maloney, Mahoney, MacNamara and Pruit

89 Prince Street
Chicago, Illinois

ATTORNEYS

Mr Walter A. Child
437 Woodlawn Drive
Panduk, Michigan

9 May 1995

Dear Mr Child

I am in possession of no information indicating that any item purchased by you from the Treasure Book Club has been returned.

I would hardly think that, if the case had been as you stated, the Treasure Book Club would have retained us to collect the amount owing from you.

If I do not receive your payment in full within three days, by 12th May 1995, we will be forced to take legal action.

Very truly yours

Hagthorpe M. Pruit, Jr

Exhibit 26

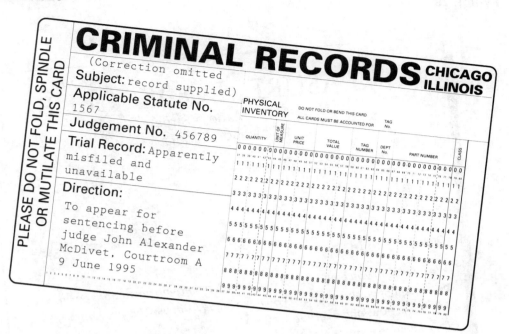

CRIMINAL RECORDS CHICAGO ILLINOIS

PLEASE DO NOT FOLD, SPINDLE OR MUTILATE THIS CARD

(Correction omitted
Subject: record supplied)

Applicable Statute No.
1567

Judgement No. 456789

Trial Record: Apparently misfiled and unavailable

Direction:

To appear for sentencing before judge John Alexander McDivet, Courtroom A 9 June 1995

PHYSICAL INVENTORY

DO NOT FOLD OR BEND THIS CARD

ALL CARDS MUST BE ACCOUNTED FOR

Exhibit 27

-FEDERAL COLLECTION OUTFIT-

88 Prince Street, Chicago, Illinois

28 February 1995

Mr Walter A. Child
437 Woodlawn Drive
Panduk, Michigan

Dear Mr Child,

Your account with the Treasure Book Club of $4.98 plus interest and charges has been turned over to our agency for collection. The amount now due is $6.83. Please send your cheque for this amount or we shall be forced to take immediate action.

Jacob N. Harshe.

Jacob N. Harshe
Vice President

Exhibit 28

TREASURE BOOK CLUB

1823 Mandy Street
Chicago, Illinois

1 February 1995

Mr Walter A. Child
437 Woodlawn Drive
Panduk, Michigan

Dear Mr Child

We have sent you a number of reminders concerning an amount owing to us as a result of book purchases you have made from us. This amount, which is $4.98, is now long overdue.

This situation is disappointing to us, particularly since there was no hesitation on our part in extending you credit at the time original arrangements for these purchases were made by you. If we do not receive payment in full by return mail, we will be forced to turn the matter to a collection agency.

Very truly yours,

Samuel P. Grimes
(Collection Mgr)

Exhibit 29

Maloney, Mahoney, MacNamara and Pruit

89 Prince Street
Chicago, Illinois

ATTORNEYS

Mr Walter A. Child
437 Woodlawn Drive
Panduk, Michigan

29th April 1995

Dear Mr Child

Your indebtedness to the Treasure Book Club has been refered to us for legal action to collect.

This indebtedness is now in the amount of $10.01. If you will send us this amount so that we may receive it before 5th May 1995, the matter may be satisfied. However, if we do not receive satisfaction in full by that date, we will take steps to collect through the courts.

I am sure you will see the advantage of avoiding a judgement against you, which as a matter of record would do lasting harm to your credit rating.

Very truly yours,

Hagthorpe M.Pruit Jr

Hagthorpe, M. Pruit, Jr
Attorney at Law

Exhibit 30

437 Woodlawn Drive
Panduk, Michigan
16 November 1994

Treasure Book Club
1823 Mandy Street
Chicago, Illinois

Dear Sirs,

I wrote you recently about the computer punch card you sent, billing me for Kim, by Rudyard Kipling. I did not open the package containing it until I had already mailed you my cheque for the amount on the card. On opening the package, I found the book missing half its pages. I sent it back to you, requesting either another copy or my money back. Instead, you have sent me a copy of Kidnapped by Robert Louis Stevenson. Will you please straighten this out?

I hereby return the copy of Kidnapped.
Sincerely yours,

Walter A. Child

Walter A. Child

Exhibit 31

TREASURE BOOK CLUB

Balance: / $4.98

Mr. Walter A. Child

For Kidnapped, by
Robert Louis
Stevenson

PLEASE DO NOT FOLD, SPINDLE
OR MUTILATE THIS CARD

PHYSICAL INVENTORY

DO NOT FOLD OR BEND THIS CARD
ALL CARDS MUST BE ACCOUNTED FOR

TAG No.

QUANTITY | UNIT OF MEASURE | UNIT PRICE | TOTAL VALUE | TAG NUMBER | DEPT No. | PART NUMBER | CLASS

SECOND NOTICE

(If remittance has been made for the above please disregard this notice)

Exhibit 32

Court of Minor Claims

CHICAGO, ILLINOIS

Name	Address
MR WALTER A. CHKD	437 WOODLAWN
DRIVE, PANDUK, MICHIGAN.	

Be informed that a judgement was taken and entered against you in this court this day of   in the amount of   including court costs.

Payment in satisfaction of this judgement may be made to this court or to the adjudged creditor. In the case of payment being made to the creditor, a release should be obtained from the creditor and filed with this court in order to free you of legal obligation in connection with this judgement.

Under the recent Reciprocal Claims Act, if you are a citizen of a different state, a duplicate claim may be automatically entered and judged against you in your own state so that collection may be made there as well as in the State of Illinois.

Exhibit 33

437 Woodlawn Drive
Panduk, Michigan
4 May 1995

Mr Hagthorpe M. Pruit, Jr
Maloney, Mahoney, MacNamara and Pruit
89 Prince Street
Chicago, Illinois

Dear Mr. Pruit,

You don't know what a pleasure it is to me in this
matter to get a letter from a live human being to whom
I can explain the situation.

The whole matter is silly. I explained it fully in
my letters to the Treasure Book Company. But I might
as well have been trying to explain to the computer
that puts out their punch cards, for all the good it
seemed to do. Briefly, what happened was I ordered a
copy of Kim by Rudyard Kipling, for $4.98. When I
opened the package they sent me, I found the book had
only half its pages, but I'd previously mailed a
cheque to pay them for the book.

I sent the book back to them, asking either for a
whole copy or my money back. Instead, they sent me a
copy of Kidnapped by Robert Louis Stevenson — which I
had not ordered; and for which they have been trying
to collect from me.

Meanwhile, I am still waiting for the money back
that they owe me for the copy of Kim that I didn't
get. That's the whole story. Maybe you can help me
straighten them out.

Relieved yours,

Walter A. Child

Walter A. Child

P.S. I also sent them back their copy of Kidnapped as
soon as I got it, but it hasn't seemed to help. They
have never even acknowledged getting it back.

Exhibit 34

TREASURE BOOK CLUB

Mr. Walter A. Child

Balance: / $4.98

PLEASE DO NOT FOLD, SPINDLE OR MUTILATE THIS CARD

Dear Customer: Enclosed is your latest book selection

Kidnapped, by Robert Louis Stevenson

PHYSICAL INVENTORY

DO NOT FOLD OR BEND THIS CARD

ALL CARDS MUST BE ACCOUNTED FOR

QUANTITY	UNIT OF MEASURE	UNIT PRICE	TOTAL VALUE	TAG NUMBER	DEPT No.	PART NUMBER	CLASS

TAG No.

Exhibit 35

-FEDERAL COLLECTION OUTFIT-

88 PRINCE STREET, CHICAGO, ILLINOIS

Mr Walter A. Child
437 Woodlawn Drive
Panduk, Michigan

8 April 1995

Dear Mr Child,

You have seen fit to ignore our courteous requests to settle your long overdue account with Treasure Book Club, which is now, with accumulated interest and charges, in the amount of $7.51. If payment in full is not forthcoming by 11 April 1995 we will be forced to turn the matter to our attorneys for immediate court action.

Ezekiel B. Harshe
President

☆

Further Assignments

English Literature

○ Use the following heading for the report in which you submit the results of your investigations to Verity Pick, chief of the missing persons department.

Pick, Sift and Scrutin, Private Investigators

Memo: Walter A. Childs	Case Number ....
	Date ....
	Investigator(s) ....

○ *Walter Childs : The Final Hours (after the story by Gordon R. Dickson)*
Imagine you are Walter Childs, in his cell on the eve of his execution. A friendly warder comes in with your final supper tray. You chat about your feelings and tell him about the extraordinary train of events which has left you just ten hours away from the electric chair.
You could write your piece either as a story or as a playscript.

English

○ *Surely There Must Be Some Mistake?*
Write your own story in which a computer or some other system puts a totally innocent person into a terrible situation from which it is very difficult to escape.
Think carefully about the train of human errors/mechanical malfunctions which could lead to the crisis.
You could treat the subject humorously or seriously.

Here are some possible scenarios :
(a) As a result of 'infallible' genetic fingerprinting, you are arrested for attempting to assassinate the Prime Minister. Write the story of your trial, in which an amazing amount of 'evidence' is accumulated to 'prove' that you had been planning the crime for many months – e.g. incriminating bits of letters to friends; lists of books with compromising titles found in your room; diary jottings which could be read as plans for 'A-day'; secretive behaviour noticed by your teachers; reports from neighbours about odd visitors to your house; bits of conversations overheard on the telephone . . .
(b) Your father has a very similar name to someone who has been involved with a brutal gang which traffics in hard drugs. One night you get home from school to learn that he has disappeared. Write about your attempts to find him.
(c) You are visiting a foreign country. At passport control, you are shown into a side room, charged with being a member of an illegal organisation and driven at high speed in a closed van to prison. Write about your experiences and fears on your first night in a cell.
(d) Your parents receive an enormous telephone bill and accuse you of bankrupting them by telephoning your boy/girlfriend who is on holiday in Australia.

You know you are innocent. How do you go about convincing everyone that there has been an error?

(e) Six weeks ago, you sent off two hundred empty crisp packets for a 'free' radio and the chance to appear on a TV chat show. You are having breakfast when there is a loud knock at the front door. You open it to find something very unwelcome on the other side . . .

(f) You receive a mysterious letter written in a shaky hand in an elaborate code. With it is a street plan of your area marked with curious symbols. Gradually you decipher more and more of the message and follow up various clues. As your investigations proceed, you begin to wonder whether anyone will ever believe what you are discovering about certain powerful and 'respectable' local citizens. Or are you going mad?

○ See if you can tell a story using no narrative, just a variety of documents such as :
letters (not always complete ones); bus tickets; maps; diagrams; pages torn from an address book; diary entries; menus; doodles; extracts from a timetable; fragments of a report; newspaper cuttings; photographs; bills; bank statements; telegrams . . .
Some possible themes:
a murder mystery; a smuggling story; the record of a love affair; a journalist's attempts to discover whether a nuclear power station is contaminating the local water supply; an account of an expedition into unknown territory . . .

Some further reading

Ray Bradbury	*Fahrenheit 451*
	The Pedestrian
Mack Reynolds	*Criminal in Utopia*
Franz Kafka	*The Trial*
Ben Elton	*Stark*

Films

Francis Coppola	*The Conversation*
James Bridges	*The China Syndrome*
John Badham	*War Games*
Steven Lisberger	*Tron*
Orson Welles	*The Trial*
Constantin Costa-Gavras	*Missing*

★

FATHERS' DAY

Assignments

English

You can work on these assignments individually or in small groups.

o *Parent of the Year Awards*
Prepare a brief news report (for a newspaper, for radio or for TV) about the first 'Parent of the Year Awards', held at your school. Use the details below but add plenty of your own ideas.

Background

All the students were asked to describe their ideal parent, listing the things they would recommend new-born babies to look for when choosing a home. From their suggestions, a committee drew up a list of ten qualities which make a parent 'good-enough' : they've rejected the idea that any parent could/should be 'perfect'.
The list might include such things as :
> finding time to talk;
> knowing when to keep out of the way;
> not dressing like a teenager *or* a geriatric;
> being firm but fair;
> having a sense of humour;
> not always being right.

Prepare your own list of ten things which you think make somebody a good parent.

Ten students nominated their parents for the award but this involved talking about their bad points as well as their good ones. An 'ideal' parent would be a bit difficult to live with.
Think what might be on the black list. Perhaps things like :
> often does the things he/she warns me not to do;
> has a habit of falling asleep and snoring like a rusty hinge when my favourite TV programme is on;
> under-/over-estimates my ability;
> no taste in shoes;
> tends to call me embarrassing names when my friends are about;
> always takes the best chocolates;
> no respect for my point of view.

Make your own list of ten things which make somebody a bad parent.

The Contest

Describe the competition – where it took place, what the students were looking for, how the three finalists were chosen – and then describe the moment when the person was voted Parent of the Year.

What sorts of thing had she/he done which the judges admired? What mistakes
had she/he made which proved she/he was human?
Describe how the winner reacted when the decision was announced.

o   *The Good-Enough Step-Parent's Handbook*
Produce a booklet giving advice to someone about to acquire a step-family.
What makes a good/bad step-parent?
Are the good/bad things the same as you'd find in all parents or does a person
need particular qualities/skills to take on somebody else's children?

You might like to use some of these headings in your booklet:
   How to Handle the First Meeting;
   What's in a Name?: what to call the kids/be called by them;
   Private Territory: what can/can't be shared;
   Making/Breaking Rules;
   Rewards and Punishments;
   Ten Things to Avoid;
   Ten Things to Do;
   The Ghastliest Possible Step-Parent;
   The Fairly Ideal Step-Parent.

☆

Read the following short story and then think about the points
which follow.

Fathers' Day

George Adams finished his coffee, mashed out his cigarette in the
saucer, and stood up. "I'm off," he said to his wife as he went to the
coat closet. "See you around six."

closet *cupboard.*

"Don't forget Bobby's school," she said.

Adams stopped, and looked at her. "What about it?" he asked.

"They're having Fathers' Day," she said. "Remember?"

"Oh, my God," Adams said. He paused, then said hurriedly, "I
can't make it. It's out of the question."

"You've got to," she said. "You missed it last year, and he was
terribly hurt. Just go for a few minutes, but you've *got* to do it. I
promised him I'd remind you."

Adams drew a deep breath and said nothing.

"Bobby said you could just come for English class," Eleanor went
on. "Between twelve twenty and one. Please don't let him down
again."

"Well, I'll try," Adams said. "I'll make it if I can."

"It won't hurt you to do it. All the other fathers do."

"I'm sure they do," Adams said. He put on his hat and went out
and rang for the elevator.

elevator *lift.*

Eleanor came to the front door. "No excuses, now!" she said.

"I said I'd do it if I could," Adams replied. "That's all I can promise
you."

Adams arrived at the school about twelve thirty, and an attendant at

the door reached out to take his hat "No, thanks," Adams said, clutching it firmly. "I'm just going to be a few minutes." He looked around and saw the cloakroom, piled high with hats and topcoats, and beyond that the auditorium, in which a number of men and boys were already having lunch. "Maybe I'm too late," he thought hopefully. "Maybe the classes are already over." To the attendant, he said, "Do you know where I'd find the sixth grade now? They're having English, I think."

"The office'll tell you," the attendant said. "Second floor."

Adams ascended a steel-and-concrete stairway to the second floor and, through the closed doors around him, heard the high, expressionless voices of reciting boys and the lower, softly precise voices of the teachers, and as he passed the open door of an empty room, he caught the smell of old wood and chalk dust and library paste. He found the office, and a middle-aged woman there directed him to a room on the floor above, and he went up and stood outside the door for a moment, listening. He could hear a teacher's voice, and the teacher was talking about the direct object and the main verb and the predicate adjective.

After hesitating a few seconds, Adams turned the knob and quietly opened the door. The first face he saw was that of his son, in the front row, and Bobby winked at him. Then Adams looked at the thin, dark-haired teacher, who seemed a surprisingly young man. He obviously had noticed Bobby's wink, and he smiled and said, "Mr Adams." Adams tiptoed to the back of the room and joined about six other fathers, who were sitting in various attitudes of discomfort on a row of folding chairs. He recognized none of them, but they looked at him in a friendly way and he smiled at them, acknowledging the bond of uneasiness that held them momentarily together.

The teacher was diagramming a sentence on the blackboard, breaking it down into its component parts by means of straight and oblique lines, and Adams, looking at the diagram, realized that, if called upon, he would be hard put to it to separate the subject from the predicate, and he prayed that the teacher wouldn't suffer a fit of whimsy and call on the fathers. As it turned out, the students were well able to handle the problem, and Adams was gratified to hear his son give correct answers to two questions that were put to him. "I'll be damned," Adams thought. "I never got the impression he knew all that."

Then the problem was completed, and the teacher glanced at the clock and said, "All right. Now we'll hear the compositions." He walked to the back of the room, sat down, and then looked around at a field of suddenly upraised hands and said, "Go ahead, Getsinger. You go first."

A thin boy with wild blond hair and a red bow tie popped out of his seat and, carrying a sheet of paper, went to the front of the room and, in a fast, singsong voice, read, "He's So Understanding. I like my Dad because he's so understanding." Several of the boys turned

101

in their seats and looked at one of the fathers and grinned as Getsinger went on, "When I ask Dad for a dime he says he'll settle for a nickel, and I say you can't get anything for a nickel any more and he says then he'll settle for six cents. Then pretty soon Mom calls and says that supper is ready, and the fight goes on in the dining room, and after a while Dad says he'll make it seven cents, and before supper is over I have my dime. That's why I say he's understanding."

Adams smiled in sympathy for Mr Getsinger, and when the next boy got up and started off, "Why I Like My Father," Adams realized with horror that all the compositions were going to be on the same subject, and he saw that his own son had a piece of paper on his desk and was waiting eagerly for his turn to read. The palms of Adams's hands became moist, and he looked at the clock, hoping that the time would run out before Bobby got a chance to recite. There was a great deal of laughter during the second boy's reading of his composition, and after he sat down, Adams looked at the clock again and saw that there were seven minutes left. Then the teacher looked around again, and five or six hands shot up, including Bobby's, and the teacher said, "All right – let's have Satterlee next," and Bobby took his hand down slowly, and Adams breathed more easily and kept his eyes riveted on the clock.

riveted *fixed.*

Satterlee, goaded by the laughter the previous student had received, read his composition with a mincing attempt to be comical, and he told how his father was unable to get any peace around the house, with his mother "chattering about the latest gossip" and his sister practising the violin. It occurred to Adams that the compositions were nothing more than the children's impressions of their own home life, and the squirming and the nervous laughter from the fathers indicated that the observations were more acute than flattering. Adams tried to think what Bobby might say, and he could remember only things like the time he had docked Bobby's allowance for two weeks, for some offence he couldn't now recall, and the way he sometimes shouted at Bobby when he got too boisterous around the apartment, and the time Bobby had threatened to leave home because he had been forbidden to go to a vaudeville show – and the time he *had* left home because of a punishment Adams had given him. Adams thought also of the night he and his wife had had an argument, and how, the next day, Bobby had asked what 'self-centered' meant, in reply to which Adams had told him it was none of his business. Then he remembered the time Bobby had been on a children's radio show and had announced that his household chores included getting out the ice for drinks, and when Adams asked him later why he had said it, Bobby had reminded him of one time Adams had asked him to bring an ice tray from the pantry into the living room. "The memories they have," Adams thought, "the diabolically selective memories."

goaded *prompted.*
mincing *pretending to be shy.*

acute *accurate.*
docked *stopped.*
allowance *pocket-money.*

boisterous *noisy.*
apartment *flat.*
vaudeville *variety.*

chores *tasks.*

diabolically *wickedly.*

Satterlee finished. The clock showed two minutes to one, and

Adams wiped his hands on his trouser legs and gripped his hat, which was getting pulpy around the brim. Then Bobby's hand went up again, almost plaintively now, and the teacher said, "All right, Adams, you're on," and Bobby bobbed up and went to the front of the room.

pulpy moist and shapeless.
plaintively sadly.

Several of the boys turned and looked at Adams as Bobby began to read, but Adams was oblivious of everything except the stocky figure in front of the blackboard, whose tweed jacket looked too small for him and who was reading fast because the bell was about to ring. What Bobby read was a list of things that Adams had completely forgotten, or that had seemed of no great importance at the time, things like being allowed to stay up late to watch a fight, and being given an old fencing mask when there was no occasion for a gift. (Adams had simply found it in a second-hand store and thought Bobby might like it), and having a model airplane made for him when he couldn't do it himself, and the time Adams had retrieved the ring from the subway grating. By the time Bobby concluded with "That's why he's OK in *my* book," Adams had recovered from his surprise and was beginning to feel embarrassed. Then the bell rang and class was dismissed, and Adams and the other fathers followed the boys out of the room.

oblivious unaware.

subway underground railway.

Bobby was waiting for him in the corridor outside. "Hi," Bobby said. "You going now?"

"Yes," said Adams. "I'm afraid I've got to."

"OK." Bobby turned and started away.

"Just a minute," Adams said, and Bobby stopped and looked back. Adams walked over to him and then hesitated a moment. "That was – ah – a good speech," he said.

"Thanks," said Bobby.

Adams started to say something else, but could think of nothing. "See you later," he finished, and quickly put on his hat and hurried down the stairs.

☆

Thinking/Talking Points

▷ Why do you think George was so reluctant to go to Fathers' Day? How do you think your parents feel about visiting school?

▷ What do you make of the way English is taught at the school? What makes it like/unlike the lessons you have?

▷ 'Then Adams looked at the thin, dark-haired teacher, who seemed a surprisingly young man.'
Why 'surprisingly'?

▷ What impression does the writer give you of the fathers, sitting at the back of the class? How do you think they feel? Why?

▷ 'Adams was gratified to hear his son give correct answers to two questions that were put to him. "I'll be damned," Adams thought, "I never got the impression he knew all that."'
Do you think your parents would be surprised if they saw the way you were treated/the way you behave in school? What are some of the ways you are a different person there from the person they know at home?

▷ 'The palms of Adams's hands became moist, and he looked at the clock, hoping that the time would run out before Bobby got a chance to recite.' What sorts of things do you think Adams is afraid he will hear?

▷ '"The memories they have," Adams thought, "the diabolically selective memories."'
(a) See if you can explain what Adams means here, in your own way.
(b) Why is this sentence funny, coming where it does?
(c) Do you think you have a tendency to remember only the good or only the bad things that happen at home?

▷ '"That's why he's OK in *my* book."'
Describe some things a parent or other adult did for you which you were very pleased about.

▷ What do you think Adams was feeling at the end of the story?
Why do you think he couldn't put it into words?

▷ How do you think your parent(s) would react if they found pages of your diary in which you described how you felt about them?
What are some of the things you would like to tell them but can't?

▷ Does your school have anything like a Fathers' Day?
Do you think it would be a good idea? Why?

Further Assignments

English

○ Rewrite *Fathers' Day* (you may prefer to call it *Mothers' Day*) as if it had been a story about your own family.
Try to give the reader a strong sense not only of the appearance, habits and personality of your mother or father but also of yourself as you think others see you. You may like to illustrate the story.

○ *Father and Son/Step-Mother and Daughter/Step-Father and Daughter/Mother and Son . . .*
Write a story (based upon your own experiences or entirely imaginary) about a parent/step-parent and teenager spending a day together.
They might be shopping; camping; fishing; at a show; visiting somebody/ somewhere.
There is something one of them wants to talk to the other about, but which it is difficult to share. Each feels a bit shy of the other; both want the relationship to

be a good one, not to do anything to spoil it. But there is something that ought to be discussed . . .

See if you can capture that tension in your story. Maybe, eventually, the 'problem' is solved; maybe it's just too difficult to be open about things. Use the outward events of the day to give the story a shape but concentrate upon the private feelings of one or both of the characters. Try to show that what people say isn't always quite what they are feeling.

English Literature

○ Essay : What do we learn about Bobby's relationship with his father in Benchley's story, *Fathers' Day*?
Refer to details which bring this out.

★

SUPERMAN AND PAULA BROWN'S NEW SNOWSUIT

What games do you remember playing at primary school?
Summer games? Autumn Games? Winter games? Spring games?

Which games did you play with a special group of friends?
Were there games you played alone?

Do you remember playing fantasy games: creating your own world, your own enemies and your own magic powers to destroy them?
Who were your childhood heroes and heroines? Who did you wish you were like?

Assignment

English

○ *A Visit to My Past*
Imagine peering through the port-hole of a time machine.
You have travelled back several years and are hovering above your old primary school. It is playtime.

Describe the scene : picture your old school. What is most striking about it?
Observe your old school mates. Describe one or two of them. What are they up to? What games are being played?
Go over and watch yourself as you were then. How do you look to a visitor?
A child with a dozy mop of ginger hair? A slight, nervous boy keeping out of trouble? A loud, breezy girl with a gang of friends . . .?
What are you wearing? What are you up to? Playing football? Nattering about Sharon? Swapping stamps? Scoffing a Mars bar? Practising handstands? Avoiding teacher? . . .

Write in the present tense.
You may like to begin something like this :

A Visit to My Past   First Call : March 15th 1983
And our camera zooms in on the playground of . . . Juniors : a prim, Victorian city school with bright blue iron railings, a red roof and a dead silver birch tree in the yard. It's playtime – all noise and movement. Balls bouncing; girls shrieking; four fat, loud boys in tatty, flapping navy anoraks with orange linings, thundering down the tarmac, being aeroplanes.
Now the camera picks out . . . who is . . .

Superman and Paula Brown's New Snowsuit

The year the war began I was in the fifth grade at the Annie F. Warren Grammar School in Winthrop, and that was the winter I won the prize for drawing the best Civil Defence signs. That was also the winter of Paula Brown's new snowsuit, and even now, thirteen years later, I can recall the changing colours of those days, clear and definite as patterns seen through a kaleidoscope.

The year the war began *the US entered the Second World War in December 1941.*

fifth grade *top juniors.*

I lived on the bay side of town, on Johnson Avenue, opposite the Logan Airport, and before I went to bed each night, I used to kneel by the west window of my room and look over to the lights of Boston that blazed and blinked far off across the darkening water. The sunset flaunted its pink flag above the airport, and the sound of waves was lost in the perpetual droning of the planes. I marvelled at the moving beacons on the runway and watched, until it grew completely dark, the flashing red and green lights that rose and set in the sky like shooting stars. The airport was my Mecca, my Jerusalem. All night I dreamed of flying.

Those were the days of my technicolour dreams. Mother believed that I should have an enormous amount of sleep, and so I was never really tired when I went to bed. This was the best time of the day, when I could lie in the vague twilight, drifting off to sleep, making up dreams inside my head the way they should go. My flying dreams were believable as a landscape by Dali, so real that I would awake with a sudden shock, a breathless sense of having tumbled like Icarus from the sky and caught myself on the soft bed just in time.

Dali *a Spanish painter of vivid, weird, dreamlike pictures.*

Icarus *the character in Greek mythology who tried to fly : the sun melted the wax which held his wings together.*

These nightly adventures in space began when Superman started invading my dreams and teaching me how to fly. He used to come roaring by in his shining blue suit with his cape whistling in the wind, looking remarkably like my Uncle Frank who was living with Mother and me. In the magic whirring of his cape I could hear the wings of a hundred sea-gulls, the motors of a thousand planes.

I was not the only worshipper of Superman in our block. David Sterling, a pale, bookish boy who lived down the street, shared my love for the sheer poetry of flight. Before supper every night, we listened to Superman together on the radio, and during the day we made up our own adventures on the way to school.

The Annie F. Warren Grammar School was a red-brick building, set back from the main highway on a black tar street, surrounded by barren gravel playgrounds. Out by the parking lot David and I found a perfect alcove for our Superman dramas. The dingy back entrance to the school was deep set in a long passageway which was an excellent place for surprise captures and sudden rescues.

parking lot *car park .*

alcove *sheltered place.*

dingy *dark, dull.*

During recess, David and I came into our own. We ignored the boys playing baseball on the gravel court and the girls giggling at dodge-ball in the dell. Our Superman games made us outlaws, yet gave us a sense of windy superiority. We even found a stand-in for a villain in Sheldon Fein, the sallow mamma's boy on our block who

recess *playtime.*

dell *small wooded hollow.*

sallow *sickly yellow colour.*

was left out of the boys' games because he cried whenever anybody tagged him and always managed to fall down and skin his fat knees.

At first, we had to prompt Sheldon in his part, but after a while he became an expert on inventing tortures and even carried them out in private, beyond the game. He used to pull the wings from flies and the legs off grasshoppers, and keep the broken insects captive in a jar hidden under his bed where he could take them out in secret and watch them struggling. David and I never played with Sheldon except at recess. After school we left him to his mamma, his bonbons, and his helpless insects.

At this time my Uncle Frank was living with us while waiting to be drafted, and I was sure that he bore an extraordinary resemblance to Superman incognito. David couldn't see his likeness as clearly as I did, but he admitted that Uncle Frank was the strongest man he had ever known, and could do lots of tricks like making caramels disappear under napkins and walking on his hands.

That same winter war was declared, and I remember sitting by the radio with Mother and Uncle Frank and feeling a queer foreboding in the air. Their voices were low and serious, and their talk was of planes and German bombs. Uncle Frank said something about Germans in America being put in prison for the duration, and Mother kept saying over and over again about Daddy, "I'm only glad Otto didn't live to see this; I'm only glad Otto didn't live to see it come to this."

In school we began to draw Civil Defence signs, and that was when I beat Jimmy Lane in our block for the fifth-grade prize. Every now and then we would practise an air raid. The fire bell would ring and we would take up our coats and pencils and file down the creaking stairs to the basement where we sat in special corners according to our colour tags, and put the pencils between our teeth so the bombs wouldn't make us bite our tongues by mistake. Some of the little children in the lower grades would cry because it was dark in the cellar, with only the bare ceiling lights on the cold black stone.

The threat of war was seeping in everywhere. At recess, Sheldon became a Nazi and borrowed a goose step from the movies, but his Uncle Macy was really over in Germany, and Mrs Fein began to grow thin and pale because she heard that Macy was a prisoner and then nothing more.

The winter dragged on, with a wet east wind coming always from the ocean, and the snow melting before there was enough for coasting. One Friday afternoon, just before Christmas, Paula Brown gave her annual birthday party, and I was invited because it was for all the children in our block. Paula lived across from Jimmy Lane on Somerset Terrace, and nobody on our block really liked her because she was bossy and stuck-up, with pale skin and long red pigtails and watery blue eyes.

She met us at the door of her house in a white organdie dress, her red hair tied up in sausage curls with a satin bow. Before we could

prompt *show him how to act.*

bonbons *sweets.*

drafted *conscripted into the army.*

incognito *in disguise.*

napkins *serviettes.*

foreboding *sense of danger coming.*

for the duration *whilst the war lasted.*

Otto *Sylvia Plath's father, who died when she was ten, was German.*

goose step *high striding marching style of the Nazi army.*

coasting *sliding.*

organdie *fine stiffened cotton fabric.*

sit down at the table for birthday cake and ice cream, she had to show us all her presents. There were a great many because it was both her birthday and Christmas time too.

Paula's favourite present was a new snowsuit, and she tried it on for us. The snowsuit was powder blue and came in a silver box from Sweden, she said. The front of the jacket was all embroidered with pink and white roses and blue-birds, and the leggings had embroidered straps. She even had a little white angora beret and angora mittens to go with it.

angora *a soft, expensive wool.*

After dessert we were all driven to the movies by Jimmy Lane's father to see the late afternoon show as a special treat. Mother had found out that the main feature was *Snow White* before she would let me go, but she hadn't realised that there was a war picture playing with it.

The movie was about Japanese prisoners who were being tortured by having no food or water. Our war games and the radio programmes were all made up, but this was real, this really happened. I blocked my ears to shut out the groans of the thirsty, starving men, but I could not tear my eyes away from the screen.

Finally, the prisoners pulled down a heavy log from the low rafters and jammed it through the clay wall so they could reach the fountain in the court, but just as the first man got to the water, the Japanese began shooting the prisoners dead, and stamping on them, and laughing. I was sitting on the aisle, and I stood up then in a hurry and ran out to the girls' room where I knelt over a toilet bowl and vomited up the cake and ice cream.

After I went to bed that night, as soon as I closed my eyes, the prison camp sprang to life in my mind, and again the groaning men broke through the walls, and again they were shot down as they reached the trickling fountain. No matter how hard I thought of Superman before I went to sleep, no crusading blue figure came roaring down in heavenly anger to smash the yellow men who invaded my dreams. When I woke up in the morning, my sheets were damp with sweat.

crusading *defeating the wicked.*

Saturday was bitterly cold, and the skies were grey and blurred with the threat of snow. I was dallying home from the store that afternoon, curling up my chilled fingers in my mittens, when I saw a couple of kids playing Chinese tag out in front of Paula Brown's house.

dallying *dawdling.*

Paula stopped in the middle of the game to eye me coldly. "We need someone else," she said. "Want to play?" She tagged me on the ankle then, and I hopped around and finally caught Sheldon Fein as he was bending down to fasten one of his fur-lined overshoes. An early thaw had melted away the snow in the street, and the tarred pavement was gritted with sand left from the snow trucks. In front of Paula's house somebody's car had left a glittering black stain of oil-slick.

We went running about in the street, retreating to the hard, brown lawns when the one who was 'It' came too close. Jimmy

110

Lane came out of his house and stood watching us for a short while, and then joined in. Every time he was 'It', he chased Paula in her powder blue snowsuit, and she screamed shrilly and looked around at him with her wide, watery eyes, and he always managed to catch her.

Only one time she forgot to look where she was going, and as Jimmy reached out to tag her, she slid into the oil-slick. We all froze when she went down on her side as if we were playing statues. No one said a word, and for a minute there was only the sound of the planes across the bay. The dull, green light of late afternoon came closing down on us, cold and final as a window blind.

Paula's snowsuit was smeared wet and black with oil along the side. Her angora mittens were dripping like black cat's fur. Slowly, she sat up and looked at us standing around her, as if searching for something. Then, suddenly, her eyes fixed on me.

"You," she said deliberately, pointing at me, "you pushed me."

There was another second of silence, and then Jimmy Lane turned on me. "You did it," he taunted. "You did it."

Sheldon and Paula and Jimmy and the rest of them faced me with a strange joy flickering in the back of their eyes. "You did it, you pushed her," they said.

And even when I shouted "I did not!" they were all moving in on me, chanting in a chorus, "Yes, you did, yes, you did, we saw you." In the well of faces moving toward me I saw no help, and I began to wonder if Jimmy had pushed Paula, or if she had fallen by herself, and I was not sure. I wasn't sure at all.

I started walking past them, walking home, determined not to run, but when I had left them behind me, I felt the sharp thud of a snowball on my left shoulder, and another. I picked up a faster stride and rounded the corner by Kelly's.

There was my dark brown shingled house ahead of me, and inside, Mother and Uncle Frank, home on furlough. I began to run in the cold, raw evening toward the bright squares of light in the windows that were home.

on furlough *on leave from the army.*

Uncle Frank met me at the door. "How's my favourite trooper?" he asked, and he swung me so high in the air that my head grazed the ceiling. There was a big love in his voice that drowned out the shouting which still echoed in my ears.

"I'm fine," I lied, and he taught me some ju-jitsu in the living-room until Mother called us for supper.

ju-jitsu *Japanese art of self-defence.*

Candles were set on the white linen table-cloth, and miniature flames flickered in the silver and the glasses. I could see another room reflected beyond the dark dining-room window where the people laughed and talked in a secure web of light, held together by its indestructible brilliance.

indestructible *unbreakable.*

All at once the doorbell rang, and Mother rose to answer it. I could hear David Sterling's high, clear voice in the hall. There was a cold draught from the open doorway, but he and Mother kept on talking, and he did not come in. When Mother came back to the

111

table, her face was sad. "Why didn't you tell me?' she said, "why didn't you tell me that you pushed Paula in the mud and spoiled her new snowsuit?"

A mouthful of chocolate pudding blocked my throat, thick and bitter. I had to wash it down with milk. Finally I said, "I didn't do it."

But the words came out like hard, dry little seeds, hollow and insincere. I tried again. "I didn't do it. Jimmy Lane did it."

"Of course we'll believe you," Mother said slowly, "but the whole neighbourhood is talking about it. Mrs Sterling heard the story from Mrs Fein and sent David over to say we should buy Paula a new snowsuit. I can't understand it."

"I didn't do it," I repeated, and the blood beat in my ears like a slack drum. I pushed my chair away from the table, not looking at Uncle Frank or Mother sitting there, solemn and sorrowful in the candlelight.

The staircase to the second floor was dark, but I went down to the long hall to my room without turning on the light switch and shut the door. A small unripe moon was shafting squares of greenish light along the floor and the window-panes were fringed with frost.

I threw myself fiercely down on my bed and lay there, dry-eyed and burning. After a while I heard Uncle Frank coming up the stairs and knocking on my door. When I didn't answer, he walked in and sat down on my bed. I could see his strong shoulders bulk against the moonlight, but in the shadows his face was featureless.

"Tell me, Honey," he said very softly, "tell me. You don't have to be afraid. We'll understand. Only tell me how it really happened."

"I told you," I said. "I told you what happened, and I can't make it any different. Not even for you I can't make it any different."

He sighed then and got up to go away. "OK, Honey," he said at the door. "OK, but we'll pay for another snowsuit anyway just to make everybody happy, and ten years from now no one will ever know the difference."

The door shut behind him and I could hear his footsteps growing fainter as he walked off down the hall. I lay there alone in bed, feeling the black shadow creeping up the underside of the world like a flood tide. Nothing held, nothing was left. The silver airplanes and the blue capes all dissolved and vanished, wiped away like the crude drawings of a child in coloured chalk from the colossal blackboard of the dark. That was the year the war began, and the real world, and the difference.

Thinking/Talking Points

▷ 'I can recall the changing colours of those days, clear and definite as patterns seen through a kaleidoscope . . .'
'I can recall those days ever so well.'

Which of these two versions of the opening of the story do you prefer? Why?

▷ 'The Annie F. Warren Grammar School was a red-brick building, set back from the main highway on a black tar street, surrounded by barren gravel playgrounds.'
This is a very simple, clear picture of the school, sharply recalled.
See if you can write a description of your present school which is about the same length and which gives the reader a simple, strong picture of the place.

▷ 'She was bossy and stuck-up, with pale skin and long red pigtails and watery blue eyes.'
How many separate bits of information does this sentence pack in?
Write a similar, one-sentence description of somebody you remember from primary school.

▷ Select half a dozen other descriptive details from the story which are particularly vivid. What do you like/dislike about the way Sylvia Plath describes people and things?

▷ Sylvia's mother would probably have prevented her daughter seeing the war film, had she known it was being shown. The girl is ill as a result of seeing it, her view of the world changed. Do you think Jimmy Lane's father was irresponsible, taking the children to the movie? Give your reasons.

▷ 'No matter how hard I thought of Superman before I went to sleep, no crusading blue figure came roaring down in heavenly anger to smash the yellow men who invaded my dreams.'
Why do you think Superman has deserted Sylvia's fantasy world?

▷ '. . .and the rest of them faced me with a strange joy flickering in the back of their eyes.'
What exactly *did* happen to ruin Paula's snowsuit?
Do you find it convincing that the other children ganged up to blame Sylvia?
Why do you think Paula, then Jimmy and finally the rest acted like that?

▷ 'But the words came out like hard, dry little seeds, hollow and insincere.'
Why do you think Sylvia can't make her version of things sound convincing?

▷ 'I lay there alone in bed, feeling the black shadow creeping up the underside of the world like a flood tide. Nothing held, nothing was left . . .'
See if you can put into your own words Sylvia's feelings at the end of the story.

Further Assignments

English

○ *'Even Now, I Can Recall the Changing Colours of Those Days'*
In her story, Sylvia Plath describes a time when she experienced some of the pains of growing up.
She begins by giving us a strong sense of herself as a child playing a child's games, cosy in her fantasy world, protected by Superman.
Then comes the shock of the war film she sees with *Snow White* and almost immediately after, the incident which upset her and which she can never

forget : being cruelly accused of something she didn't do and being unable to make anyone believe in her innocence.

Use this structure to write an extended story about your own childhood.

(a) Begin by giving the reader a strong sense of yourself in a safe, innocent world. Use plenty of descriptive details to make the setting and some of the people you knew then vivid.

(b) Then describe something which happened which made you realise that life could be ugly, less cosy than you used to think it was. (For example, perhaps you saw a road accident or overheard a conversation which shocked you.)

and/or

(c) Then describe an incident in which you felt deserted by your friends and/or family, felt all alone in a cold, cruel world. (For example, perhaps you were caught/suspected of doing something wrong; perhaps you were told something about somebody in your family which changed the way you saw them; perhaps you had to face some danger alone for the first time.)

○ *Get Lost!*
Write a story about a child finding himself/herself pushed out by his/her friends.
Write as if the events are happening to you.
You may like to base the story on something which actually happened.

English Literature

○ Examine the way Sylvia Plath captures her changing outlook on life as a result of what happens in *Superman and Paula Brown's New Snowsuit*. Quote from different parts of the story to show how her view of the world alters and describe how the powerful language she uses helps you to share and understand the girl's experiences.

○ Write the conversation Uncle Frank and Sylvia's mother have whilst she tries to get off to sleep at the end of the story.

Some further reading

Sylvia Plath   *The Bell Jar* (her autobiographical novel)
William Golding   *Free Fall*
Mary Lavin   *The Living*
John Wain   *A Message from the Pigman*

★

What is your most treasured possession?

Is it the most expensive?

Do you own anything which no amount of money would make you sell?

How do you think you would feel if when you got home tonight that thing was gone and there was a cheque in its place?

A Cap for Steve

Dave Diamond, a poor man, a carpenter's assistant, was a small, wiry, quick-tempered individual who had learned how to make every dollar count in his home. His wife, Anna, had been sick a lot, and his twelve-year-old son, Steve, had to be kept in school. Steve, a big-eyed, shy kid, ought to have known the value of money as well as Dave did. It had been ground into him.

But the boy was crazy about baseball, and after school, when he could have been working as a delivery boy or selling papers, he played ball with the kids. His failure to appreciate that the family needed a few extra dollars disgusted Dave. Around the house he wouldn't let Steve talk about baseball, and he scowled when he saw him hurrying off with his glove after dinner.

When the Phillies came to town to play an exhibition game with the home team and Steve pleaded to be taken to the ball park, Dave, of course, was outraged. Steve knew they couldn't afford it. But he had got his mother on his side. Finally Dave made a bargain with them. He said that if Steve came home after school and worked hard helping to make some kitchen shelves he would take him that night to the ball park.

Steve worked hard, but Dave was still resentful. They had to coax him to put on his good suit. When they started out Steve held aloof, feeling guilty, and they walked down the street like strangers; then Dave glanced at Steve's face and, half-ashamed, took his arm more cheerfully.

As the game went on, Dave had to listen to Steve's recitation of the batting average of every Philly that stepped up to the plate; the time the boy must have wasted learning these averages began to appal him. He showed it so plainly that Steve felt guilty again and was silent.

After the game Dave let Steve drag him onto the field to keep him company while he tried to get some autographs from the Philly players, who were being hemmed in by gangs of kids blocking the way to the club-house. But Steve, who was shy, let the other kids block him off from the players. Steve would push his way in, get blocked out, and come back to stand mournfully beside Dave. And Dave grew impatient. He was wasting valuable time. He wanted to get home; Steve knew it and was worried.

Then the big, blond Philly outfielder, Eddie Condon, who had been held up by a gang of kids tugging at his arm and thrusting their score cards at him, broke loose and made a run for the club-house. He was jostled, and his blue cap with the red peak, tilted far back on his head, fell off. It fell at Steve's feet, and Steve stooped quickly and grabbed it. "Okay, son," the outfielder called, turning back. But Steve, holding the hat in both hands, only stared at him.

"Give him his cap, Steve," Dave said, smiling apologetically at the big outfielder who towered over them. But Steve drew the hat closer to his chest. In an awed trance he looked up at big Eddie

---

dollar *worth about 50p (the story is set in the USA).*

appreciate *realise.*

scowled *frowned.*

the Phillies *a baseball team from Philadelphia.*

held aloof *kept apart.*

recitation *recital.*
plate *a flat piece of white rubber at which the batter stands.*

outfielder *deep fielding position in a baseball team.*

jostled *pushed.*

in an awed trance *lost in admiration.*

116

Condon. It was an embarrassing moment. All the other kids were watching. Some shouted, "Give him his cap."

"My cap, son," Eddie Condon said, his hand out.

"Hey, Steve," Dave said, and he gave him a shake. But he had to jerk the cap out of Steve's hands.

"Here you are," he said.

The outfielder, noticing Steve's white, worshipping face and pleading eyes, grinned and then shrugged. "Aw, let him keep it," he said.

"No, Mister Condon, you don't need to do that," Dave protested.

"It's happened before. Forget it," Eddie Condon said, and he trotted away to the club-house.

Dave handed the cap to Steve; envious kids circled around them and Steve said, "He said I could keep it, Dad. You heard him, didn't you?"

"Yeah, I heard him," Dave admitted. The wonder in Steve's face made him smile. He took the boy by the arm and they hurried off the field.

On the way home Dave couldn't get him to talk about the game; he couldn't get him to take his eyes off the cap. Steve could hardly believe in his own happiness. "See," he said suddenly, and he showed Dave that Eddie Condon's name was printed on the sweat-band. Then he went on dreaming. Finally he put the cap on his head and turned to Dave with a slow, proud smile. The cap was away too big for him; it fell down over his ears. "Never mind," Dave said. "You can get your mother to take a tuck in the back."

take a tuck *put in a pleat.*

When they got home Dave was tired and his wife didn't understand the cap's importance, and they couldn't get Steve to go to bed. He swaggered around wearing the cap and looking in the mirror every ten minutes. He took the cap to bed with him.

swaggered *showed off by strutting around.*

Dave and his wife had a cup of coffee in the kitchen, and Dave told her again how they had got the cap. They agreed that their boy must have an attractive quality that showed in his face, and that Eddie Condon must have been drawn to him — why else would he have singled Steve out from all the kids?

But Dave got tired of the fuss Steve made over that cap and of the way he wore it from the time he got up in the morning until the time he went to bed. Some kid was always coming in, wanting to try on the cap. It was childish, Dave said, for Steve to go around assuming that the cap made him important in the neighbourhood, and to keep telling them how he had become a leader in the park a few blocks away where he played ball in the evenings. And Dave wouldn't stand for Steve's keeping the cap on while he was eating. He was always scolding his wife for accepting Steve's explanation that he'd forgotten he had it on. Just the same, it was remarkable what a little thing like a ball cap could do for a kid, Dave admitted to his wife as he smiled to himself.

scolding *telling off.*

One night Steve was late coming home from the park. Dave didn't realize how late it was until he put down his newspaper and

117

watched his wife at the window. Her restlessness got on his nerves.

"See what comes from encouraging the boy to hang around with those park loafers," he said.

"I don't encourage him," she protested.

"You do," he insisted irritably, for he was really worried now.

A gang hung around the park until midnight. It was a bad park. It was true that on one side there was a good district with fine, expensive apartment houses, but the kids from that neighbourhood left the park to the kids from the poorer homes. When his wife went out and walked down to the corner it was his turn to wait and worry and watch at the open window. Each waiting moment tortured him. At last he heard his wife's voice and Steve's voice, and he relaxed and sighed; then he remembered his duty and rushed angrily to meet them.

"I'll fix you, Steve, once and for all," he said. "I'll show you you can't start coming into the house at midnight."

"Hold your horses, Dave," his wife said. "Can't you see the state he's in?' Steve looked utterly exhausted and beaten.

"What's the matter?" Dave asked quickly.

"I lost my cap," Steve whispered; he walked past his father and threw himself on the couch in the living-room and lay with his face hidden.

"Now, don't scold him, Dave," his wife said.

"Scold him? Who's scolding him?" Dave asked, indignantly. "It's his cap, not mine. If it's not worth his while to hang on to it, why should I scold him?" But he was implying resentfully that he alone recognized the cap's value.

"So you are scolding him," his wife said. "It's his cap. Not yours. What happened, Steve?"

Steve told them he had been playing ball and he found that when he ran the bases the cap fell off; it was still too big despite the tuck his mother had taken in the band. So the next time he came to bat he tucked the cap in his hip pocket. Someone had lifted it, he was sure.

"And he didn't even know whether it was still in his pocket," Dave said sarcastically.

"I wasn't careless, Dad," Steve said. For the last three hours he had been wandering around to the homes of the kids who had been in the park at the time; he wanted to go on, but he was too tired. Dave knew the boy was apologizing to him, but he didn't know why it made him angry.

"If he didn't hang on to it, it's not worth worrying about now," he said, and he sounded offended.

After that night they knew that Steve didn't go to the park to play ball; he went to look for the cap. It irritated Dave to see him sit around listlessly, or walk in circles, trying to force his memory to find a particular incident which would suddenly recall to him the moment when the cap had been taken. It was no attitude for a growing, healthy boy to take, Dave complained. He told Steve firmly

loafers *lazy people.*

apartment houses *flats.*

implying *suggesting.*

lifted *stolen.*

listlessly *without any energy.*

once and for all that he didn't want to hear any more about the cap.

One night, two weeks later, Dave was walking home with Steve from the shoemaker's. It was a hot night. When they passed an ice-cream parlour Steve slowed down. "I guess I couldn't have a soda, could I?" Steve said.

"Nothing doing," Dave said firmly. "Come on now," he added as Steve hung back, looking in the window.

"Dad, look!" Steve cried suddenly, pointing at the window. "My cap! There's my cap! He's coming out!"

A well-dressed boy was leaving the ice-cream parlour; he had on a blue ball cap with a red peak, just like Steve's cap. "Hey, you!" Steve cried, and he rushed at the boy, his small face fierce and his eyes wild. Before the boy could back away Steve had snatched the cap from his head. "That's my cap!" he shouted.

"What's this?" the bigger boy said. "Hey, give me my cap or I'll give you a poke on the nose."

Dave was surprised that his own shy boy did not back away. He watched him clutch the cap in his left hand, half crying with excitement as he put his head down and drew back his right fist: he was willing to fight. And Dave was proud of him.

"Wait, now," Dave said. "Take it easy, son," he said to the other boy, who refused to back away.

"My boy says it's his cap," Dave said.

"Well, he's crazy. It's my cap."

"I was with him when he got this cap. When the Phillies played here. It's a Philly cap."

"Eddie Condon gave it to me," Steve said. "And you stole it from me, you jerk."

"Don't call me a jerk, you little squirt. I never saw you before in my life."

"Look," Steve said, pointing to the printing on the cap's sweat-band. "It's Eddie Condon's cap. See? See, Dad?"

"Yeah. You're right, Son. Ever see this boy before, Steve?"

"No," Steve said reluctantly.

The other boy realized he might lose the cap. "I bought it from a guy," he said. "I paid him. My father knows I paid him." He said he got the cap at the ball park. He groped for some magically impressive words and suddenly found them. "You'll have to speak to my father," he said.

"Sure, I'll speak to your father," Dave said. "What's your name? Where do you live?"

"My name's Hudson. I live about ten minutes away on the other side of the park." The boy appraised Dave, who wasn't any bigger than he was and who wore a faded blue windbreaker and no tie. "My father is a lawyer," he said boldly. "He wouldn't let me keep the cap if he didn't think I should."

"Is that a fact?" Dave asked belligerently. "Well, we'll see. Come on. Let's go." And he got between the two boys and they walked along the street. They didn't talk to each other. Dave knew the

soda *fizzy drink.*

appraised *summed up.*
windbreaker *warm jacket.*

belligerently *aggressively.*

119

Hudson boy was waiting to get to the protection of his home, and Steve knew it, too, and he looked up apprehensively at Dave. And Dave, reaching for his hand, squeezed it encouragingly and strode along, cocky and belligerent, knowing that Steve relied on him.

apprehensively *fearfully*.

The Hudson boy lived in that row of fine apartment houses on the other side of the park. At the entrance to one of these houses Dave tried not to hang back and show he was impressed, because he could feel Steve hanging back. When they got into the small elevator Dave didn't know why he took off his hat. In the carpeted hall on the fourth floor the Hudson boy said, "Just a minute," and entered his own apartment. Dave and Steve were left alone in the corridor, knowing that the other boy was preparing his father for the encounter. Steve looked anxiously at his father, and Dave said, "Don't worry, Son," and he added resolutely, "No one's putting anything over on us."

elevator *lift*.

encounter *meeting*.
resolutely *determinedly*.
putting anything over on us *taking advantage of us*.

A tall balding man in a brown velvet smoking-jacket suddenly opened the door. Dave had never seen a man wearing one of those jackets, although he had seen them in department-store windows. "Good evening," he said, making a deprecatory gesture at the cap Steve still clutched tightly in his left hand. "My boy didn't get your name. My name is Hudson."

a deprecatory gesture at the cap *showing that he didn't think the cap was very important*.

"Mine's Diamond."

"Come on in," Mr Hudson said, putting out his hand and laughing good-naturedly. He led Dave and Steve into his living-room. "What's this about that cap?" he asked. "The way kids can get excited about a cap. Well, it's understandable, isn't it?"

"So it is," Dave said, moving closer to Steve, who was awed by the broadloom rug and the fine furniture. He wanted to show Steve he was at ease himself, and he wished Mr Hudson wouldn't be so polite. That meant Dave had to be polite and affable, too, and it was hard to manage when he was standing in the middle of the floor in his old windbreaker.

affable *friendly*.

"Sit down, Mr Diamond," Mr Hudson said. Dave took Steve's arm and sat him down beside him on the chesterfield. The Hudson boy watched his father. And Dave looked at Steve and saw that he wouldn't face Mr Hudson or the other boy; he kept looking up at Dave, putting all his faith in him.

chesterfield *sofa*.

"Well, Mr Diamond, from what I gathered from my boy, you're able to prove this cap belonged to your boy."

"That's a fact," Dave said.

"Mr Diamond, you'll have to believe my boy bought that cap from some kid in good faith."

"I don't doubt it," Dave said. "But no kid can sell something that doesn't belong to him. You know that's a fact, Mr Hudson."

"Yes, that's a fact," Mr Hudson agreed. "But that cap means a lot to my boy, Mr Diamond."

"It means a lot to my boy, too, Mr Hudson."

"Sure it does. But supposing we called in a policeman. You know what he'd say? He'd ask you if you were willing to pay my boy what he paid for the cap. That's usually the way it works out," Mr Hudson said, friendly and smiling, as he eyed Dave shrewdly.

"But that's not right. It's not justice," Dave protested. "Not when it's my boy's cap."

"I know it isn't right. But that's what they do."

"All right. What did you say your boy paid for the cap?" Dave said reluctantly.

"Two dollars."

"Two dollars!" Dave repeated. Mr Hudson's smile was still kindly, but his eyes were shrewd, and Dave knew the lawyer was counting on his not having the two dollars; Mr Hudson thought he had Dave sized up; he had looked at him and decided he was broke. Dave's pride was hurt, and he turned to Steve. What he saw in Steve's face was more powerful than the hurt to his pride: it was the memory of how difficult it had been to get an extra nickel, the talk he heard about the cost of food, the worry in his mother's face as she tried to make ends meet, and the bewildered embarrassment that he was here in a rich man's home, forcing his father to confess that he couldn't afford to spend two dollars. Then Dave grew angry and reckless. "I'll give you the two dollars," he said.

Steve looked at the Hudson boy and grinned brightly. The Hudson boy watched his father.

"I suppose that's fair enough," Mr Hudson said. "A cap like this can be worth a lot to a kid. You know how it is. Your boy might want to sell – I mean be satisfied. Would he take five dollars for it?"

"Five dollars?" Dave repeated. "Is it worth five dollars, Steve?" he asked uncertainly.

Steve shook his head and looked frightened.

"No, thanks, Mr Hudson," Dave said firmly.

"I'll tell you what I'll do," Mr Hudson said. "I'll give you ten dollars. The cap has a sentimental value for my boy, a Philly cap, a big-leaguer's cap. It's only worth about a buck and a half really," he added. But Dave shook his head again. Mr Hudson frowned. He looked at his own boy with indulgent concern, but now he was embarrassed. "I'll tell you what I'll do," he said. "This cap – well, it's worth as much as a day at the circus to my boy. Your boy should be recompensed. I want to be fair. Here's twenty dollars," and he held out two ten-dollar bills to Dave.

"That much money for a cap," Dave thought, and his eyes brightened. But he knew what the cap had meant to Steve; to deprive him of it now that it was within his reach would be unbearable. All the things he needed in his life gathered around him; his wife was there, saying he couldn't afford to reject the offer, he had no right to do it; and he turned to Steve to see if Steve thought it wonderful that the cap could bring them twenty dollars.

"What do you say, Steve?" he asked uneasily.

"I don't know," Steve said. He was in a trance. When Dave smiled, Steve smiled too, and Dave believed that Steve was as impressed as he was, only more bewildered, and maybe even more aware that

shrewdly *knowingly.*

nickel *five-cent coin.*

reckless *rash.*

buck *dollar.*

with indulgent concern *caring about his feelings.*

recompensed *repaid.*
bills *notes.*

deprive *take away from.*

they could not possibly turn away that much money for a ball cap.

"Well, here you are," Mr Hudson said, and he put the two bills in Steve's hand. "It's a lot of money. But I guess you had a right to expect as much."

With a dazed, fixed smile Steve handed the money slowly to his father, and his face was white.

Laughing jovially, Mr Hudson led them to the door. His own boy followed a few paces behind.

In the elevator Dave took the bills out of his pocket. "See, Stevie," he whispered eagerly. "That windbreaker you wanted! And ten dollars for your bank! Won't Mother be surprised?"

"Yeah," Steve whispered, the little smile still on his face. But Dave had to turn away quickly so their eyes wouldn't meet, for he saw that it was a scared smile.

Outside, Dave said, "Here, you carry the money home, Steve. You show it to your mother."

"No, you keep it," Steve said, and then there was nothing to say. They walked in silence.

"It's a lot of money," Dave said finally. When Steve didn't answer him, he added angrily, "I turned to you, Steve. I asked you, didn't I?"

"That man knew how much his boy wanted that cap," Steve said.

"Sure. But he recognized how much it was worth to us."

"No, you let him take it away from us," Steve blurted.

"That's unfair," Dave said. "Don't dare say that to me."

"I don't want to be like you," Steve muttered, and he darted across the road and walked along on the other side of the street.

"It's unfair," Dave said angrily, only now he didn't mean that Steve was unfair, he meant that what had happened in the prosperous Hudson home was unfair, and he didn't know quite why. He had been trapped, not just by Mr Hudson, but by his own life. Across the road Steve was hurrying along with his head down, wanting to be alone. They walked most of the way home on opposite sides of the street, until Dave could stand it no longer. "Steve," he called, crossing the street. "It was very unfair. I mean, for you to say . . ." but Steve started to run. Dave walked as fast as he could and Steve was getting beyond him, and he felt enraged and suddenly he yelled, "Steve!" and he started to chase his son. He wanted to get hold of Steve and pound him, and he didn't know why. He gained on him, he gasped for breath and he almost got him by the shoulder. Turning, Steve saw his father's face in the street light and was terrified; he circled away, got to the house, and rushed in, yelling, "Mother!"

"Son, Son!" she cried, rushing from the kitchen. As soon as she threw her arms around Steve, shielding him, Dave's anger left him and he felt stupid. He walked past them into the kitchen.

"What happened?" she asked anxiously. "Have you both gone crazy? What did you do, Steve?"

"Nothing," he said sullenly.

122

"What did your father do?"

"We found the boy with my ball cap, and he let the boy's father take it from us."

"No, no," Dave protested. "Nobody pushed us around. The man didn't put anything over us." He felt tired and his face was burning. He told what had happened; then he slowly took the two ten-dollar bills out of his wallet and tossed them on the table and looked up guiltily at his wife.

It hurt him that she didn't pick up the money, and that she didn't rebuke him. "It is a lot of money, Son," she said slowly. "Your father was only trying to do what he knew was right, and it'll work out, and you'll understand." She was soothing Steve, but Dave knew she felt that she needed to be gentle with him, too, and he was ashamed.

When she went with Steve to his bedroom, Dave sat by himself. His son had contempt for him, he thought. His son, for the first time, had seen how easy it was for another man to handle him, and he had judged him and had wanted to walk alone on the other side of the street. He looked at the money and he hated the sight of it.

His wife returned to the kitchen, made a cup of tea, talked soothingly, and said it was incredible that he had forced the Hudson man to pay him twenty dollars for the cap, but all Dave could think of was "Steve was scared of me."

Finally, he got up and went into Steve's room. The room was in darkness, but he could see the outline of Steve's body on the bed, and he sat down beside him and whispered, "Look, Son, it was a mistake. I know why. People like us – in circumstances where money can scare us. No, no," he said, feeling ashamed and shaking his head apologetically; he was taking the wrong way of showing the boy they were together; he was covering up his own failure. For the failure had been his, and it had come out of being so separated from his son that he had been blind to what was beyond the price in a boy's life. He longed now to show Steve he could be with him from day to day. His hand went out hesitantly to Steve's shoulder. "Steve, look," he said eagerly. "The trouble was I didn't realize how much I enjoyed it that night at the ball park. If I had watched you playing for your own team – the kids around here say you could be a great pitcher. We could take that money and buy a new pitcher's glove for you, and a catcher's mitt. Steve, Steve, are you listening? I could catch you, work with you in the lane. Maybe I could be your coach . . . watch you become a great pitcher." In the half-darkness he could see the boy's pale face turn to him.

Steve, who had never heard his father talk like this, was shy and wondering. All he knew was that his father, for the first time, wanted to be with him in his hopes and adventures. He said, "I guess you do know how important that cap was." His hand went out to his father's arm. "With that man the cap was – well it was just something he could buy, eh Dad?" Dave gripped his son's hand hard. The wonderful generosity of childhood – the price a boy was willing to pay to be able to count on his father's admiration and approval – made him feel humble, then strangely exalted.

★

123

Thinking/Talking Points

▷ Read the opening paragraph of *A Cap for Steve* again.
Think about how the author has developed the whole story from those first details.

▷ 'When they started out Steve held aloof, feeling guilty, and they walked down the street like strangers; then Dave glanced at Steve's face and, half-ashamed, took his arm more cheerfully.'
See if you can explain just why Steve felt 'guilty' and why his father felt 'half-ashamed' as they walked to the game.

▷ '. . .it was remarkable what a little thing like a ball cap could do for a kid, Dave admitted to his wife as he smiled to himself.'
How would you explain the effect owning the hat has had on Steve?
What does the detail 'he smiled to himself' tell you about Dave's feelings?

▷ 'Dave knew the boy was apologising to him, but he didn't know why it made him angry.
 "If he didn't hang on to it, it's not worth worrying about now," he said, and he sounded offended.' (page 118)
See if you can explain why Dave is feeling like this.

▷ 'He groped for some magically impressive words and suddenly found them.
"You'll have to speak to my father," he said.' (page 119)
See if you can explain how the Hudson boy knows that these words will be 'magically impressive'.

▷ Why do you think Dave took off his hat in the lift?

▷ Pick out a couple of details which give you a strong impression
(a) of Mr Hudson and (b) of the Hudsons's flat.

▷ '". . .that cap means a lot to my boy, Mr Diamond."
"It means a lot to my boy, too, Mr Hudson."' (page 120)
(a) What do you think the two fathers are feeling about owning the cap at this point in the story?
(b) How do you imagine the expressions on the two boys' faces?

▷ '"Two dollars!" Dave repeated. Mr Hudson's smile was still kindly, but his eyes were shrewd . . .'
How do you explain Mr Hudson's expression?
How do you think he would describe Dave Diamond to his wife?

▷ Read again from 'Steve looked at the Hudson boy and grinned brightly . . .' to 'Laughing jovially, Mr Hudson led them to the door. His own boy followed a few paces behind.' (page 122)
What do you feel about Dave's behaviour here?
Would you have acted like him? Give your reasons.

▷ 'He had been trapped, not just by Mr Hudson but by his own life.' (page 122)
See if you can explain what the author means here.

▷ 'Finally he got up and went into Steve's room.'
Imagine you are Dave. How are you feeling at this point in the story?

▷ Read the final paragraph of the story again.
See if you can describe in your own words the change in Steve's feelings at the end.

▷ '"With that man the cap was – well it was just something he could buy, eh Dad?"'
Do you think there is a sense in which the Hudson boy is poorer than Steve at the end of the story? Why?
What do you feel the story shows us about 'the value of money'?
Read through the story again now before choosing your assignment.
Have you had any experience similar to Steve's?

Assignments

English

○ *A Scarf/Letter/Sticker/Autograph/Photo/Date/Gig for* . . .
Write your own story about a child and parent falling out over something which is very valuable to one of them. Tell the story as if you are *either* the parent *or* the child.
Perhaps, as in *A Cap for Steve*, the upset brings to the surface some other problems in the relationship : things which haven't been faced before, feelings which haven't been talked about.
Maybe the crisis finally helps the relationship to improve.
You may like to write from your own experience.

○ Write about your own most treasured possession.
What does it look like? Where did it come from? Why is it so special to you? Where do you keep it?
How would you feel if your mother or father wanted you to sell it, give it away or just throw it out?

○ This is an activity which could be attempted in pairs.
Here are the openings of two stories. Think about how the details could be developed.
Either improvise some scenes and then write them up as a playscript *or* use one of the paragraphs as the opening of a story of your own.

(a) Life was very hard for the Whipples. It was hard to feed all the hungry mouths, it was hard to keep the children in flannels during the winter, short as it was : "God knows what would become of us if we lived north," they would say ; keeping them decently clean was hard. "It looks like our luck won't never let up on us," said Mr Whipple, but Mrs Whipple was all for taking what was sent and calling it good, anyhow when the neighbours were in earshot. "Don't ever let a soul hear us complain," she kept saying to her husband. She couldn't stand to be pitied . . . "Nobody's going to get a chance to look down on us." (Katherine Anne Porter *He*)

(b) Emma Woodhouse, handsome, clever and rich, with a comfortable home and happy disposition, seemed to unite some of the best blessings of existence; and had lived nearly twenty-one years in the world with very little to distress or vex her. (Jane Austen *Emma*)

English Literature

o Essay:'For the failure had been his, and it had come out of being so separated from his son that he had been blind to what was beyond the price in a boy's life.'
Do you feel that this sums up what happens in the story? Is Dave entirely to blame?
Write an essay about the relationship between father and son in *A Cap for Steve*. Begin by talking about their relationship at the beginning of the story. Then describe how it alters as a result of their going to the ball game and then when Steve loses the cap. Finally talk about their relationship at the end of the story. Don't retell too much of the plot; concentrate upon Steve's and Dave's feelings about each other at different moments. Talk about how you would feel/behave in a similar situation.
Select a dozen or so *brief* quotations around which to build your essay.

o For discussion (in pairs) or writing :
Imagine that, instead of going home after the cap had been sold to the Hudsons, Steve had run to his grandfather's house and explained to him what had happened.
Improvise or write their conversation.
It's up to you to decide what sort of man the grandfather is. Does he try to see Dave's point of view or does he just feel sorry for the boy?

o For discussion (in pairs) or writing:
Imagine you are the Hudson boy telling his mother/best friend the story of his cap. Use details from *A Cap for Steve* but add plenty of your own ideas.
Try to bring out the boy's feelings at different moments in the story — particularly what he thought of Dave and Steve Diamond.

Some further reading

John Wain   *Manhood*
Franz Kafka   *A Letter to my Father*
J.D. Salinger   *Catcher in the Rye*

★

Tsushima
MISSING

De Hann
ABSENT

According to the Children's Society, in Britain an estimated 100,000 children run away from home every year.
What do you think are some of the reasons for their running away?

Have you ever thought seriously about leaving home?
How do you think your parents would react if you did, tomorrow?

This story is set in Japan but the situation is universal.

Missing

After more than half an hour standing in bemusement under the light, the mother firmly turned the switch. At once the brightness of the mercury-vapour streetlamps and neon signs outside surged in through the glass as if barely able to hold back till the room was dark. Alarmed, the mother hurriedly flicked the switch on again and restored about herself the narrow ring of light to which her eyes were accustomed, while beyond the window the proper darkness of night returned. The mother gazed around her daughter's room, which she had just cleaned an hour ago; no matter how many times she looked, it remained too neat. Bending towards the window she peered at the wooden fence half-hidden by shrubs, then, having first taken a deep breath, she turned the switch off once more and sat down like a deflated balloon.

For some time the mother listened tensely for any stirrings outside. The only sounds that reached her ears, however, were those of cars speeding like ambulances down the main street, the violent din of road works, and the muffled barking of what must be an old dog.

When she tired of straining her whole body in expectation of something – the click of heels on the paving, perhaps – the mother leaned forward and with the nail of her little finger painstakingly picked out scraps of rubbish wedged deep in the crevices between the tatami mats on which she was sitting. There were all sorts of oddments: the seed of a summer tangerine, pencil shavings, hairs, a nail paring, cracker crumbs, lint, an unidentifiable black pellet

bemusement *confusion.*

surged in *poured in like huge waves.*

to which her eyes were accustomed *which her eyes were used to.*

deflated *with the air let out.*

din *noise.*

painstakingly *taking great care and time.*
crevices *narrow gaps.*
tatami mats *rush mats.*
paring *clipping.*
cracker *biscuit.*

127

(possibly the breath freshener Jintan) . . . She set the scraps, one by one, in a row along the border of the tatami. Odd that they hadn't caught her eye while the room was light. She'd swept so thoroughly, too. Now she'd have to get the vacuum cleaner and give it another going-over.

Picking up a bit of sky-blue thread and placing it on the palm of her hand, the mother sighed. One person's daily round had thrown up this much debris from somewhere – though the girl had had this room next to the entrance hall to herself for only five years. The mother's hand, pale in the light from outside, was shaking like a withered leaf in the wind. Seeing the distinct shadow it cast on the tatami, she was again surprised at how bright it was out there.

The last train must have returned to the depot hours ago. She didn't need to see a clock, she could tell by the ache at the back of her eyes. Already more than eight hours – one-third of a day – had elapsed since she'd come home. By this time she would normally be so sound asleep that cats and dogs could brawl beside her pillow and she wouldn't know it. This thought helped to make up for the two big yawns she'd let out, one right after the other, an hour or so earlier. She wasn't used to this business of staying up all night – not like her girl. Children these days (children who insisted they weren't children any more) seemed to make a habit of it.

After yawning in spite of herself the mother had none the less felt both shame and weariness. And she began to be bothered by the glow of the electric bulb whose reddish tinge seemed to lure and compel her towards sleep. Whatever happened, she mustn't sleep on a night when she didn't know where her daughter was. That was what parenthood meant.

Before she did her daughter's room, the mother had cleaned the house from top to bottom. She had polished the kitchen floor and washed every window in sight. She had laundered the curtains and sheets, though she hadn't hung them out in the yard – they were still in the spin dryer. She'd never believed in drying the washing at night, as she'd heard the children wouldn't stop wetting their beds if she did. But hadn't the laundry and the housecleaning made far too much noise for the middle of the night? Remembering, the mother blushed. Wouldn't the neighbours have noticed? Besides, what if her daughter had come home and caught her busily wiping windowpanes? How she'd have laughed – she was such a tease. "At this hour? What's the matter? Been having nightmares? And why are you still wearing black? . . ."

Her daughter's imagined inquiry startled her. It was true, she hadn't as much as taken off her formal white socks since arriving home from the memorial service. She hadn't omitted to make dinner, and close the shutters, and even neatly shine several pairs of shoes that her daughter had left, and yet she'd overlooked her own costume like some absent-minded child forgetting her schoolbag – as her daughter had twice done in second grade. The sleeve of her black kimono was, she saw, already speckled with dust. But the mother didn't feel like changing her clothes. Not unless she could change into her nightdress.

She must be more tired than she realised, thought the mother as she straightened the dishevelled neckline of her kimono. She had been on the move since early morning, travelling to a seaside town two hours distant where the seventh anniversary service was to be held in memory of her sister; it was the longest trip she'd made in years. On reaching the temple, she was at once ushered through to the back, where her aunt asked her to prepare tea and cakes for thirty people. There were two girls as helpers, but they were more useless than her own daughter. (She gathered they were the daughters of the eldest son of the family into which her late sister had married, but didn't recall having seen them before.) And what's more they appeared to have taken the memorial service for some kind of party, for whenever they spotted an unknown boy of their own age among the distant relatives they whispered together with stifled mirth.

Her own daughter had surely learned only too well, through the mother herself, what worthless creatures men were. A man was the sort who'd sire any number of children and then run off when the mood took him (when a young woman gave him a suggestive smile). The sort who was capable of amusing himself with some young floozy while his wife washed nappies. And then anonymously sending senseless expensive toys. At times, though, the mother would fall to wondering whether it was not so much that men were worthless, but that the women attracted to the fellows were fools. At her son's wedding three years ago she'd looked over the bride, who was even plainer than her daughter, with mixed feelings. But never mind her son, it was her daughter she needed to watch over. In bringing her up the mother had taken pains to speak ill of the husband who had deserted them and of men in general. Thanks to her efforts, her daughter hadn't yet made a single male friend. At least, not as far as she knew. For the time being the mother was satisfied. Her mind was made up: she must never allow her to follow in her own footsteps.

Had her daughter been packing her bags in this room about the time the mother was thinking these thoughts in the seaside town? What expression could she have been wearing? A pout and a frown? Or was she in tears? No, that she couldn't imagine: why leave home if it made her cry? She must have set out as if going on nothing more than a hiking trip. But who with? It was unthinkable that her daughter, who'd been minding the house, would simply go off of her own accord.

In the temple hall, seated opposite her brother-in-law, who'd remarried, and the children, the mother had let her attention stray from the reading of the sutras to memories of her sister, dead of cancer after a brief six months' stay in the hospital. In their schooldays the mother, who was the younger of the two, had enjoyed being shown the notes her sister often received from younger girls. Her sister liked to detect errors in their spelling and grammar. She wanted to be a language teacher or a reporter for a women's magazine. The mother felt a growing pity for the sister who'd only succeeded in becoming the parent of three grubby children before she died; the pity was stronger than it had been seven years ago, and coming on top of the memory of her own marriage it brought tears to her eyes. As for the bereaved husband, before the seventh anniversary he'd got himself a young wife from somewhere, impregnated her without delay, and was the picture of fond contentment. The mother had headed for home in a gloomy frame of mind, further convinced that women were the losers every time.

As she slipped off her lacquered wooden sandals in the hallway she'd called to her daughter, eager for a sight of the girl who had, after all, led a quiet life so far. She called loudly four or five times, but her daughter, who was supposed to be looking after things on her own, didn't answer. Disgruntled, the mother went into the living room. What a neglectful girl she was. A newspaper, a cup, and a bottle of digestive medicine was still on the low table where they'd been that morning; there too was the extra big round cushion that went by an English-sounding name, 'floor cushion' or some such thing, which the daughter had bought for herself – but not the daughter. She took a look in the kitchen, in the daughter's room, in her own bedroom, and upstairs in what had been her husband's preserve. The girl wasn't anywhere.

Back in the living room the mother pondered for a while, then went slowly and deliberately to the hallway and opened the shoe cupboard. On the two shelves reserved for her daughter's use there was an empty space between the boxes holding her old school shoes and her galoshes. At least three pairs were missing. Among them would be the black patent leather shoes she had bought only last month. Picking up the white sandals her daughter had kicked off at the entrance and placing them neatly alongside her own, she returned once more to the living room, where she clenched the hand whose minute trembling she had only just noticed and pressed it to her teeth.

For the next ten minutes the mother bit her hand.

"To go off to the cinema like that and not even lock up?"

Having taken her hand from her mouth to snap these words at her daughter's floor cushion, the mother was so unnerved by the loudness of her voice that she sat down beside the table. Then she clumsily opened the morning paper, which she hadn't had time to read. She was remembering her daughter's tearful face when, at fourteen, she wasn't allowed to see a film with a friend. The mother couldn't understand why she would want to go out specially to a cinema when there was the television, and furthermore, she was proposing to go with a mysterious friend whose name the mother had never even heard. Of course the mother, who could only associate cinemas with darkness, hadn't given permission. With

lacquered *painted*.

disgruntled *in a bad temper*.

preserve *territory*.
pondered *thought about things*.

galoshes *over-shoes worn in wet weather*.

unnerved *frightened*.

131

tears forming in her eyes the daughter had submitted and apologised. She may very well have gone in secret all the same. Mothers could be fooled in any number of ways . . .

Suddenly turning pale, the mother threw the newspaper aside and rushed to the daughter's room. She surveyed it slowly, calling to mind how it had appeared before. Since she didn't look in every day – the daughter always propped the door shut from inside – her memory was vague, but she could tell that an assortment of items had disappeared. The red alarm clock the girl had treasured as a graduation present from a friend, the contents of the letter holder, the pennant from the design school she'd been attending since the spring, a large ruler, bottles of toilet water, a hairbrush, several photograph albums dating back to childhood, a black patent leather handbag that matched the shoes, the cloth shoulder bag she'd used since high school . . . The portable stereo and stack of records bought with her wages from a part-time job must have proved too bulky; these she'd had to do without. Drums and trumpets would often blare from the daughter's room in the middle of the night.

With a groan, the mother sat down heavily beside the stereo. She couldn't bring herself to open the wardrobe. It was enough that the hairbrush and the photograph albums were gone. She'd been careless in spite of having feared this very thing. Why, oh why, did children choose to imitate only their parents' folly? The frustration, slow in rising, came welling up now.

Slipping her trembling hand into the breast of her kimono, she began to examine the three black faces pictured on the jacket of one of her daughter's records. The three faces were three different shades of black: one was near indigo, one was dark brown, one verged on a deep green. Were black people's skin colours each so different? Which did they like best themselves? The mother deliberated as earnestly as she did when unable to decide the menu for the evening meal. Every time there was a sound outside the window (car horns, a drunk singing), the mother abused her unseen daughter, her face twisting. "Fancy not even being capable of minding the house properly! And playing at running off, just like your father's tomfoolery . . ."

A premonition had made her shiver many times before now. When her daughter was supposedly at kindergarten she'd been picked up by the police way over by the breakwater. While at primary school, she'd once locked herself in the garden shed, from the inside, and stayed in hiding the whole day. The mother had asked more and more urgently what was the matter, but could get no answer but crying. And then – was it around the end of high school? – without warning the girl had come home intoxicated one night, after eleven o'clock. The mother had given her a lecture that lasted fully an hour, to which the daughter had responded coolly, "You don't have to make such a dreadful scene. I'm home now, so why all the fuss?" Beside herself with rage, the mother had grabbed at the girl, who'd stuck out a hand and quite effortlessly pushed her

submitted *given in.*

graduation *ceremony to mark leaving school.*

pennant *flag.*

folly *stupidity.*

frustration *sense of helplessness.*

deliberated as earnestly *thought about it as seriously.*

abused *criticised.*

tomfoolery *silliness.*

premonition *a feeling that something bad was going to happen.*

kindergarten *nursery school.*

breakwater *stone structure which protects a harbour from the force of the waves.*

132

over, then lurched into her room. "Bacteria, that's what does it," muttered the mother, and she gripped her right breast with the hand she'd tucked into the front of her kimono. Clearly, bacteria which would poison her whole system in an unguarded moment had taken hold in the girl's body – caught from her father, of course.

The mother remained seated for perhaps an hour or more. Then, leaping up as though someone had thundered in her ear, she rushed into the kitchen and began washing rice and vegetables for dinner. By the time she realised what she was doing she'd prepared quantities that would take the two of them a good three days to eat. As soon as she had carried the meal to the table and covered it with a cloth, she set to work polishing the kitchen floor. Next came the bench, then the sideboard. Halfway through this another idea struck her and she took down the living-room curtains and piled them into the washing machine. While she was doing that her eye fell on the stained tiles of the bathroom wall, and she went at them with a scrubbing brush. No sooner was one thing done than the dirt in some other place assailed her. As if dodging this way and that in the path of whatever was bearing down on her, the mother darted about the house with her rags and broom. Although the lights were on she might as well have been cleaning in the dark.

The last room she did was her daughter's. This was the only one with a window on the west side of the house; as it faced onto the alley, one could keep watch on anyone who opened the gate and came to the door. While she was busily cleaning, the mother's attention was gradually drawn to the window and what might be outside. She had a notion the daughter was lurking behind the fence; she'd have made it as far as the gate hours earlier, but finding the house lit up she'd be hiding, watching her mother's movements. Wasn't she stuck in the alley, biting her lower lip and thinking, "All I did was join a friend at the pictures, and here's Mother in a fit, tearing my room apart. Anyone would think I'd run away from home." Once this thought struck her she was unable to move a finger, clutching her broom . . .

But where *could* she be at this time of night? Rubbing her aching eyes, the mother posed the question to the bits and pieces she'd lined up along the edge of the tatami.

Over the row of scraps a scene gradually took shape: the figure of her daughter in some entertainment district bouncing like a puppy along a pavement illuminated by colourful neon signs and strings of fairy lights. No doubt she's just come out of a cinema or café. A young man the mother has never set eyes on is chatting to her, one arm encircling her shoulders. He has his hair long and permed, rimless dark glasses, and clothes fringed like an American Indian's. The daughter is wearing baggy red and black slacks that the mother doesn't recognise, and she too has on dark glasses.

Everything in sight is lit up like a Christmas display in a toyshop window. Even the night sky scintillates like silver lamé. Music mingles with the city's noise, and jingling sleigh bells ring in Santa

bacteria *germs.*

scintillates *glitters.*
silver lamé *material made with silver thread.*
ring in *announce.*

133

Claus. Laughing (whenever her eyes meet the youth's) as innocently as when a child, the daughter is singing a song. Probably
black music – not a Negro spiritual, but that soul rock or whatever it
is . . .

People throng the pavements. Red faces, blue faces, yellow faces,
all laughing with mouths wide open. Everybody in the district is
undoubtedly drunk. The bacteria known as alcohol hang in the air
like dust clouds. Therefore the daughter and her companion – who
is that young man? – must also be drunk. Seen from behind they
appear to be doing a folk dance. In the streets people lie flat on their
backs, huddle over, leap into the air. How can her daughter bear the
place, how can she not get dizzy? She's just a child; perhaps her
head is filled with the novelty of it.

The daughter and the young man come to a stop in front of a great
box of red glass. He gives her a push and they go in. A good-natured,
gullible girl like her can't turn anyone down. The red glass box is
packed with jostling Santa Clauses. Reindeer, too, with tumblers of
whiskey in hand. Glass beads snow from the ceiling, glinting every
colour of the rainbow. In the midst of the snowstorm, swinging on a
trapeze, are dwarves who might have stepped out of a fairy tale,
while beyond them a motorcycle team dives through flaming hoops.
The daughter gazes enraptured at the box of bedlam. Before she
knows it, the youth at her side has also donned a Santa costume.

A reindeer approaches and hands them each a whiskey. They
drink a toast with the beast, draining their glasses dry. Whereupon
the youthful Santa Claus gives some sort of order to the daughter.
Laughing ticklishly she strips off her clothes, underwear and all.
Then she mounts the reindeer's back. Next the young man mounts.
As he's about to give the deer a flick of the whip he takes off his dark
glasses and reveals his face. A face familiar from somewhere
(narrow eyes like the daughter's, a flared nose): the face of her
husband . . .

Instantly the mother was on her feet, shaking all over. For her
husband's face, of all things, to appear – she doubted her own
reason. What had come over her? Santa Clauses, and her daughter
naked? Where had things gone wrong? With a brisk shake of her
head, as if to throw off an animal clinging to her hair, she leaned out
of the window and whispered to the fence in a quivering voice:

". . . Are you . . . there, dear?"

There wasn't a rustle, nor, of course, an answer.

Again the mother sat down in the middle of the darkened room.
She told herself to wait, not to think any more – which only gave
rise to a great many more thoughts, keeping her busy brushing
them off. Like a swarm of flies – she'd no sooner kill one than a new
one would buzz in her face. The mother closed her eyes and blocked
her ears and the other flies disappeared from view, leaving only her
baby daughter. She was drawing up her stubby arms and legs and
bawling till perspiration stood out on her half-bald head. With her
turned-up nose and eyes aslant – her father's features – no one

throng *crowd.*

gullible *too trusting, naïve.*

**enraptured at the box of
bedlam** *delighted by,
intoxicated with the mad goings
on.*

donned *put on.*

quivering *trembling.*

bawling *howling.*

134

could have called her a pretty baby.

When she had just started school, the daughter often wanted to hear about her babyhood.

"How did I sound when I cried?"

"Exactly like a cat."

"Did I have dimples when I smiled?"

"Dimples? Oh, no, you were like a little mouse."

"Did I sleep in a cradle?"

"In the daytime I put you down on a cushion."

"Did I really wear nappies?"

"I had to keep you in nappies until after your second birthday, you know."

"Did everyone cuddle me?"

"Who's everyone?"

"My brother, and grandmother, and father . . ."

". . . Only me. I was the only one who cuddled you."

"Only you?"

"That's right. Isn't that good enough for you?"

The mother stood up, watching her shadow on the tatami as she did so, and flicked the light switch. The shadow that had extended towards the desk vanished and another formed like a cat curled at her feet. She rubbed her eyes at the returning burst of light, dealt the rubbish on the mat's edge a kick that sent it flying, and stumbled out to the hallway. In the corner where she'd forgotten them were the rags and bucket. She put the rags in the bucket and, carrying the lot outside, emptied the dirty water under the shrubbery. The rags slopped out as well. Setting the bucket down beside the two humps they made – which put her in mind of dead moles – the mother opened the gate and stepped into the alley. The telephone poles and a TV aerial on the house opposite cast oblique shadows. Softly, she began to walk.

oblique *sloping, diagonal.*

So near dawn, it was natural that every house should be dark and quiet, yet there was one window lighted like her daughter's. It was in the new block of flats at the end of the alley. What, the mother thought suspiciously, could they be doing up at this hour? Were they waiting for someone? In front of the house three doors down, a quoit set lay in pieces. The mother fitted the peg back on the stand and placed it carefully against the wall.

quoit set *a game in which rings are thrown onto pegs.*

She came to the main street, where the mercury-vapour lamps shone wastefully bright, the neon signs winked gaily away with no one there to see, and cars flashed by, now black, now white, on a road which looked broader in that light than in the light of day. The unexpected brightness eased the mother's mind. She wished she'd come out sooner. Her daughter must surely be in this same bright light. Releasing a deep breath – part sigh and part yawn – the mother squatted in front of the shuttered door of the corner rice store. She couldn't miss her here. Would she come home on foot or by taxi? Because of all that luggage – how much would it amount to? – she might have to come by taxi.

Hugging her knees and resting her chin on them, the mother waited for a shadowy figure to run up to her. A figure holding a cloth bundle in each hand and wearing a rucksack: a little girl in a short skirt, or a teenager, or her husband looking gaunt and tired. The figure could have been any of these. She was no longer sure who she was waiting for.

Before long, the drowsiness she'd pressed back behind her eyes began infiltrating the mother's body, dissolving from the inside. Dreamily, she found herself playing house with her six-year-old sister. Her sister, being older, was hostess. Their fruit juice was crushed from morning glories, and the stems of foxtails did for straws. From polite conversation about the weather, the sisters moved on to gossip about the neighbours.

Their mother's voice was heard.

". . . What are you doing?"

Her sister and the juice were gone in a flash. She faltered a reply:

". . . Waiting."

"What a useless little thing you are . . ."

"But . . . what else can I do?"

"Such a fool of a child. I'm disappointed in you."

". . . Tell me, how exciting is it to go out on the town?"

". . . You should give it a try . . ."

By some trick the voice had turned into those of her husband and her daughter. The mother said the words over again to herself. As she murmured them, tears brimmed in her eyes.

". . . But there's nowhere for me to enjoy myself. Not now."

"You disappoint me, you really do. Why have my children had such bad luck, the pair of you?"

Bad luck: that was it. The mother went on saying these words over to herself. The sounds gradually worked loose, drifted distinctly into the air, and faded away in different directions.

When the sounds had gone, leaving her plumped there with her bottom on the pavement and her chin buried between her knees, the mother was so fast asleep that she wouldn't have woken at once if a policeman on the beat had hailed her or a cat licked her cheek.

drowsiness *sleepiness.*

infiltrating *invading.*

morning glories, foxtails
types of flower.

Thinking/Talking Points

▷ Why do you think the mother in this story spends so much time and effort cleaning?

▷ 'Children these days (children who insisted they weren't children any more) seemed to make a habit of it.'
Which details in the story suggest that the mother does not want her daughter to grow up?

136

▷ 'Her own daughter had surely learned only too well, through the mother herself, what worthless creatures men were.'
What does this detail suggest to you:
(a) about the family situation?
(b) about the conversations the mother and her daughter may have had about boyfriends?
Find the passage later in the story where we learn more about how the mother has tried to influence her daughter's attitude towards men. What do you think of the mother's behaviour?

▷ 'But never mind her son, it was her daughter she needed to watch over.'
Why do you think the mother in the story is more anxious about one child than the other? Do you think she is right to feel differently about them?

▷ '"To go off to the cinema like that and not even lock up!"'
How do you know that when she says this, the mother does not really think her daughter has gone to the cinema? Why do you think she says it? See if you can find another example of the mother talking to herself like this.

▷ 'The daughter always propped the door shut from inside . . . Drums and trumpets would often blare from the daughter's room in the middle of the night.'
Look at these details and at the list of things the girl has taken with her. What picture of her do they give you?

▷ '"Bacteria, that's what does it" . . . Clearly bacteria which would poison her whole system . . . caught from her father, of course.'
How serious do you think the mother is being here? What would be your own 'diagnosis'?

▷ Read again the part of the story which begins:
'Over the row of scraps a scene gradually took shape' and ends 'the face of her husband.'
What does this passage reveal to you about the mother's deepest fears? Which details do you find most interesting? Do you feel sympathetic towards the mother or critical of her at this point? Why?

▷ Read again the paragraph which begins:
'Hugging her knees and resting her chin on them, the mother waited for a shadowy figure to run up to her.'
How does this paragraph alter the way we see the woman's feelings about her husband?

▷ Read again the imaginary conversation the woman has with her own mother at the end of the story. It begins '". . . What are you doing?"'
The woman seems to be facing something about herself in this passage which she has not considered before. What do you think it is?

▷ 'The mother, the daughter, the sister, the husband . . .'
Why do you think the author chose not to give any of her characters names?
Do you think the story would be better if she had?
Give your reasons.
To what extent do you agree that, although set in Japan, the story is universal?

Read through the story again before choosing an assignment.
The story is very carefully written. Notice how each detail the writer gives us adds to our understanding of the people involved.

Role-play (working in threes)

○ Two days later, the daughter is found by a policeman. When she returns to the house, she is accompanied by a social worker. The social worker explains to the mother that her daughter will come back home only if certain things are sorted out between them.
Improvise the conversation which follows.
Think about the small and the big things which need to be discussed. How does the mother react to being put in this situation? How does the social worker use his/her experience to help them see what needs talking about? Are mother and daughter able to come to a new understanding?

Assignments

English

○ *Leaving Home*
Someone of your age is trying to decide whether the time has come to leave home.
Present his/her thoughts as a poem, as a short story or as a letter to his/her parents.

○ Write a series of diary entries by someone who has run away from home. The four or five entries should cover a period of about six months. Try to give the reader a strong sense of the writer's changing feelings about (a) home (b) her/himself (c) the world outside.

○ *A Woman's Place*
'The mother felt a growing pity for the sister who'd only succeeded in becoming the parent of three grubby children before she died; the pity was stronger than it had been seven years ago, and coming on top of the memory of her own marriage it brought tears to her eyes . . . The mother had headed for home in a gloomy frame of mind, further convinced that women were the losers every time.'

What does this story make you feel about the lives of women in modern society? Do you think that they are still at a disadvantage compared with men? What do you think prevents them enjoying equal rights, an equal chance to be happy and fulfilled?
How do you think marriage can (a) help (b) hinder a woman from being a 'winner'?

English Literature

○ *The Daughter's Story*
'Had her daughter been packing her bags in this room about the time the mother was . . . in the seaside town? What expression could she have been wearing? A pout and a frown? Or was she in tears? . . . She must have set out as if going on nothing more than a hiking trip. But who with? It was

138

unthinkable that her daughter, who'd been minding the house, would simply go off of her own accord.'

From what you have understood of the atmosphere in the family, and about the girl's personality, write the story of the girl's last hour in the house as if *she* were describing it.
What does she feel about her mother, about her life in the house, about her own future?
Why does she leave? Does she have a definite plan? Where is she going? What are her hopes and fears? Is she going alone or with somebody? What are her feelings as she closes the door behind her? Does she think she will ever return?

○ When the mother returns home, she finds a letter from her daughter wrapped in her nightdress. Write that letter. Think carefully about the mood you think the girl was in when she wrote it.

○ 'Mothers Could Be Fooled in Any Number of Ways . . ."
Write about an earlier incident when the daughter and mother in the story had disagreed about her going out somewhere. How did the daughter trick her mother? How did she feel about it?

○ *A Premonition*
'A premonition had made her shiver many times before now. When her daughter was supposedly at kindergarten she'd been picked up by the police way over by the breakwater. While at primary school she'd once locked herself in the garden shed, from the inside, and stayed in hiding the whole day. The mother had asked more and more urgently what was the matter, but could get no answer but crying. And then – was it around the end of high school? – without warning the girl had come home intoxicated one night, after eleven o'clock . . .'
Write about one of those earlier incidents when the daughter's behaviour had alarmed her mother, *either* from the mother's *or* from the daughter's point of view.

○ Essay: 'Whatever happened, she mustn't sleep on a night when she didn't know where her daughter was. That was what parenthood meant.'
What has this story told you about being a parent? At what points in the story do you feel sorry for the mother? Can you suggest why her daughter may have left home?
Refer to a dozen or so particular details from the story in your answer.

Some further reading

Yuko Tsushima   *The Shooting Gallery and Other Stories*
Edna O'Brien   *Cords*

☆

Here is a story with a similar theme, written by Tui De Hann, a student at North Westminster Community School in London. In Tui De Hann's story, we see the situation both from the boy's and from his mother's point of view. Think about the advantages and disadvantages of this technique compared with Yuko Tsushima's way of telling her tale. It's an approach you may like to experiment with in some of your own writing.

Absent

A wave of nausea swept over him. He scrambled to his feet, his mind still asleep, his body cocooned in his own staleness. He stumbled into the bathroom.

Ten minutes later he was scrubbing the sink with an old toothbrush, trying to wear away the sick stains and the stench. Discarding the now beige toothbrush, he stretched, and studied his face in the cracked, brown-splattered mirror before him. His pupils were large and clouded. He pulled a face.

He wasn't actually quite sure, he thought, as he squeezed a spot on his forehead, he wasn't quite sure how he got to be standing in a strange, dirty bathroom somewhere in North London, with a sprinkling of people he had never seen before, and probably would never see again. The night before was a blank. Snatches were still clear, the small, plastic square, the key to the undiscovered labyrinths of his mind. He rooted in his jeans for a cigarette and found none. Sighing, he left the bathroom.

Out in the unfamiliar hall, the floor was scattered with comatose bodies, contorted with sleep and alcohol. The air was thick with putrid, poisonous light and the night before's cigarette smoke. A face jerked into life; a cough, a yawn, dry-tongued and scarlet-eyed. Picking his feet over the semi-living figures around him, he made his way back to the living room.

The scent hit him immediately. His head began to rise, and spin slowly, as he sat down on the floor, quietly blending into the surroundings again. A small, thin, white object was shoved into his hand. Automatically, he raised it to his lips, and drew in his breath deeply, swallowing and filling the base of his throat with the sweet heavy smoke. Almost immediately, his body began to tingle; his limbs became heavy, liquid; his perception clouded and hazed.

It was Tuesday morning, similar to any other.

She woke with a start. There was a shooting pain in her neck as she raised her head from the kitchen table, where it had fallen, unknown to her, the night before. The room was icy cold. Outside the grey, dull light of early morning gone, the newly fallen snow a chilling brightness. She shuddered.

The hum of the milkfloat outside brought her to her feet. Absently, she straightened her rumpled slept-in clothes and patted her hair, put on the kettle, and placed two slices of bread in the toaster.

He hadn't come home.

In vain, she attempted to push the thought to the back of her mind. But to no avail. It was the third time this month. He would stumble in some time in the afternoon, silent and bitter, and disappear to his room. Helpless and sad, she would long for a link, the breaking of the barriers. But, just when she had worked up enough courage to approach him, enough resolution to work up some optimism, he would dart out of the door again calling, "Off out, Mum", and she would be alone, alone while she cried bitter tears over him, the small, happy baby with the bluest eyes.

She didn't really want to know what he did with his time; ignored the enlarged pupils, the empty whisky bottles in his room, the scars on his wrists. She was consumed with the fear of him. The guilt of fearing him. The guilt of her weakness, the all-destroying guilt that weighted her down, stifled them both. What had gone wrong? she thought to herself. Why did they not seem able to communicate any more? He was a stranger, encased in an impenetrable block of ice. She was helpless.

And then there was the school. She knew he didn't go in much. But there was nothing she could do, she reasoned with herself. "After all, he's nearly old enough to leave, and it is his decision entirely." But when the official-headed letters came through the door at regular intervals, her heart sank. When she went for meetings with the Headmaster – the conspicuous click of her shoes echoing down the corridors, the young eyes whispering, smirking, the hot rush that flooded her head when a sympathetic, smiling face told her gently that her son was a failure, a bully, a bad influence – all fed on her conscience, until she would run out, her face in her hands, as far away as possible. Then the shame would descend on her, partly on his behalf, but mostly because she had not been strong enough for him.

After all, she was on his side. Wasn't she?

He felt a twinge of guilt as he looked at the clock. School would be preparing for the insanity of the lunch-hour row, with stocky, red-faced and white-coated women barricading themselves against the torrent of the mass of bodies which threw itself at the piles of food like piranhas. He had always hated that part of the day, and consequently would stroll out of the building instead, secure in his own company, with a joint in his hand and the open sky in his eyes.

Then, unable to face the hordes again in the afternoon, he would wander away, all resolutions dulled by the fragrant smoke, and return home much, much later, guilty and tired. Sometimes he felt as if his life was spiralling down, to an unknown, unimaginable destination. The distance from his mother was by now so far that a reconciliation appeared impossible. He smiled to himself. The distance was safe.

The soothing, warm liquid spilled down his throat. He cupped his hands around the filthy mug, warming his fingers from its heat. Outside, the whiteness had turned grey-brown, distorted by the trampling of people's feet and the sick, yellow light that thudded down from the thick storm-clouds. The small, shabby kitchen was bare, the only food available being a very old tin of tuna and some crispbread, or at least crumbs of crispbread. With a sigh, he set about the tiresome task of getting some sort of meal for himself.

It didn't really bother him much, food. He was used to going without, more often than not living on cigarettes and four-packs for days at a time. Involuntarily, the memory of his mother's food crossed his mind. She had been proud of her cooking, and it had probably been the deciding element in her marriage to his father. And with him, as he grew up, she had introduced him to the love of food. She hadn't usually had much money, but she always managed to conjure up something; rich, thick, aromatic stews, flavoured with the cheap bones the butcher rejected, the huge bowls of porridge, thick, steaming and filling.

His mouth was watering, unnoticed. He looked down at the array of stale food and chipped crockery before him. The tuna almost definitely had a tinge of green, and the tin was so old that the picture on the wrapper had faded to a single shade of orange. Repulsed, he tipped the tin into the bin and strode out of the kitchen.

Out in the hall, the majority of people were awake, propped up against the decaying walls as if the survival of the house's structure depended on it. He sat down amongst them. Looking about he studied the faces that surrounded him: the greed that lit up their features, the coldness of their laughter and their smiles. They resembled a crowd of sleepy, yet money-hungry vultures around a roulette wheel. But the stakes were high, and the chips small squares of treated plastic that would unleash your mind and send your senses soaring. As, one by one, they placed the tabs in their mouths, one by one they seemed to disappear from reach. He felt alone.

The bitterness descended on him, with the memories and the hope that died so young. The sadness of his existence penetrated his core, desperate and helpless. But what could he do? Was he in fact able to pick up where he left off? Go back to school, and his mother, return to the mundaneness of suburbia? He was no longer sure. But could he stay as he was? Neither was an option really.

He looked at a young girl lying motionless beside him. An icy hand lightly fingered his spine. He shuddered. Her eyes, the only part of her that seemed alive, were inside, staring at some indetermined spot on the opposite wall. And the blankness, the cold un-dead quality of her expression scared him. She was young, too young to be capable of such a look. His mind was made up for him. He could not continue as he was, to become no more than a body, a mass of flesh that was totally reliant on the artificiality of drugs or anything else.

He stood, and before he had a chance to wonder what he was doing, walked out the door.

She felt a surge of hope each time the phone rang.

But as the hours passed she felt the hopelessness returning, the feeling of him being out of reach.

Was she going about this in the wrong way? She didn't know. There was simply the block he'd set up between them. But she wanted him back so badly she felt as if her heart would be eaten away with the pain. The determination was fading with the light outside.

Absently she begun preparing the supper.

As she chopped the vegetables, she reasoned with herself. He needed her too, he must do. A compromise could be reached with time.

But first they needed to get to know each other again. And they could do. Her train of thought was broken on the door. Silhouetted in the glass were the outlines of two tall men. The silver sheen of a policeman's badge penetrated the darkness of the hall. Hesitatingly, she peered round the door.

"Mrs Pearson?"

"Yes."

"We regret to inform you that a boy identified as your son has been killed in a motorbike accident. Apparently, according to the autopsy, he was under the influence of LSD. We are sincerely sorry."

Their faces were totally expressionless. And inwardly, she let a note of pure pain pierce the air.

★

What do you understand by the word 'separation'?
(Think about how it can describe a stage in a relationship.)
What is good/bad about children separating/being separated from their parents?

Many children are sent away from home to boarding school.
What are some of the reasons why this happens?
What do you think might be gained/lost by sending a child away from home to school?
Would you like such an arrangement? Why?

Have you ever been separated from your parents for more than a day or so?
If you had to spend a long time away from home (e.g. in hospital, on an educational exchange, at boarding school) how do you think the separation would affect (a) you (b) them?

How do you think you would feel as a parent if one of your children won a competition which meant a year's education in Australia or in America?

A Red-Letter Day

The hedgerow was beaded with silver. In the fog the leaves dripped with a deadly intensity, as if each falling drop were a drop of acid.

Through the mist cabs came suddenly face to face with one another, passing and repassing between station and school. Backing into the hedges — twigs, withered berries striking the windows — the drivers leaned out to exchange remarks, incomprehensible to their passengers, who felt oddly at their mercy. Town parents especially shrank from this malevolent landscape — wastes of rotting cabbages, flint cottages with rakish privies, rubbish heaps, grey napkins dropping on clotheslines, the soil like plum cake. Even turning in at the rather superior school gates, the mossy stone, the smell of fungus, still dismayed them. Then, as the building itself came into view, they could see Matron standing at the top of the steps, fantastically white, shaming nature, her hands laid affectionately upon the shoulders of such boys as could not resist her. The weather was put in its place. The day would take its course.

Tory was in one of the last of the cabs. Having no man to exert authority for her, she must merely take her turn, standing on the slimy pavement, waiting for a car to come back empty. She stamped her feet, feeling the damp creeping through her shoes. When she left home she had thought herself suitably dressed; even for such an early hour her hat was surely plain enough? One after another she had tried on, and had come out in the end leaving hats all over the bed, so that it resembled a new grave with its mound of wreathed flowers.

One other woman was on her own. Tory eyed her with distaste. Her sons (for surely she had more than one? She looked as if she had what is often called a teeming womb; was like a woman in a pageant symbolizing maternity), her many sons would never feel the lack of a father, for she was large enough to be both to them. Yes, Tory thought, she would have them out on the lawn, bowling at them by the hour, coach them at mathematics, oil their bats, dubbin their boots, tan their backsides (she was working herself up into a hatred of this woman, who seemed to be all that she herself was not) — one love affair in her life, or, rather, mating. "She has probably eaten her husband now that her childbearing days are over. He would never have dared to ask for a divorce, as mine did." She carried still her 'mother's bag' — the vast thing which, full of napkins, bibs, bottles of orange juice, accompanies babies out to tea. Tory wondered what was in it now. Sensible things: a Bradshaw, ration books, a bag of biscuits, large clean handkerchiefs, a tablet of soap, and aspirins.

A jolly manner. "I love young people. I feed on them," Tory thought spitefully. The furs on her shoulders made her even larger; they clasped paws across her great authoritative back like hands across the ocean. Tory lifted her muff to hide her smile.

Nervous dread made her feel fretful and vicious. In *her* life all was

---

Red-Letter Day *an exciting day to remember.*

cabs *taxis.*

incomprehensible *meaningless.*

malevolent *evil, hostile.*

rakish privies *outside lavatories which the people from towns think are indecent.*

napkins *nappies.*

dismayed *made them feel unhappy.*

Matron *person responsible for the boys' welfare in the school's boarding house.*

shaming nature *putting nature to shame for being so unwelcoming.*

eyed her *looked at her.*

teeming *producing lots of children.*

pageant *a type of play.*

symbolizing maternity *representing motherhood.*

bats *cricket bats.*

dubbin *grease used to waterproof leather.*

tan *beat.*

Bradshaw *book containing railway timetables for the whole of Great Britain.*

ration books *the story is set shortly after World War Two when some foods were still in short supply.*

muff *warm soft covering for the hands, usually made of fur.*

vicious *cruel.*

frail, precarious; emotions fleeting, relationships fragmentary. Her life with her husband had suddenly loosened and dissolved, her love for her son was painful, shadowed by guilt — the guilt of having nothing solid to offer, of having grown up and forgotten, of adventuring still, away from her child, of not being able to resist those emotional adventures, the tenuous grasping after life; by the very look of her attracting those delicious secret glances, glimpses, whispers, the challenge, the excitement — not deeply sexual, for she was flirtatious; but not, she thought, watching the woman rearranging her furs on her shoulders, not a great featherbed of oblivion. Between Edward and me there is no premise of love, none at all, nothing taken for granted as between most sons and mothers, but all tentative, agonized. We are indeed amateurs, both of us — no tradition behind us, no gift for the job. All we achieve is too hard come by. We try too piteously to please each other, and if we do, feel frightened by the miracle of it. I do indeed love him above all others. Above all others, but not exclusively.

Here a taxi swerved against the curb, palpitated as she stepped forward quickly, triumphantly, before Mrs Hay-Hardy (whose name she did not yet know), and settled herself in the back.

"Could we share?" Mrs Hay-Hardy asked, her voice confident, melodious, one foot definitely on the running board. Tory smiled and moved over much farther than was necessary, as if such a teeming womb could scarcely be accommodated on the seat beside her.

Shifting her furs on her shoulders, settling herself, Mrs Hay-Hardy glanced out through the filming windows, undaunted by the weather, which would clear, she said, would lift. Oh, she was confident that it would lift by midday.

"One is up so early, it seems midday now," Tory complained.

But Mrs Hay-Hardy had not risen until six, so that naturally it still seemed only eleven to her, as it was.

She will share the fare, Tory thought. Down to the last penny. There will be a loud and forthright women's argument. She will count out coppers and make a fuss.

This did happen. At the top of the steps Matron still waited with the three Hay-Hardys grouped about her, and Edward, who blushed and whitened alternately with terrible excitement, a little to one side.

To this wonderful customer, this profitable womb, the headmaster's wife herself came into the hall. Her husband had sent her, instructing her with deft cynicism from behind his detective novel, himself one of those gods who rarely descend, except, like Zeus, in a very private capacity.

"This is the moment I marked off on the calendar," Edward thought. "Here it is. Every night we threw one of our pebbles out of the window — a day gone." The little stones had dropped back onto the gravel under the window, quite lost, untraceable, the days of their lives.

frail *fragile.*

precarious *very uncertain.*

fleeting *quickly changing.*

fragmentary *incomplete.*

tenuous *half-hearted.*

oblivion *forgetfulness, not thinking.*

premise *assumption.*

tentative *unsure.*

piteously *deserving people's pity.*

exclusively *keeping all others out.*

palpitated *her heart beat quickly.*

running board *step which runs along the side of a car.*

accommodated *fitted in.*

filming *misting over.*

undaunted *not discouraged.*

this profitable womb *it is a fee-paying school.*

deft cynicism *expert, calculating way of treating people to get what he wants.*

Zeus *the supreme god of the Ancient Greeks.*

in a very private capacity *for purely selfish reasons.*

As smooth as minnows were Mrs Lancaster's phrases of welcome; she had soothed so many mothers, mothered so many boys. Her words swam all one way in unison, but her heart never moved. Matron was always nervous; the results of her work were so much on the surface, so checked over. The rest of the staff could hide their inefficiency or shift their responsibility; she could not. If Mrs Hay-Hardy cried, "Dear boy, your teeth!" to her first-born, as she did now, it was Matron's work she criticized, and Matron flushed. And Mrs Lancaster flushed for Matron; and Derrick Hay-Hardy flushed for his mother.

"Perhaps I am not a born mother," Tory thought, going down the steps with Edward. They would walk back to the Crown for lunch, she said. Edward pressed her arm as the taxi, bulging with Hay-Hardys, went away again down the drive.

"Do you mean you wanted to go with them?" she asked.

"No."

"Don't you like them?"

"No."

"But why?"

"They don't like me."

Unbearable news for any mother, for surely all the world loves one's child, one's only child? Doubt set in, a little nagging toothache of doubt. You *are* happy? she wanted to ask. "I've looked forward so much to this," she said instead. "*So* much."

He stared ahead. All round the gateposts drops of moisture fell from one leaf to another; the stone griffins were hunched up in misery.

"But I imagined it being a different day," Tory added. "Quite different."

"It will be nice to get something different to eat," Edward said.

They walked down the road towards the Crown as if they could not make any progress in their conversation until they had reached this point.

"You *are* warm enough at night?" Tory asked, when at last they were sitting in the hotel dining room. She could feel her question sliding away off him.

"Yes," he said absently, and then, bringing himself back to the earlier, distant politeness, added, "Stifling hot."

"Stifling? But surely you have plenty of fresh air?"

"*I* do," he said reassuringly. "My bed's just under the window. Perishing. I have to keep my head under the bedclothes or I get earache."

"I am asking for all this," she thought. When the waiter brought her pink gin she drank it quickly, conscious that Mrs Hay-Hardy, across the hotel dining room, was pouring out a nice glass of water for herself. She was so full of jokes that Tory felt she had perhaps brought a collection of them along with her in her shopping bag. Laughter ran round and round their table above the glasses of water. Edward turned once, and she glimpsed the faintest quiver

minnows *little fishes.*

in unison *together.*

flushed *blushed.*

the Crown *a hotel.*

griffins *statues of mythical beasts, half eagle, half lion.*

absently *not concentrating on what's being said.*

pink gin *gin flavoured with bitters.*

under one eye, and an answering quiver on the middle Hay-Hardy's face.

She felt exasperated. Cold had settled in her; her mouth, her heart too, felt stiff.

"What would you like to do after lunch?" she asked.

"We could look round the shops," Edward said, nibbling away at his bread as if to keep hunger at arm's length.

The shops were in the Market Square. At the draper's the hats were steadily coming round into fashion again. "I could astonish everyone with one of these," Tory thought, setting her own hat right by her reflection in the window. Bales of apron print rose on both sides; a wax-faced little boy wore a stiff suit, its price ticket dangling from his yellow, broken fingers, his painted blue eyes turned mildly upon the street. Edward gave him a look of contempt and went to the shop door. Breathing on the glass in a little space among suspended bibs and jabots and parlourmaids' caps, he watched the cages flying overhead between cashier and counter.

The Hay-Hardys streamed by, heading for the open country.

Most minutely, Tory and Edward examined the draper's shop, the bicycle shop, the family grocer's. There was nothing to buy. They were just reading the postcards in the newsagent's window when Edward's best friend greeted them. His father, a clergyman, snatched off his hat and clapped it to his chest at the sight of Tory. When she turned back to the postcards she could see how unsuitable they were — jokes about bloomers, about twins; a great seaside world of fat men in striped bathing suits; enormous women trotted down to the sea's edge; crabs humorously nipped their behinds; farcical situations arose over bathing machines, and little boys had trouble with their water. She blushed.

The afternoon seemed to give a litle sigh, stirred itself, and shook down a spattering of rain over the pavements. Beyond the Market Square the countryside, which had absorbed the Hay-Hardys, lowered at them.

"Is there anything you want?" Tory asked desperately, coveting the warm interiors of the shops.

"I could do with a new puncture outfit," Edward said.

They went back to the bicycle shop. "My God, it's only three o'clock!" Tory despaired, glancing secretly under her glove at her watch.

The Museum Room at the Guildhall was not gay, but at least there were Roman remains, a few instruments of torture, and half a mammoth's jawbone. Tory sat down on a seat among all the broken terra-cotta and took out a cigarette. Edward wandered away.

"No smoking, please," the attendant said, coming out from behind a case of stuffed deer.

"Oh, please!" Tory begged, She sat primly on the chair, her feet together, and when she looked up at him her violet eyes flashed with tears.

---

draper's *shop which sells cloth and clothes.*

apron print *practical, cheap cotton material.*

jabots *decorative frills for shirts and blouses.*

cages flying overhead between cashier and counter *some shops used to have an elaborate system of overhead wires along which little boxes containing money and receipts were propelled.*

clapped *held tightly.*

bloomers *women's long baggy knickers, fashionable in the late nineteenth century.*

farcical *ridiculous, silly.*

bathing machines *cabins on wheels in which people used to change their clothes at the seaside.*

lowered *scowled, looked threateningly.*

coveting *longing for.*

gay *cheerful.*

terra-cotta *pottery.*

primly *in a very respectable way.*

The attendant struck a match for her, and his hand, curving round it, trembled a little.

"It's the insurance," he apologized. "I'll have this later, if I may," and he put the cigarette she had given him very carefully in his breast pocket, as if it were a lock of her hair.

"Do you have to stay here all day long with these dull little broken jugs and things?" she asked, looking round.

He forgave her at once for belittling his life's work, only pointing out his pride, the fine mosaic on the wall.

belittling *scorning.*

"But floor should be lying down," she said naïvely — not innocently.

Edward came tiptoeing back.

"You see that quite delightful floor hanging up there?" she said. "This gentleman will tell you all about it. My son adores Greek mythology," she explained.

"Your son!" he repeated, affecting gallant disbelief, his glance stripping ten or fifteen years from her. "This happens to be a Byzantine mosaic," he said and looked reproachfully at it for not being what it could not be. Edward listened grudgingly. His mother had forced him into similar situations at other times: in the Armoury of the Tower of London; once at Kew. It was as if she kindled in men a little flicker of interest and admiration which her son must keep fanned, for she would not. Boredom drew her away again, yet her charm must still hold sway. So now Edward listened crossly to the story of the Byzantine mosaic, as he had last holidays minutely observed the chasing on Henry VIII's breastplate, and in utter exasperation the holidays before that watched curlews through field glasses ("Edward is so very keen on birds") for the whole of a hot day while Tory dozed elegantly in the heather.

affecting gallant disbelief *flattering her, pretending that he could not believe she was old enough to have a son.*

Byzantine *from medieval Byzantium (now Istanbul).*

grudgingly *resentfully.*

Kew *the botanical gardens near Richmond, Surrey.*

kindled *lit.*

keep fanned *sustain.*

chasing *decoration.*

breastplate *part of a suit of armour.*

"Ordinary days perhaps are better," Edward thought. Sinking down through him were the lees of despair, which must at all costs be hidden from his mother. He glanced up at every clock they passed and wondered about his friends. Alone with his mother, he felt unsafe, wounded and wounding; saw himself in relation to the outside world, oppressed by responsibility. Thoughts of the future, and even, as they stood in the church porch to shelter from another little gust of rain, of death, seemed to alight on him, brushed him, disturbed him, as they would not do if he were at school, anonymous and safe.

lees *dregs.*

oppressed *weighed down.*

alight *land.*

anonymous *part of the crowd.*

Tory sat down on a seat and a read a notice about missionaries, chafing her hands inside her muff while all her bracelets jingled softly.

chafing *rubbing.*

Flapping, black, in his cassock, a clergyman came hurrying through the graveyard, between the dripping umbrella trees. Edward stepped guiltily outside the porch as if he had been trespassing.

cassock *a churchman's long black robe.*

"Good afternoon," the vicar said.

"Good afternoon," Tory replied. She looked up from blowing the fur of her muff into little divisions, and her smile broke warmly, beautifully, over the dark afternoon.

Then, "The weather —" both began ruefully, broke off and hesitated, then laughed at each other.

It was wonderful; now they would soon be saying good-bye. It was over. The day they had longed for was almost over — the polite little tea among the chintz, the wheel-back chairs of the Copper Kettle; Tory frosty and imperious with the waitresses, and once Edward beginning, "Father —" at which she looked up sharply before she could gather together the careful indifference she always assumed at this name. Edward faltered. "He sent me a parcel."

"How nice!" Tory said, laying ice all over his heart. Her cup was cracked. She called the waitress. She could not drink tea from riveted china, however prettily painted. The waitress went sulkily away. All around them sat other little boys with their parents. Tory's bracelets tinkled as she clasped her hands tightly together and leaned forward. "And how," she asked brightly, indifferently, "how is your father's wife?"

Now the taxi turned in at the school gates. Suddenly the day withdrew; there were lights in the ground-floor windows. She thought of going back in the train, a lonely evening. She would take a drink up to her bedroom and sip it while she did her hair, the gas fire roaring in its white ribs, Edward's photograph beside her bed.

The Hay-Hardys were unloading at the foot of the steps; flushed from their country walk and all their laughter, they seemed to swarm and shout.

Edward got out of the taxi and stood looking up at Tory, his new puncture outfit clasped tightly in his hand. Uncertainly, awaiting a cue from her, he tried to begin his good-bye.

Warm, musky-scented, softly rustling, with the sound of her bracelets, the touch of her fur, she leaned and kissed him. "So lovely, darling!" she murmured. She had no cue to give him. Mrs Hay-Hardy had gone into the school to have a word with Matron, so she must find her own way of saying farewell.

They smiled gaily as if they were greeting each other.

"See you soon."

"Yes, see you soon."

"Good-bye, then, darling."

"Good-bye."

She slammed the door and, as the car moved off, leaned to the windows and waved. He stood there uncertainly, waving back, radiant with relief; then, as she disappeared round the curve of the drive, ran quickly up the steps to find his friends and safety.

☆

ruefully *sadly.*

chintz *cotton cloth printed with bright coloured patterns.*

imperious *arrogant.*

riveted *mended with a metal pin.*

indifferently *without feeling anything.*

cue *lead.*

radiant *full of joy.*

Thinking/Talking Points

▷ 'this malevolent landscape'
Which details in the first two paragraphs help to create the idea of a malevolent landscape?
What sort of story does the atmosphere created in the opening paragraphs make you expect?
See if you can find a couple of details from later in the story which develop this impression of the day and the countryside.

▷ How do you picture the school, the staff and the boys' lives there?
Which details in the story give you that impression?

▷ Read again the two paragraphs which begin
'One other woman was on her own' and end
'Tory lifted her muff to hide her smile.' (page 145)
We see the woman through Tory's eyes.
Which details here tell us more about Tory than about the woman she is looking at?

▷ 'Nervous dread made her feel fretful and vicious.'
How would you describe Tory's state of mind here?
From what we are told in the rest of this paragraph, see if you can explain why she is feeling like this.

▷ What impression of Mrs Hay-Hardy (the woman Tory had been looking at) and her family do you get from the moment when she approaches the cab to the end of the story?
Which details do most to give you that impression?

▷ '"My God, it's only three o'clock!" Tory despaired, glancing secretly under her glove at her watch.'
Why do you think she 'despaired'?

▷ '"But the floor should be lying down," she said *naïvely – not innocently.*'
Explain the words in italics.

▷ What do you think Edward feels his mother is doing by telling the man that her son 'adores Greek mythology'?

▷ Read again the paragraph which begins
'"Ordinary days perhaps are better," Edward thought.' (page 149)
See if you can describe how Edward is feeling here.
Why do you think he is feeling like that?
What does this sentence suggest about how Edward had felt before his mother arrived?

▷ '. . . and once Edward beginning, "Father –," at which she looked up sharply before she could gather together the careful indifference she always assumed at this name.'
See if you can explain what the writer means by 'careful indifference' here.
What does this detail add to the way you see Tory?

▷ '"And how," she asked brightly, indifferently, "how is your father's wife?"'
Why do you think Tory asks this question?
Why do you think she chooses those particular words?
How do you think the question makes Edward feel?

▷ 'Warm, musky-scented, softly rustling, with the sound of her bracelets, the touch of her fur, she leaned and kissed him.'
What does the way Tory is described here suggest about how Edward feels about her?

▷ How 'separate' are Edward and his mother?
Which details in the story as a whole do you think show this?

Reread the story carefully now, before selecting an assignment. Notice which details tell us most about Edward's feelings.

Assignments

English

○ You are twelve.
Your parents have separated, home is in chaos, it is the Summer holidays and 'while things are sorted out', you have been sent to stay with a relative or to a holiday camp.
You haven't been told very much by your parents, and what one has said has not always tallied with what the other has told you.

Write a series of diary entries and/or letters home in which we can see the story unfolding, your feelings changing. In some letters, the problems of home may seem to have disappeared into the background, as you get excited about something which has happened on holiday. In others, you may feel hostile to one or both of your parents or you may try to push them into 'making everything all right again'.
Write your first entry/letter as if you are travelling, perhaps leaving home for the first time without your parents.
What do you see, hear?
What are you feeling excited about? Nervous about? Muddled about?
Are you pleased with your new 'freedom' or frightened by it?
How much do you understand of what is happening?

○ *Disneyland Here I Come*
Unknown to your parent(s), you have entered a cornflakes competition. The first prize is a fortnight's supervised holiday in California, including lots of time and money to spend at Disneyland.
A letter in a red envelope arrives, telling you that you have won a first prize and will be joining six other lucky winners on the Holiday of a Lifetime in August.

Write a short story or a short play about this situation.
You may like to limit the piece to a conversation over breakfast after the letter arrives. Bring out the way people's first reactions of surprise, delight, amazement, change as everyone begins to realise what will be involved – changing plans already made, buying clothes and suitcases, being apart for the first time ever . . .

You could include a couple more scenes (e.g. going shopping, your parents talking in the kitchen) in which we see people's attitudes gradually changing. The final scene could be the parting at the airport.

Think about the mixture of feelings each person might have in this situation:
parent(s) – concerned about safety; pleased/sorry to see you growing up and becoming independent; envious/proud/surprised; looking forward to a break themselves . . .
you – excited/nervous; wanting them to let you go and to stop you going; hoping they will be all right without you; wondering if you will be all right without them . . .

English Literature

○ What impression of Tory's situation and her personality does the story give you?
Do you feel sorry for her and/or for her son? Give your reasons.
(Select a dozen or so brief quotations to give you a framework around which to shape your essay.)

○ Rewrite this story but so that we see things from Edward's point of view. Instead of telling the reader about Tory's feelings, concentrate upon her son's. Describe people and things (e.g. the Hay-Hardys, the museum, the school) as he would see them. Use details from the story but add plenty of your own ideas.
You may choose to write
either as if Edward is telling the story. For example,
   Mother's cab was the last one to arrive, I was beginning to wonder whether she had missed the train again . . .
or as if you are somebody observing him. For example,
   As Edward stood shivering a bit on the school steps, he began to wonder if his mother were coming after all . . .

○ Imagine you are Edward writing a letter to thank your father for the parcel. Tell him about school, about your mother's visit, about how you are looking forward to the holidays.

Some further reading

Doris Lessing   *Through the Tunnel*

★

Lots of children spend time apart from one parent or both.

What problems can arise from seeing a parent just occasionally
(a) for the child (b) for the parents?

In this story, a father collects his daughter from the home he has left, to take
her for a day out.
Before you read it, think about how each of the people involved – the father,
his former wife and his ten year-old daughter – might be feeling about the day
ahead.

Mine on Thursdays

To begin with, it took more than two hours to drive from Boston to
Monument, twice the usual time, because of an accident near
Concord that caused a traffic backup that turned a three-mile line of
cars into a giant metal caterpillar, inching ponderously forward.
Meanwhile, I had a splitting headache, my eyes were like raw
onions and my stomach lurched on the edge of nausea, for which I
fully accepted the blame. Ordinarily, the night before my Thursdays
with Holly, I took it easy, avoided involvements and went to bed
early. But yesterday afternoon, I'd had a futile clash with McClafflin
– all arguments with employers are futile – and had threatened to
quit, an empty gesture that caused him to smile because he knew
about all my traps. This led to a few solitary and self-pitying drinks
at the bar across the street, leaving me vulnerable to an invitation to
a party in Cambridge, a party that turned out to be nothing more
than pseudo-intellectual talk, plus liquor, the effect of which was
pseudo: promising so much and delivering little except a clanging
hangover and the familiar and desperate taste of old regrets.
Somehow, I managed to survive the morning and left at my usual
hour, aware that McClafflin was watching my painful progress
through the office. And I thought: "The hell with you, Mac. You
think I'm going to leave her waiting uselessly, while I take a cold
shower and sleep it off. But Holly expects me and I'll be there."

I *was* there, late maybe but present and accounted for, and Holly
leaped with delight when she saw me drive into her street. I made a
reckless U-turn, knowing that Alison would be watching from the
window, frowning her disapproval. The scarlet convertible was
sufficient to insult her cool grey New England eyes and my lateness
was an affront to her penchant for punctuality (she'd been a teacher

**Boston, Monument,
Concord, Vermont** *towns
in New England, USA.*

backup *jam.*

ponderously *slowly,
sluggishly.*

**my stomach lurched on
the edge of nausea** *I felt I
was going to be sick.*

futile *pointless.*

quit *resign.*

solitary *lonely.*

vulnerable *easily persuaded.*

pseudo-intellectual
pretending to be clever.

liquor *alcohol.*

pseudo *false, phoney.*

**present and accounted
for** *like a soldier on parade.*

convertible *a car whose roof
can be folded down.*

affront *challenge, snub.*

penchant for punctuality
*expecting people to keep to
timetables.*

before our marriage and still loved schedules and timetables). Anyway, the brakes squealed as I pulled up in front of the house on the sedate street. On impulse, I blew the horn, long and loud. I always did things like that, to provoke her, killing myself with her, or killing whatever was left of what we'd had together, like a dying man hiding the medicine in the palm of his hand instead of swallowing the pill that might cure him.

Holly came streaking off the porch, dazzling in something pink and lacy and gay. Holly, my true love, the one person who could assuage my hangovers, comfort my aching limbs and give absolution to my sins.

"Oh, Daddy, I knew you'd come. I just knew it," she said, flinging herself at me.

I dug my face into her shampoo-scented hair and clutched the familiar geography of her bones and flesh. "Did I ever stand you up?" Then, laughing: "Don't answer that." Because there had been times, of course, when it had been impossible for me to come.

"Wonder World today, Dad?" she asked.

The sun hurled its rays against my eyeballs, penetrating the dark glasses, and the prospect of those whirling rides at the amusement park spread sickness through my veins. But aware that Alison was there behind the white curtains, I assured Holly: "Whatever you say, baby, whatever you say." Wanting Alison to know that somebody loved me. "The sky's the limit."

Holly was mine on Thursdays, and during the two years of our Thursdays together, we had made the circuit many times – shopping trips to fancy stores, movie matinees, picnics on Moosock Ridge, bowling, Wonder World in season – all the things an adult can do with a child. I'd always been careful to indulge her, basking in her delight. We shared the unspoken knowledge that we were playing a special kind of hooky, each of us a truant, she from that well-regulated and orderly world of her mother's and I from the world of too many martinis, too many girls, too many long shots that had never come in.

For some reason, I thought of my father. Occasionally, Holly and I journeyed out to the cemetery where I stood at his grave and tried to recall him. I most often remembered the time, a few weeks before he died, when we sat together at the nursing home. After long minutes of silence, he'd said: "The important thing, Howie, is to be a man."

He began to cry, tears overflowing his red-rimmed eyes, and I pitied him, pitied all the old people who could only look back, look back. After a while, I asked: "What's a man, Dad?" Not really curious but wanting to say something.

My poor father. Who'd had too much booze and too little love and no luck at all, at cards or dice or all those jobs. And all the deals that had collapsed.

"To be a man," my father said, wiping his cheeks, "is to look at the wreckage of your life and to confront it all without pity for yourself.

---

schedules *lists, plans.*

sedate *quiet, sober, prim and proper.*

On impulse *without thinking.*

provoke *taunt.*

streaking *racing.*

assuage *heal.*

give absolution to my sins *forgive my mistakes.*

penetrating *going through.*

prospect *looking forward to.*

movie matinees *afternoons at the cinema.*

bowling *ten-pin bowling.*

indulge *spoil.*

basking *warming myself.*

hooky *playing truant.*

martinis *cocktails.*

long shots that never came in *gambles which didn't come off.*

curious *interested.*

confront *face.*

Without alibis. And to go on. To endure . . ."

It had been a long day and I had been impatient to get away from the ancient abandoned man who called himself my father. I left shortly afterwards, thinking: he'd always had a way with words, hadn't he? And what had it got him in the end? A wife whose early death had given him an excuse to drown himself in bottle after bottle, while his son, whose birth was the cause of that death, was shunted from uncle to aunt to cousin. Yet, he had tried hard to be a father, in his way, always showing up on holidays, bundled with gifts and stories of great adventures in the cities he visited on his sales routes.

Now, Holly and I drove along soft-shaded Spruce Street and I was relieved that a trip to the cemetery was not on the agenda that day. Holly chatted gaily. She told me about the neighbourhood carnival she and her friends had staged and how their names had appeared in the newspaper because they'd donated the proceeds to charity. She described the shopping trips for school clothes, because September loomed ahead. She brought me up to date on all the things that make up the life and times of a ten-year-old girl, and I barely listened, taking pleasure in her presence alone. She wore pigtails, and she was dark, unlike Alison, who was blond, and this secretly delighted me. Holly prattled on: there was a fabulous new ride at Wonder World, "The Rocket Trip to the Moon," that all the kids were crazy about, and could we go on it, Dad, could we, huh, please?

"Why not?" I asked. All the "why nots" I had tossed her on Thursdays, like bouquets of love. I agreed so quickly because I knew she would change her mind at the last moment. Holly was shy, timid, and she usually avoided the more adventurous and perilous rides. Ordinarily, she was content to stroll through the park at my side while we made up stories about people passing by. She liked the merry-go-round and the distorted mirrors in the fun-house and she was reluctant to attempt such daring exploits as the roller coaster or the loop-the-loop. For which I was grateful. Particularly on days such as this when my head pounded and my stomach revolted at the slightest movement.

"How's your mother?" I asked, the question ritual.

Usually, the answer was ritual, too. "Fine" or "swell." As if Holly'd received instructions. But today, she hesitated, sighed, and said: "Tired."

"Tired?" I was searching for a parking place in the busy Wonder World lot.

"Oh, she's been on a committee to get blood donors —"

That was Alison. Conscientious and community-minded and always willing to help. She had a desire for service to others and she dearly loved Monument and had no wish to venture to other places. Which was part of our trouble, or at least the beginning of it all. I had always regarded Monument as a starting point, not a destination. Alison and I had met the summer I'd been planning to leave,

alibis *excuses.*

agenda *plan for the day.*

prattled *chatted about trivial things.*

perilous *dangerous.*

exploits *daring adventures.*

ritual *formality.*

lot *car park.*

conscientious and community-minded *taking her responsibilities as a citizen very seriously.*

venture to *explore.*

156

ready to knock on a thousand doors in New York City, seeking a job, something, anything — just to get away. But Alison had been so beautiful and I had loved her so incredibly that I'd remained in Monument, writing obituaries and other equally dismal stories for the town newspaper. However, I was always aware of the world outside Monument and I had wanted to see it, to know a million people, visit a million places, all of which was ridiculous, of course, and eminently impractical. Sometimes, my frustration would burst out. "Alison," I'd plead, "let's try, let's pack up and take our chances. I don't mean to go to the other side of the world. But somewhere. The world's so big and Monument's so small, our lives are so small . . ."

Alison had held up little Holly, who smiled at me in her infant innocence. "Is she so small, too, that you can't be a father to her?"

Defeated, I remained in Monument but spent more and more time away from that confining claustrophobic apartment. In a bar or cocktail lounge, there were kind shadows and when you'd consumed just the right amount of beer or rye or whatever, all the sharp edges blurred and Monument itself receded. Inevitably, if you go often enough to a bar, a girl walks in. And, finally, Sally arrived. She was a member of a television unit dispatched to Monument by a Boston station to capture, on tape, the one-hundred-and-fifth birthday of Harrison Shanks, the oldest man in the county. Sally and I had a drink or two; she confessed that she was only a secretary for the film crew, an errand girl, really. Laughing, she reversed the cliché and wondered what a fellow like me was doing in a place like that. Meaning Monument, of course. She leaned against me warmly, a frankness about her body. Alison hid herself in tailored suits or loose, comfortable sweaters while Sally wore clothes that made me constantly aware that she was a woman. Sitting beside her on that first night, before I had said two dozen words to her, I felt as though I had known her body before, probably in a thousand adolescent dreams.

The television people were in Monument only two days. I served as their unofficial guide, arranging the interview with Harrison Shanks, who sat bewildered in a wicker chair on the porch of his ancient house, croaking monosyllabic answers to the inane questions placed by the interviewer. "How does it feel to be one hundred and five years old?" The old man, confused by time and place, kept muttering about the banks closing and Herbert Hoover, which caused a few laughs and quips off camera, and I felt myself tightening inside. Someone pressed my arm.

"You're a sensitive one, aren't you?" Sally asked.

"He's an old man. I've known him all my life."

"Poor boy," she said, touching the tip of my nose with a delicate finger. "You need a little tender loving care."

The interview with Harrison Shanks used up only ninety-three seconds of a special show dealing with the problems of the aged but my alliance with Sally lasted much longer than that. But not long

obituaries *newspaper account of the life of someone who has just died.*

dismal *sad, dreary.*

eminently impractical *obviously impossible.*

claustrophobic *stifling.*

apartment *flat.*

rye *a kind of whiskey.*

receded *moved into the background.*

dispatched *sent.*

cliché *a clever phrase which has become stale.*

frankness *openness.*

monosyllabic *one-word.*

inane *foolish.*

Herbert Hoover *elected US President in 1928.*

quips *jokes.*

off camera *behind the scenes, not recorded on film.*

alliance *relationship.*

157

enough. That was the terrible part: leaving Alison and Holly for Sally and all the bright promises of Boston, to dislocate our lives and make Holly that pitiable object – the child of a broken home – to do all that and then to end up alone, after all. Sally found other sensitive men upon whom to bestow her tender loving care. Her care wasn't really loving, I had learned, and I drifted from one job to another, sideways, not upwards. To go upwards demanded more than talent. It demanded ruthlessness and cunning, the necessity for sitting up nights plotting the next day's manoeuvre, the next day's presentation. But I found more allure in a drink or two, which became three or four, and then, what the hell, let's have a party, let's have some fun. And then it wasn't fun any more.

"Daddy, you look kooky," Holly said now, giggling uncontrollably.

"You're not exactly Cinderella at the ball," I retorted.

We were regarding ourselves in the fun-house mirrors: Holly suddenly short and fat as if invisible hands had clapped her head down into her body, and I ludicrously tall and thin, pencil-like, my head a soiled eraser. Then we moved and exchanged grotesqueries, laughing some more at our reversed roles. At one point, I picked her up and whirled her around, basking in the gaiety of her laughter, despite the pain that stabbed my head. Dizziness overtook me and I set her down. "Let's rest awhile, baby." But she was carried on the momentum of her excitement and pulled me on. "The Rocket Ride, Dad, the Rocket Ride."

I let myself be led through the sun-dazzled park, telling myself to hold out for a little while. There was a small bar across the street and maybe I could duck in there for a cool one while Holly went on the rocket. On those Thursdays with Holly, I had seldom cheated that way, had devoted all my time to her, perhaps to show Alison that I wasn't completely without a conscience. When I had first called her after finding my loneliness intolerable, she'd been sceptical.

"We've been doing nicely, thanks," she said, cool and crisp. "Don't upset things, Howie. We haven't seen you for – how long? Three years? – and we've arranged our lives. It doesn't hurt any more."

"You mean, you don't need me," I said.

When she didn't answer, I took the plunge. "But I need you."

Her laughter infuriated me. I wanted to hurt her. "All right, maybe not you. But Holly. I need her. She's mine, too. My blood runs . . ."

"I know. Your blood runs in her veins. But nothing else, I hope."

I was startled by her bitterness but, upon reflection, I saw that she was justified. When the divorce had become final, I hadn't made any particular demands about Holly. Alison had been generous enough to leave the terms open: I could see the child whenever and however I wished. Terms that I did not take her up on, because I was too intoxicated with my freedom and Sally and later the others. Until that day I called, alone and desperate in that hotel room,

dislocate *disrupt.*

pitiable *sad.*

manoeuvre *tactics.*

allure *temptation.*

eraser *rubber.*

grotesqueries *distorted pictures.*

momentum *forward movement.*

sceptical *suspicious, not willing to believe in me.*

abandoned by everyone, needing somebody. And so we decided, over the telephone, that Holly would be mine on Thursdays. Thursday afternoon to be precise. Those first few weeks, I clutched at those hours with Holly as if they were gulps of oxygen in an airless world. We made the rounds, stiff and awkward at first, but finally Holly began to laugh at my jokes and eventually she accepted me. Alison remained distant, however, and never ventured out of the house. I was not invited inside, of course.

One day she addressed me through the screen door as I met Holly at the porch. She told Holly to go to the car.

"You know what you're doing?" she asked. But it wasn't a question: more an accusation.

"What?"

"Disrupting her life, her routine. Cruising in here every week like a year-round Santa Claus."

"Are you jealous? Or don't you think a kid needs a little fun now and then?"

She recoiled as if I'd slapped her or had stumbled upon the truth, and I felt a twist of triumph.

recoiled *flinched.*

"Here we are, Dad," Holly said.

"My God," I cried, confronted by the huge and elaborate piece of machinery rising from the ground in front of us. Ordinarily, the rides in amusement parks all resemble one another, but the Rocket Ride seemed to be an exception, a roaring and revolving device that emitted billows of smoke and showers of sparks. Circular in design, the machinery contained small, simulated rockets with room for two or three people in each rocket. As the entire device moved in circular motion, the individual rockets swung up and down and occasionally poised daringly fifty feet above the ground before descending in a roar of smoke and flame. As we watched the ride was apparently completing its circuit. I realized, finally, that the smoke was simulated and that the flames were actually paper streamers cunningly devised to resemble the real thing.

emitted *let out.*
billows *clouds.*
simulated *imitation.*

poised *suspended.*

"Isn't it cool, Dad?" Holly asked.

I chuckled at my shy little girl, who had yet to find the courage for a trip on the roller coaster.

"You're not going on *this*, are you?" Although the ride was not as awesome as it had seemed at first glance, there was still a fifty-foot swoop.

awesome *terrifying.*

"All the kids have," Holly said, eyes blazing with challenge. "If I don't they'll think I'm –" she groped for the alien word – "chicken."

alien *unfamiliar.*

My poor sweet. So small and worried, risking an encounter with the monster to prove to her friends that she was not afraid. The ride came to a stop with screams and shouts and bellows and a muffled explosion. The pain between my eyes increased, my stomach rose.

bellows *roars.*

"Please, Daddy?"

"Tickets," called the attendant.

"Boy, oh boy," exulted a fellow coming off the ramp, his arm around a small blond girl who was flushed and excited, her body

160

ripe and full. Somehow, our eyes met. She was young, but her eyes held the old message, the ancient code I had deciphered a thousand times.

"Can I, Daddy?" Holly's voice was poised on the edge of victory, interpreting my sudden preoccupation as acquiescence.

I watched the blond and her boyfriend as they made their way to a nearby refreshment stand. As a test. Sure enough, her eyes found their way to mine.

Holly had been leading me to the ticket booth, and I found myself with wallet in hand.

"You really want to go on this thing?" I asked, thinking that perhaps she had started to grow up, beginning to leave childhood behind. And yet I doubted her endurance. She was still only a baby.

"Oh, Daddy," she said impatiently, the woman emerging from the girl, a hint of the future.

I thought of a tall cool one in the bar across the street. Or maybe an approach to the blond. Handing a dollar to the cashier, I said: "One."

"Child or adult?"

"Child," I answered. Adult? What sane adult would risk a ride on that terrible parody of a rocket shot?

"Aren't you coming with me?" Holly asked.

"Look, Holly, your daddy's getting old for these kinds of capers. Rocket ships are for the young." Leading her toward the entrance, I urged: "Better hurry. You won't get a seat."

"Do you think I should go on the ride alone?" she asked, doubts gathering, almost visible in her eyes.

I squinted at the mechanism, conjuring up the vision of myself, complete with pounding head and queasy stomach, being tossed and turned and lifted and dashed down. Ridiculous. It was impossible for me to accompany her. I was not equipped for Rocket Rides, with or without a hangover. Blond or no blond.

The crowd jostled us, pushing forward, carrying us to the entrance. Placing the ticket in Holly's hand, I waved her on. She was swept along in the crowd and then emerged on the ramp leading to the platform where customers entered the individual capsules. The attendant on the platform took her ticket. I hoped he would realize how young she was and guide her to a rocket where other people would be near her. He led her to a small rocket, a capsule with enough room for only one person, installed no doubt for those who preferred to ride alone. She hesitated for a moment and then entered the compartment. She seemed small and wan and abandoned. She snapped a thin bar in place – her only protection from falling out. But, of course, nobody ever fell out of those things. Did they? I told myself to stop being melodramatic; it was only a lousy ride in an amusement park and she wasn't a child any longer.

Damn it. I walked over to the cashier's booth, drawing my wallet. But I was halted in my tracks by the attendant's cry: "All aboard. We're off to the moon."

deciphered *read and understood.*

preoccupation *interest in something else, distraction.*

aquiescence *agreeing to do what she wanted.*

endurance *stamina.*

parody *imitation.*

capers *games.*

queasy *unsettled.*

jostled *pushed against.*

emerged *came out.*

wan *pale, sickly.*

melodramatic *behaving as if things are worse than they are.*

"You can just make it, mister," the cashier offered.

But I'd look foolish scurrying up the ramp. And, besides, all the rockets were probably filled.

scurrying *rushing*.

A belch of smoke escaped the rocket, the roar of an engine filled the air and the entire mechanism seemed to come alive. I ran back near the entrance, eager to see Holly before the ride began. She was sitting erect in her seat, as if she were a dutiful fifth-grader being obedient for her teacher. Her hands were folded on her lap. Our eyes met and I garlanded my face with a smile, assuring her that she was going to have fun. She nodded back, sighed a little, and with a roar and swish and booms, the trip started.

dutiful fifth-grader *obedient pupil (Holly is ten years old).*

garlanded *decorated.*

It all resembled a merry-go round gone mad, the rockets whirling madly and individually, rising and falling and twisting, often at crazy impossible angles. I was grateful for my restraint, for having refused to go with Holly; I'd have been sick as a dog already. I glanced toward the refreshment stand; the blond was gone. Like so many others.

restraint *holding back.*

When I turned back to the ride again, it was in full swing. People screamed, those peculiar screams of terror and delight. The machinery *whooshed* and I sought Holly. At first, I couldn't find her in the nightmare of motion and colour and sound. And then the small rocket swung into view and I spotted her. Her eyes were wide with surprise, her body tense, her hands clinging to the bar. Then she was gone, whisked away out of sight. The other people passed like blurs before my eyes. On the next turn, Holly's eyes were closed and her face resembled melted wax, as if a mad sculptor had moulded her flesh into a mask of fright. As she began to rise, far up, I wondered whether there was an element of danger, after all. Suppose she lost her grip on the bar. I walked toward the attendant who stood at bored attention near the entrance, but I finally decided not to bother him. "Stop dramatizing," I told myself. Then Holly swept by, her eyes wild with horror, terrible eyes, agonized. I hurried to the attendant and asked him how long the ride went on.

"What?" he shouted above the din.

"How long's the ride?"

"Five minutes. They get their money's worth," he yelled.

Stalking to my vantage point, I cursed myself. A moment later, she came into view, her eyes closed once more, her body crouched and tense, pitifully small and vulnerable. I remembered that as a child of three or so she'd been subject to nightmares. And she'd been afraid of thunder and lightning. I thought of all the thunderstorms she had endured and how I hadn't been there to comfort her.

stalking to my vantage point *moving stealthily like a hunter to watch his prey.*

vulnerable *at risk.*

endured *put up with.*

Now, the rocket swept around again and began the long ascent. Her eyes were open, in a gaze of desperation. She looked downward and saw me. Her lips were pressed tight, her cheeks taut. In that precious moment I tried to hold her in my view. I smiled, more than smiled: I attempted to inject courage and love and protection into

ascent *climb.*

taut *tense.*

162

my smile. And our eyes met for a long moment – and then she was gone. Up and away. Around and around. And I closed my own eyes.

The ride finally ended and I rushed to the exit to greet her, arms ready to welcome her, happy to have her safe at last. I watched as she carefully let herself out of the rocket. She walked, one foot after the other, across the ramp, a little unsteady, perhaps, but determined. I held out my arms as she approached.

"Holly!" I cried.

She looked up thoughtfully, startled, as if she were surprised to find me there.

"Say, that was quite a trip, wasn't it?" I inquired. "Holy mackerel, I was ready to rip off my clothes, show my Superman outfit and leap to the rescue."

She smiled distantly. But not at my words. She was smiling at something else. It was a terrible smile. Private. The kind of smile that didn't belong on the face of a child.

"Are you all right?" I asked.

"I'm fine," she said.

"I'm sorry you were alone. Too bad you couldn't have got into a rocket with somebody else. I was afraid you might fall out."

"I'm safe and sound," she said.

But she wasn't looking at me.

"Well," I said, "what's next on the schedule?" Trying to induce enthusiasm into my voice.

induce coax.

"I think I'd like to go home, please," she replied, in her best polite-little-girl manner.

"It's early," I pointed out. "How about something to eat?" Ordinarily, she was ravenous for the things I bought her: popcorn and candy floss and triple-header ice-cream cones.

ravenous very hungry.

"I'm not hungry," she said.

We were passing the fun-house. I thought of those crazy mirrors inside and grimaced at the thought of myself bloated and distorted. With Holly walking beside me – beside me and yet getting farther and farther away with every step we took – I wondered if the mirrors weren't true reflections, after all. "Forget it," I ridiculed myself, "stop thinking of yourself as a poor man's Dorian Gray."

grimaced winced.

"Look, Holly, it's early. You said school's starting. How about a trip downtown? To Norton's? For some new clothes?" Everybody went to Norton's and I was sure that I would be able to charge purchases there without any fuss.

Dorian Gray a character in a story by Oscar Wilde whose portrait reveals the true state of his mind.
charge purchases get goods on credit.

She blew air out of the side of her mouth. "I think I'd rather just go home," she said. "Besides, Mom isn't feeling too well, I might be able to help her."

"Your wish is my command," I said, keeping it light, keeping it gay.

And Alison. How tired did she get? And why wasn't she feeling well? Should I have inquired once in a while? But who inquired about me?

163

We made our way to the car under a sky suddenly subdued with clouds. The brilliance of the sun was muted, for which my eyes were thankful.

Once in the car, I asked: "Sure you want to go right home?" Clinging to her presence.

She looked straight ahead, I realized she hadn't looked at me directly since she'd emerged from the Rocket Ride.

"Oh, Daddy," she said.

Oh, Daddy. Without anguish, without any reprimand. *Oh, Daddy.* With a tired, weary acceptance that echoed a thousand other acceptances that had marked my life. A comment on all my defections.

"Next Thursday," I said, "we should do something different, something crazy." Thinking wildly. "Maybe your mother would let you come in to Boston. We could really do the town."

"I don't know," she said. "I think there's something special going on next Thursday. At school. Orientation Day – getting ready for September."

"But –" I began. And then stopped. I'd been about to say: You are mine on Thursdays. But I saw, of course, that she was not actually mine, not on Thursdays or any other day of the week, or the year. We'd been playing truant, sure enough, but not as father and daughter, merely as adult and child. All those *why nots* I had tossed her – not bouquets of love, but bribes. I glanced at her as we drove along. She sat erect, composed, that elegance of Alison's so much in evidence, and I ached with love and longing and tenderness, knowing that she was more Alison than me, despite the dark hair. Where was I in her? Was I there at all?

I turned the car away from Spruce Street. "I'd like to drive by the cemetery," I told her.

"All right," she said, eyes still on the road ahead.

I stopped the car at the comfortless place of grey and green, slab and grass, and I thought of my father and what he had said that time about being a man and confronting the débris of your dreams. Without self-pity.

"Holly," I said.

Finally, she turned toward me – those lovely eyes, that curve of cheek. I had wondered before whether I was anywhere in her and now I hoped I wasn't.

"Yes?" she asked, mildly interested.

I wanted to say: I'm sorry. I'm sorry for playing Santa Claus when I should have been a father. I'm sorry for wanting the whole world when I should have wanted only those who loved me. I'm sorry for the Rocket Ride – and all the Rocket Rides of your life that I didn't share.

Instead, I said: "I won't be coming to Monument for a while." I didn't allow her to answer but began to improvise quickly. "See, I've been thinking of leaving Boston, getting away from the rat race. I heard of a small-town newspaper up in Vermont – a weekly – that's

subdued *dull.*

anguish *pain.*
reprimand *telling off.*

defections *betrayals.*

composed *stiff, keeping her feelings to herself.*

débris *wreckage.*

improvise *invent things.*

164

looking for a man. Maybe I'll give it a whirl."

"That sounds interesting," she said, as if we were strangers on a plane.

"And if it works out, who knows? Maybe the Monument *Times* might have an opening someday.

Don't you see, my darling, what I'm trying to say?

"And I'll come home for good," I ventured.

She looked out over the cemetery, her face as bleak as any tombstone.

"Wouldn't you like that?" I asked.

At last, she looked at me again. "Yes," she said, For a moment, something raced across her face, something appeared in her eyes, perhaps an echo of the child I had known a long time ago. Then it faded. And the eyes were old. I knew I had done this to her. "Yes, that would be nice," she said, in that correct manner.

We drove away from the cemetery and to Spruce Street, and I parked in front of that house that once had been home. She kissed me dutifully on the cheek. I didn't blow the horn to provoke Alison or as a last attempt at amusing Holly. I drove away slowly, and I kept telling myself desperately that I wasn't saying goodbye.

Thinking/Talking Points

▷ 'The familiar and desperate taste of old regrets.'
   What impression does this phrase give you of Howie's outlook on life?

▷ 'Killing myself with her, or killing whatever was left of what we'd had together, like a dying man hiding the medicine in the palm of his hand instead of swallowing the pill that might cure him.'
   See if you can put Howie's confused feelings here into your own words.

▷ What do Holly's first words suggest may have been going on in the house before her father arrived?

▷ 'We were playing a special kind of hookey.'
   What do you think (a) Holly and (b) her father were truanting from?

▷ How far do you agree with Howie's father's definition of 'a man'?
   How do you think Howie's relationship with his father influenced the way he grew up?

▷ '"I know. Your blood runs in her veins. But nothing else, I hope."'
   What do you think Alison meant by that? Why did she say it?

▷ '"Cruising in here every week like a year-round Santa Claus."'
   Why 'cruising'? Do you feel sympathy with Alison's point of view?
   Give your reasons.

▷ 'All the "why nots" I had tossed her on Thursdays, *like bouquets of love*.'
   What do you think this phrase reveals about Howie's feelings for Holly?

▷ See if you can explain what led Howie to spend more and more time in bars and then get involved with Sally.

▷ 'Handing a dollar to the cashier, I said: "One" . . . It was impossible for me to accompany her.'
What do you think were the reasons for Howie making this crucial decision?
Do you sympathise with him at this point? Why?

▷ How do you think Holly was feeling as she took her place in the capsule?
See if you can imagine how things would look to her as the machine gathered speed.

▷ 'And our eyes met for a long moment.'
How do you imagine Holly's expression? What do you think she is feeling?

▷ How would you describe Howie's mixed feelings as he watches Holly on the Rocket Ride?

▷ Read again the conversation between Holly and Howie after she gets off the Rocket. How do you think each of them is feeling here?
Which details bring out the distance between them?

▷ 'We'd been playing truant, sure enough, but not as father and daughter, merely as adult and child.'
See if you can explain in your own way what Howie means.

▷ Why do you think Howie decided, after all, to visit the cemetery?

▷ '"Don't you see, my darling, what I'm trying to say?"'
What do you think Howie is trying to say here?
Why can't he find the right words?

▷ From what you've understood of the situation, do you think Howie will be seeing Holly again?
What are your feelings about him at the end of the story?

Assignments

English

○ *It Happened Nearly a Year Ago . . .*
Use this phrase to begin a story of your own about an occasion on which a child feels let down/cheated/abandoned by a parent, or both parents.
Decide first if you will tell the story from the child's point of view or through the parent's eyes. See if you can bring out the private thoughts of the storyteller: the things he/she doesn't say but would like to. Try to show how what people say isn't always what they really feel.

Maybe the rift will be quickly mended. Or perhaps the incident will mark a final turning point in a relationship which has been under strain for some time. It could be that the sense of being let down is based upon a misunderstanding – in which case, the story could turn out to be amusing instead of serious like Robert Cormier's piece.

Choose an interesting setting for the story. Include descriptive details which will bring the place to life and help make the story convincing. Here are some ingredients you might use:
   a visit to the zoo, to the cinema, to a restaurant, to a concert;

a meeting with "a very special person I've been wanting you to meet for some time";
a child coming home to find some new, unexpected arrangement . . .;
a promise which isn't kept in the way the child expected . . .;
"There's something you ought to know . . .".

English Literature

○ *His on Thursdays* (after *Mine on Thursdays* by Robert Cormier)
How would this story read if Holly or Alison were telling it?

Holly's account would include many of the same incidents but they would be seen through very different eyes.
How did she feel, waiting for the sound of her father's car?
What/who did she notice as they walked round the fairground?
How did she 'read' her father's mood as she chatted to him?
Was she thinking more about her mother than she showed?
Were there other things on Holly's mind she couldn't tell her father about?
How did she really feel as she climbed onto the Rocket?
At what point did she lose faith in her father and decide to reject him?
Was her rejection as firm as it seemed to be?
What was she feeling/hoping as she heard him drive away?

Alison would experience only the events at the beginning and at the end of the story directly. She would have to piece together what had happened at the park from what Holly was willing to tell her when she got back. But there would be her own suspicions and knowledge of her ex-husband. She would have been thinking about the visit well in advance.
How did she feel when the car arrived?
And as she saw her daughter and ex-husband drive off?
What was she imagining/fearing whilst the two were away?
Was she pleased when they returned early?
How did she really feel about Howie three years after the divorce?

Choose just part of this story to rewrite, as if Holly or Alison were telling it.
Keep to the hard facts of Robert Cormier's original story but think carefully about how the new storyteller's version will be different from Howie's.
Add plenty of details of your own which help to bring out Holly's (or Alison's) personality and outlook – particularly the way she sees Howie.

○ Essay: Would you agree that it is difficult to feel sorry for Howie in Robert Cormier's story, *Mine on Thursdays*?
Describe why you think Holly behaves as she does at the end.
Do you think her father deserves to be treated like that?
Quote briefly from the story to illustrate the points you are making.

Some further reading

Robert Cormier   *8 + 1*
                          I Am the Cheese
Donald Gallo (editor)   *Sixteen*

★

THE RAIN HORSE
THE HAWK IN THE RAIN

Do you like to think about your past?

Which place from your past would you most like to revisit?

Have you ever returned to somewhere you once knew well but which has become unfamiliar?

Can you remember how you expected things to be? And what they were actually like?

In this story, a man returns to a place he has not visited for twelve years. He does not know what he expects to happen but it's certainly not what *does* happen.

Most of the action takes place in open countryside in terrific rain. Before you see how Ted Hughes wrote his story, jot down some words and phrases you might use:

(a) to describe the various ways rain falls;

(b) to convey the feeling of being drenched, with nowhere to shelter;

(c) to describe the appearance and movements of a wild horse.

The Rain Horse

As the young man came over the hill, the first thin blowing of rain met him. He turned his coat-collar up and stood on top of the shelving rabbit-riddled hedgebank, looking down into the valley.

shelving *sloping gently.*

rabbit-riddled *full of rabbit holes.*

He had come too far. What had set out as a walk along pleasantly remembered tarmac lanes had turned dreamily by gate and path and hedge-gap into a cross-ploughland trek, his shoes ruined, the dark mud of the lower fields inching up the trouser legs of his grey suit where they rubbed against each other. And now there was a raw, flapping wetness in the air that would be downpour again at any minute. He shivered, holding himself tense against the cold.

trek *a long, hard journey.*

downpour *heavy rain.*

This was the view he had been thinking of. Vaguely, without really directing his walk, he had felt he would get the whole thing from this point. For twelve years, whenever he had recalled this scene, he had imagined it as it looked from here. Now the valley lay sunken in front of him utterly deserted, shallow bare fields, black and sodden as the bed of an ancient lake after the weeks of rain.

sodden *water-logged.*

Nothing happened. Not that he had looked forward to any very transfiguring experience. But he had expected something, some pleasure, some meaningful sensation, he didn't quite know what.

transfiguring experience *something happening which changes your whole outlook.*

So he waited, trying to nudge the right feelings alive with the details – the surprisingly familiar curve of the hedges, the stone

nudge *coax.*

169

gate-pillar and iron gatehook let into it that he had used as a target, the long bank of the rabbit-warren on which he stood and which had been the first thing he ever noticed about the hill when twenty years ago, from the distance of the village, he had said to himself, "That looks like rabbits".

Twelve years had changed him. This land no longer recognized him, and he looked back at it coldly, as at a finally visited home-country, known only through the stories of a grandfather; felt nothing but the dullness of feeling nothing. Boredom. Then, suddenly, impatience, with a whole exasperated swarm of little anxieties about his shoes, and the spitting rain and his new suit and that sky and the two-mile trudge through the mud back to the road.

It would be quicker to go straight forward to the farm a mile away in the valley and behind which the road looped. But the thought of meeting the farmer – to be embarrassingly remembered or shouted at as a trespasser – deterred him. He saw the rain pulling up out of the distance, dragging its grey broken columns, smudging the trees and the farms.

A wave of anger went over him: anger against himself for blundering into this mud-trap and anger against the land that made him feel so outcast, so old and stiff and stupid. He wanted nothing but to get away from it as quickly as possible. But as he turned, something moved in his eye-corner. All his senses startled alert. He stopped.

Over to his right, a thin, black horse was running across the ploughland towards his hill, its head down, neck stretched out. It seemed to be running on its toes like a cat, like a dog up to no good.

From the high point on which he stood the hill dipped slightly and rose to another crested point fringed with the tops of trees, three hundred yards to his right. As he watched it the horse ran up to that crest, showed against the sky – for a moment like a nightmarish leopard – and disappeared over the other side.

For several seconds he stared at the skyline, stunned by the unpleasantly strange impression the horse had made on him. Then the plastering beat of icy rain on his bare skull brought him to himself. The distance had vanished in a wall of grey. All around him the fields were jumping and streaming.

Holding his collar close and tucking his chin down into it he ran back over the hilltop towards the town-side, the lee-side, his feet sucking and splashing, at every stride plunging to the ankle.

This hill was shaped like a wave, a gently rounded back lifting out of the valley to a sharply crested, almost concave frcnt hanging over the river meadows towards the town. Down this front, from the crest, hung two small woods separated by a fallow field. The near wood was nothing more than a quarry, circular, full of stones and bracken, with a few thorns and nondescript saplings, foxholes and rabbit holes. The other was rectangular, mainly a planting of scrub oak trees. Beyond the river smouldered the town like a great heap of blue cinders.

rabbit-warren *system of burrows.*

a whole exasperated swarm of little anxieties *lots of little irritating worries.*

trudge *slow, tiring walk.*

trespasser *somebody who has no right to be there.*

deterred him *put him off.*

blundering *acting rashly, foolishly, clumsily.*

startled alert *were suddenly ready for anything.*

crested point *high point with trees which look like the ornament on a helmet.*

crest *high point.*

lee-side *side sheltered from the wind.*

concave *hollowed, curving inwards.*

fallow *land which has been ploughed but not sown.*

nondescript *uninteresting, not memorable.*

saplings *young trees.*

scrub *stunted, undergrown.*

cinders *remains of burnt-out coal.*

He ran along the top of the first wood and finding no shelter but the thin, leafless thorns of the hedge, dipped below the crest out of the wind and jogged along through thick grass to the wood of oaks. In blinding rain he lunged through the barricade of brambles at the wood's edge. The little crippled trees were small choice in the way of shelter, but at a sudden fierce thickening of the rain he took one at random and crouched down under the leaning trunk.

Still panting from his run, drawing his knees up tightly, he watched the bleak lines of rain, grey as hail, slanting through the boughs into the clumps of bracken and bramble. He felt hidden and safe. The sound of the rain as it rushed and lulled in the wood seemed to seal him in. Soon the chilly sheet lead of his suit became a tight, warm mould, and gradually he sank into a state of comfort that was all but trance, though the rain beat steadily on his exposed shoulders and trickled down the oak trunk on to his neck.

All around him the boughs angled down, glistening, black as iron. From their tips and elbows the drops hurried steadily, and the channels of the bark pulsed and gleamed. For a time he amused himself calculating the variation in the rainfall by the variations in a dribble of water from a trembling twig-end two feet in front of his nose. He studied the twig, bringing dwarfs and continents and animals out of its scurfy bark. Beyond the boughs the blue shoal of the town was rising and falling, and darkening and fading again, in the pale, swaying backdrop of rain.

He wanted this rain to go on forever. Whenever it seemed to be drawing off, he listened anxiously until it closed in again. As long as it lasted he was suspended from life and time. He didn't want to return to his sodden shoes and his possibly ruined suit and the walk back over that land of mud.

All at once he shivered. He hugged his knees to squeeze out the cold and found himself thinking of the horse. The hair on the nape of his neck prickled slightly. He remembered how it had run up to the crest and showed against the sky.

He tried to dismiss the thought. Horses wander about the countryside often enough. But the image of the horse as it had appeared against the sky stuck in his mind. It must have come over the crest just above the wood in which he was now sitting. To clear his mind, he twisted around and looked up the wood between the tree stems, to his left.

At the wood top, with the silvered grey light coming in behind it, the black horse was standing under the oaks, its head high and alert, its ears pricked, watching him.

A horse sheltering from the rain generally goes into a sort of stupor, tilts a hind hoof and hangs its head and lets its eyelids droop, and so it stays as long as the rain lasts. This horse was nothing like that. It was watching him intently, standing perfectly still, its soaked neck and flank shining in the hard light.

He turned back. His scalp went icy and he shivered. What was he to do? Ridiculous to try driving it away. And to leave the wood, with

lunged *thrust forward.*

bracken *coarse undergrowth.*
brambles *thorny shrubs, wild blackberry bushes.*
lulled *lessened.*

boughs *thick arms of trees.*

scurfy *flaky.*
shoal *like a submerged sandbank.*

stupor *daze.*
hind *rear.*

171

the rain still coming down full pelt, was out of the question. Meanwhile the idea of being watched became more and more unsettling until at last he had to twist around again, to see if the horse had moved. It stood exactly as before.

This was absurd. He took control of himself and turned back deliberately, determined not to give the horse one more thought. If it wanted to share the wood with him, let it. If it wanted to stare at him, let it. He was nestling firmly into these resolutions when the ground shook and he heard the crash of a heavy body coming down the wood. Like lightning his legs bounded him upright and about face. The horse was almost on top of him, its head stretching forwards, ears flattened and lips lifted back from the long yellow teeth. He got one snapshot glimpse of the red-veined eyeball as he flung himself backwards around the tree. Then he was away up the slope, whipped by oak twigs as he leapt the brambles and brush-wood, twisting between the close trees till he tripped and sprawled. As he fell, the warning flashed though his head that he must at all costs keep his suit out of the leaf-mould, but a more urgent instinct was already rolling him violently sideways. He spun around, sat up and looked back, ready to scramble off in a flash to one side. He was panting from the sudden excitement and effort. The horse had disappeared. The wood was empty except for the drumming, slant grey rain, dancing the bracken and glittering from the branches.

He got up, furious. Knocking the dirt and leaves from his suit as well as he could, he looked around for a weapon. The horse was evidently mad, had an abscess on its brain or something of the sort. Or maybe it was just spiteful. Rain sometimes puts creatures into queer states. Whatever it was, he was going to get away from the wood as quickly as possible, rain or no rain.

Since the horse seemed to have gone on down the wood, his way to the farm over the hill was clear. As he went, he broke a yard length of wrist-thick dead branch from one of the oaks, but immediately threw it aside and wiped the slime of rotten wet bark from his hands with his soaked handkerchief. Already he was thinking it incredible that the horse could have meant to attack him. Most likely it was just going down the wood for better shelter and had made a feint at him in passing − as much out of curiosity or playfulness as anything. He recalled the way horses menace each other when they are galloping around in a paddock.

The wood rose to a steep bank topped by the hawthorn hedge that ran along the whole ridge of the hill. He was pulling himself up to a thin place in the hedge by the bare stem of one of the hawthorns when he ducked and shrank down again. The swelling gradient of fields lay in front of him, smoking in the slowly crossing rain. Out in the middle of the first field, tall as a statue, and a ghostly silver in the under-cloud light, stood the horse, watching the wood.

He lowered his head slowly, slithered back down the bank and crouched. An awful feeling of helplessness came over him. He felt certain the horse had been looking straight at him. Waiting for him?

resolutions *decisions.*

bounded him *shoved him.*

sprawled *lay spread out on the ground.*

abscess *ulcer.*

feint *swerve.*

menace *threaten.*

paddock *small field where horses are exercised.*

hawthorn *thorny tree.*

swelling gradient *rising slope.*

172

Was it clairvoyant? Maybe a mad animal can be clairvoyant. At the same time he was ashamed to find himself acting so inanely, ducking and creeping about in this way just to keep out of sight of a horse. He tried to imagine how anybody in their senses would just walk off home. This cooled him a little, and he retreated farther down the wood. He would go back the way he had come, along under the hill crest, without any more nonsense.

The wood hummed and the rain was a cold weight, but he observed this rather than felt it. The water ran down inside his clothes and squelched in his shoes as he eased his way carefully over the bedded twigs and leaves. At every instant he expected to see the prick-eared black head looking down at him from the hedge above.

At the woodside he paused, close against a tree. The success of this last manoeuvre was restoring his confidence, but he didn't want to venture out into the open field without making sure that the horse was just where he had left it. The perfect move would be to withdraw quietly and leave the horse standing out there in the rain. He crept up again among the trees to the crest and peeped through the hedge.

The grey field and the whole slope were empty. He searched the distance. The horse was quite likely to have forgotten him altogether and wandered off. Then he raised himself and leaned out to see if it had come in close to the hedge. Before he was aware of anything, the ground shook. He twisted around wildly to see how he had been caught. The black shape was above him, right across the light. Its whinnying snort and the spattering whack of its hooves seemed to be actually inside his head as he fell backwards down the bank, and leapt again like a madman, dodging among the oaks, imagining how the buffet would come and how he would be knocked headlong. Half-way down the wood the oaks gave way to bracken and old roots and stony rabbit diggings. He was well out into the middle of this before he realized that he was running alone.

Gasping for breath now and cursing mechanically, without a thought for his suit he sat down on the ground to rest his shaking legs, letting the rain plaster the hair down over his forehead and watching the dense flashing lines disappear abruptly into the soil all around him as if he were watching through thick plate glass. He took deep breaths in the effort to steady his heart and regain control of himself. His right trouser turn-up was ripped at the seam and his suit jacket was splashed with the yellow mud of the top field.

Obviously the horse had been farther along the hedge above the steep field, waiting for him to come out at the woodside just as he had intended. He must have peeped through the hedge – peeping the wrong way – within yards of it.

However, this last attack had cleared up one thing. He need no longer act like a fool out of mere uncertainty as to whether the horse was simply being playful or not. It was definitely after him. He picked up two stones about the size of goose eggs and set off towards the bottom of the wood, striding carelessly.

clairvoyant *a mind reader.*
inanely *foolishly.*

manoeuvre *plan.*
venture *take the risk of going.*

buffet *blow.*

173

A loop of the river bordered all this farmland. If he crossed the little meadow at the bottom of the wood, he could follow the three-mile circuit, back to the road. There were deep hollows in the river-bank, shoaled with pebbles, as he remembered, perfect places to defend himself from if the horse followed him out there.

shoaled partly filled.

The hawthorns that choked the bottom of the wood – some of them good-sized trees – knitted into an almost impassable barrier. He had found a place where the growth thinned slightly and had begun to lift aside the long spiny stems, pushing himself forward, when he stopped. Through the bluish veil of bare twigs, he saw the familiar shape out in the field below the wood.

But it seemed not to have noticed him yet. It was looking out across the field towards the river. Quietly, he released himself from the thorns and climbed back across the clearing towards the one side of the wood he had not yet tried. If the horse would only stay down there he could follow his first and easiest plan, up the wood and over the hilltop to the farm.

Now he noticed that the sky had grown much darker. The rain was heavier every second, pressing down as if the earth had to be flooded before nightfall. The oaks ahead blurred and the ground drummed. He began to run. And as he ran he heard a deeper sound running with him. He whirled around. The horse was in the middle of the clearing. It might have been running to get out of the terrific rain except that it was coming straight for him, scattering clay and stones, with an immensely supple and powerful motion. He let out a tearing roar and threw the stone in his right hand. The result was instantaneous. Whether at the roar or the stone the horse reared as if against a wall and shied to his left. As it dropped back on its fore-feet he flung his second stone, at ten yards' range, and saw a bright mud blotch suddenly appear on the glistening black flank. The horse surged down the wood, splashing the earth like water, tossing its long tail as it plunged out of sight among the hawthorns.

whirled spun.

supple flowing.

shied swerved suddenly in fear.

surged rushed like a huge wave.

He looked around for stones. The encounter had set the blood beating in his head and given him a savage energy. He could have killed the horse at that moment. That this brute should pick him and play with him in this malevolent fashion was more than he could bear. Whoever owned it, he thought, deserved to have its neck broken for letting the dangerous thing loose.

malevolent fashion evil, cruel way.

He came out at the woodside, in open battle now, still searching for the right stones. There were plenty here, piled and scattered where they had been ploughed out of the field. He selected two, then straightened and saw the horse twenty yards off in the middle of the steep field, watching him calmly. They looked at each other.

"Out of it!" he shouted, brandishing his arm. "Out of it! Go on!" The horse twitched its pricked ears. With all his force he threw. The stone soared and landed beyond with a soft thud. He re-armed and threw again. For several minutes he kept up his bombardment without a single hit, working himself into a despair and throwing more and more wildly, till his arm began to ache with the unaccus-

brandishing waving aggressively.

tomed exercise. Throughout the performance the horse watched him fixedly. Finally he had to stop and ease his shoulder muscle. As if the horse had been waiting for just this, it dipped its head twice and came at him.

He snatched up two stones and roaring with all his strength flung the one in his right hand. He was astonished at the crack of the impact. It was as if he had struck a tile – and the horse actually stumbled. With another roar he jumped forward and hurled his other stone. His aim seemed to be under superior guidance. The stone struck and rebounded straight up into the air, spinning fiercely, as the horse swirled away and went careering down towards the far bottom of the field, at first with great, swinging leaps, then at a canter, leaving deep churned holes in the soil.

under superior guidance *as if a god were helping him.*

swirled *spun.*

canter *gentle gallop.*

It turned up the far side of the field, climbing till it was level with him. He felt a little surprise of pity to see it shaking his head, and once it paused to lower its head and paw over its ears with its fore-hoof as a cat does.

"You stay there!" he shouted. "Keep your distance and you'll not get hurt."

And indeed the horse did stop at that moment, almost obediently. It watched him as he climbed to the crest.

The rain swept into his face and he realized that he was freezing, as if his very flesh were sodden. The farm seemed miles away over the dreary fields. Without another glance at the horse – he felt too exhausted to care now what it did – he loaded the crook of his left arm with stones and plunged out onto the waste of mud.

waste *wasteland.*

He was half-way to the first hedge before the horse appeared, silhouetted against the sky at the corner of the wood, head high and attentive, watching his laborious retreat over the three fields.

laborious retreat *exhausting way back.*

The ankle-deep clay dragged at him. Every stride was a separate, deliberate effort, forcing him up and out of the sucking earth, burdened as he was by his sogged clothes and load of stone and limbs that seemed themselves to be turning to mud. He fought to keep his breathing even, two strides in, two strides out, the air ripping his lungs. In the middle of the last field he stopped and looked around. The horse, tiny on the skyline, had not moved.

At the corner of the field, he unlocked his clasped arms and dumped the stones by the gatepost, then leaned on the gate. The farm was in front of him. He became conscious of the rain again and suddenly longed to stretch out full-length under it, to take the cooling, healing drops all over his body and forget himself in the last wretchedness of the mud. Making an effort, he heaved his weight over the gate-top. He leaned again, looking up at the hill.

Rain was dissolving land and sky together like a wet water-colour as the afternoon darkened. He concentrated, raising his head, searching the skyline from end to end. The horse had vanished. The hill looked lifeless and desolate, an island lifting out of the sea, awash with every tide.

Under the long shed where the tractors, plough, binders and the

water-colour *painting done in water-colours.*

desolate *empty and sad.*

binders *machines for binding straw.*

rest were drawn up, waiting for their seasons, he sat on a sack thrown over a petrol drum, trembling, his lungs heaving. The mingled smell of paraffin, creosote, fertilizer, dust – all was exactly as he had left it twelve years ago. The ragged swallows' nests were still there tucked in the angles of the rafters. He remembered three dead foxes hanging in a row from one of the beams, their teeth bloody.

creosote *liquid used for waterproofing wood.*

The ordeal with the horse had already sunk from reality. It hung under the surface of his mind, an obscure confusion of fright and shame, as after a narrowly escaped street accident. There was a solid pain in his chest, like a spike of bone stabbing, that made him wonder if he had strained his heart on that last stupid burdened run. Piece by piece, he began to take off his clothes, wringing the grey water out of them, but soon he stopped that and just sat staring at the ground, as if some important part had been cut out of his brain.

obscure confusion *strange mixture.*

Thinking/Talking Points

▷ What seems to you to be the man's attitude to the place he is revisiting? Pick out some details which suggest this.
What can you make out about his life since he left there?
Suggest why he is anxious not to run into the farmer.

▷ Do you think his feelings about being there influence what happens to him in the story? Give your reasons.

▷ Select half a dozen descriptive details which give you a vivid sense of the rain. What do you find effective about each of them?

▷ Which words and phrases make the horse seem real and frightening?

▷ Could any of the details you have chosen which describe the horse be used to describe the rain (or vice versa)?

▷ ' . . . but soon he stopped that and just sat staring at the ground, as if some important part had been cut out of his brain.'
How do you think the man is feeling at the end of the story?

Assignments

Role-play (working in pairs)

○ A few minutes later, the farmer comes across the man resting in his barn.
Does he recognise him? Is he the farmer who was there twelve years ago?
How much does each of them reveal about the past and about what has happened since?
How does the man explain being in the barn? The state of his clothes?
Does he tell the farmer what happened in the rain? Is he angry? Secretive? Distressed? Embarrassed?

176

How does the farmer treat him? With sympathy? Rudely? Is he pleased to see the man in such a state?

Whose horse was it anyway? . . . If it was a horse.

Improvise this scene (try it twice, swapping roles).

You may like to develop your experiments into a script which could be included in your English file.

Alternatively, you could write about this meeting as a story, a sequel to *The Rain Horse*.

English

○ *A Waking Nightmare*

Write a story of your own about a similar experience.

(a) You are in the countryside or at the seaside or abroad. You are in a strange town or in a part of the country where you don't feel at home. Or perhaps you are revisiting a place which once was home.

Give the reader a vivid sense of the place, the time, and the season by choosing a few powerful descriptive details: of buildings, landscape, people.

(b) You feel uneasy – it's getting late, you're not certain of the way back to where you agreed to meet your friends or family. You've wandered off the beaten track despite various warnings . . .

(c) The weather is turning. In your story perhaps it's not rain but stuffy heat or a thunderstorm or wind or cold which adds to your discomfort . . .

Give yourself time to describe the way the weather changes. And the way that affects you.

(d) Suddenly, all your vague discomfort and fears give way to terror as you find yourself confronted by . . . a stray dog, a farm animal, some unfriendly looking strangers . . . whatever/whoever you most dread meeting. At first you're not sure whether it/they mean you any harm or whether you are imagining things.

It/they come and go in the half-light . . . may have noticed you, may be quite unaware of your existence . . .

Concentrate upon conveying to your reader your own feelings of panic, fear, confusion. Not only your eyes but your ears too may be playing tricks on you. Avoid too much actually happening. Keep the reader uncertain about whether the danger is real or just in your head.

See if you can leave the ending of the story as uncertain as Ted Hughes did in *The Rain Horse*.

English Literature

○ From the details we are given in the story, see if you can produce a map of the young man's movements.

○ Draw a picture strip suggested by the story.

○ Essay: With a dozen or so brief quotations from the story, show how Ted Hughes keeps us puzzled about what really happens in *The Rain Horse*. Which descriptive details make the setting and the experiences of the man seem 'real'?

Which details suggest that his fears may be playing tricks on him?
Do you think the story is exciting? Did you find it convincing? How did you
feel after you read it?
Discuss particular details which impressed you.

○ Essay: Compare and contrast the situation in *The Rain Horse* with the one in the
following poem, which is also by Ted Hughes.
How are the situations of the people similar?
What is similar/different about the way the horse and the hawk are described?
What is different about the speakers' attitudes to the other creatures?
Which of the two works did you enjoy more? Give your reasons.

The Hawk in the Rain

I drown in the drumming ploughland, I drag up
Heel after heel from the swallowing of the earth's mouth,
From clay that clutches my each step to the ankle
With the habit of the dogged grave, but the hawk

dogged *tenacious, determined.*

Effortlessly at height hangs his still eye.
His wings hold all creation in a weightless quiet,
Steady as a hallucination in the streaming air.
While banging wind kills these stubborn hedges,

hallucination *illusion.*

Thumbs my eyes, throws my breath, tackles my heart,
And rain hacks my head to the bone, the hawk hangs
The diamond point of will that polestars
The sea-drowner's endurance: and I,

polestars *acts like the pole star by which sailors navigate.*

Bloodily grabbed dazed last-moment-counting
Morsel in the earth's mouth, strain towards the master-
Fulcrum of violence where the hawk hangs still.
That maybe in his own time meets the weather

morsel *scrap of food.*
master-fulcrum *pivot.*

Coming the wrong way, suffers the air, hurled upside down,
Fall from his eye, the ponderous shires crash on him,
The horizon trap him; the round angelic eye
Smashed, mix his heart's blood with the mire of the land.

suffers *allows.*
ponderous *weighty.*

mire *muck.*

Some further reading

Ted Hughes   *Wodwo* (the anthology of poetry and stories from which
                    The Rain Horse comes)
                    Capturing Animals
                    Moortown
Martin Armstrong   *The Poets and the Housewife*

★

Thinking/Talking Points

▷ What do you think is the difference between a 'horror story' and a 'horrible story'?

What do you understand by the phrase 'the pornography of violence'?

Sometimes people laugh at scenes which, if they were real, would involve great pain and suffering.

Do you think that people can/do distinguish between a horrible story on the news and what they read in a horror magazine or see in a horror film?

▷ What effects do you think seeing acts of cruelty has on people?

See if you can recall seeing/reading a *particular* horrible scene.

Do you think you saw things from the point of view of the person who was suffering or from the point of view of the person who was causing the suffering?

Which, if any, of the following feelings do you think the incident gave you: fear; excitement; pleasure; anger; a sense of powerlessness; a sense of power; frustration; anxiety; hatred; love; amusement; indifference; shock; disbelief; confusion . . .

Add some words of your own to those you have selected.

▷ Some people argue that there should be controls over what the public is allowed to read and allowed to see on television, on videos and in films. Do you believe that people should be allowed to make films:

(a) which dramatise horrible things which people have really suffered? (e.g. a film about slavery or cruelty to children);

(b) which explore horror and cruelty in a fantasy style? (e.g. a story about vampires or vicious monsters from outer space);

(c) which record actual suffering – to people or to animals? (e.g. a film of a bull fight or of somebody committing suicide).

What guidelines do you think should be given to film makers about what kinds of suffering can and cannot be shown?

▷ Why do you think horror films and stories are so popular?

Do you think violence on the streets and in the family is linked to what people see on television? Give your reasons.

What controls (if any) will you exercise upon what your own children read/listen to/watch? Explain why.

▷ Many items on the news are about horrible things: war; famine; murder; rape; accidents; disease.

Do you think seeing and hearing about these things makes people more or less aware of how victims feel?

Do you think such news helps to bring about an end to people's suffering?

Consider the following examples:
   pictures of children starving;
   a documentary about somebody facing the death penalty;
   an Amnesty International report about the torture of political prisoners;
   a news item about a family murdered by someone who is mentally ill;
   a story about someone needing an operation which he/she cannot afford.
What do you think the editors of newspapers/television news programmes should ask themselves before they decide to tell the public about such things?

▷ You are the editor of a national newspaper.
You have been handed an eye-witness account (with photographs) of the torturing of children by security forces in a named foreign country. You must decide if you will publish the material, as it stands or as a news report.
What considerations would come in?
What good might publishing the story do?
Are there any ways in which it might do harm?
How would you defend your decision from those who object:
either
(a) that publishing such stories is just an unpleasant way of selling newspapers since people read such things only to get a thrill of sadistic horror, not because they care about the victims.
or
(b) that by keeping the public ignorant of the horrible facts, such cruelty will continue and get worse.

▷ During the Second World War, many people in Europe were unaware of what was happening in the concentration camps. Even today, many people know very little about what really happened there.
Here we include a story about that experience. It is very disturbing, and you may prefer to turn to something else.

If you decide to read the story, *The Shawl*, consider the points we have been discussing. What are you expecting from the story? Is there any good reason to keep such stories in print? How does reading this one affect you? Do you think *The Shawl* is 'a horror story' or 'a horrible story'? Is it literature or pornography?

The Shawl

Stella, cold, cold the coldness of hell. How they walked on the roads together, Rosa with Magda curled up between sore breasts, Magda wound up in the shawl. Sometimes Stella carried Magda. But she was jealous of Magda. A thin girl of fourteen, too small, with thin breasts of her own, Stella wanted to be wrapped in a shawl, hidden away, asleep, rocked by the march, a baby, a round infant in arms. Magda took Rosa's nipple, and Rosa never stopped walking, a walking cradle. There was not enough milk; sometimes Magda sucked air; then she screamed. Stella was ravenous. Her knees were tumors on sticks, her elbows chicken bones.

ravenous *desperately hungry.*

tumors *swellings caused by disease.*

181

Rosa did not feel hunger; she felt light, not like someone walking but like someone in a faint, in trance, arrested in a fit, someone who is already a floating angel, alert and seeing everything, but in the air, not there, not touching the road. As if teetering on the tips of her fingernails. She looked into Magda's face through a gap in the shawl: a squirrel in a nest, safe, no one could reach her inside the little house of the shawl's windings. The face, very round, a pocket mirror of a face: but it was not Rosa's bleak complexion, dark like cholera, it was another kind of face altogether, eyes blue as air, smooth feathers of hair nearly as yellow as the Star sewn into Rosa's coat. You could think she was one of *their* babies.

Rosa, floating, dreamed of giving Magda away in one of the villages. She could leave the line for a minute and push Magda into the hands of any woman on the side of the road. But if she moved out of line they might shoot. And even if she fled the line for half a second and pushed the shawl-bundle at a stranger, would the woman take it? She might be surprised, or afraid; she might drop the shawl, and Magda would fall out and strike her head and die. The little round head. Such a good child, she gave up screaming, and sucked now only for the taste of the drying nipple itself. The neat grip of the tiny gums. One mite of a tooth tip sticking up in the bottom gum, how shining, an elfin tombstone of white marble gleaming there. Without complaining, Magda relinquished Rosa's teats, first the left, then the right; both were cracked, not a sniff of milk. The duct crevice extinct, a dead volcano, blind eye, chill hole, so Magda took the corner of the shawl and milked it instead. She sucked, and sucked, flooding the threads with wetness. The shawl's good flavor, milk of linen.

It was a magic shawl, it could nourish an infant for three days and three nights. Magda did not die, she stayed alive, although very quiet. A peculiar smell, of cinnamon and almonds, lifted out of her mouth. She held her eyes open every moment, forgetting how to blink or nap, and Rosa and sometimes Stella studied their blueness. On the road they raised one burden of a leg after another and studied Magda's face. "Aryan," Stella said, in a voice grown as thin as a string; and Rosa thought how Stella gazed at Magda like a young cannibal. And the time that Stella said "Aryan," it sounded to Rosa as if Stella had really said "Let us devour her".

But Magda lived to walk. She lived that long, but she did not walk very well, partly because she was only fifteen months old, and partly because the spindles of her legs could not hold up her fat belly. It was fat with air, full and round. Rosa gave almost all her food to Magda, Stella gave nothing; Stella was ravenous, a growing child herself, but not growing much. Stella did not menstruate. Rosa did not menstruate. Rosa was ravenous, but also not; she learned from Magda how to drink the taste of a finger in one's mouth. They were in a place without pity, all pity was annihilated in Rosa, she looked at Stella's bones without pity. She was sure that Stella was waiting for Magda to die so she could put her teeth into the little thighs.

arrested *caught, stuck.*

teetering *walking unsteadily.*

cholera *a deadly disease.*

the Star *the Nazis forced Jews to identify themselves by sewing a yellow star onto their clothing.*

elfin *tiny.*

relinquished *let go of.*

Aryan *in Nazi politics, someone of north European descent, not Jewish.*

menstruate *have periods.*

annihilated *wiped out.*

182

Rosa knew Magda was going to die very soon; she should have been dead already, but she had been buried away deep inside the magic shawl, mistaken there for the shivering mound of Rosa's breasts; Rosa clung to the shawl as if it covered only herself. No one took it away from her. Magda was mute. She never cried. Rosa hid her in the barracks, under the shawl, but she knew that one day someone would inform; or one day, someone, not even Stella, would steal Magda to eat her. When Magda began to walk Rosa knew that Magda was going to die very soon, something would happen. She was afraid to fall asleep; she slept with the weight of her thigh on Magda's body; she was afraid she would smother Magda under her thigh. The weight of Rosa was becoming less and less; Rosa and Stella were slowly turning into air.

Magda was quiet, but her eyes were horribly alive, like blue tigers. She watched. Sometimes she laughed – it seemed a laugh, but how could it be? Magda had never seen anyone laugh. Still, Magda laughed at her shawl when the wind blew its corners, the bad wind with pieces of black in it, that made Stella's and Rosa's eyes tear. Magda's eyes were always clear and tearless. She watched like a tiger. She guarded her shawl. No one could touch it; only Rosa could touch it. Stella was not allowed. The shawl was Magda's own baby, her pet, her little sister. She tangled herself up in it and sucked on one of the corners when she wanted to be very still.

Then Stella took the shawl away and made Magda die.

Afterward Stella said: "I was cold."

And afterward she was always cold, always. The cold went into her heart: Rosa saw that Stella's heart was cold. Magda flopped onward with her little pencil legs scribbling this way and that, in search of the shawl; the pencils faltered at the barracks opening, where the light began. Rosa saw and pursued. But already Magda was in the square outside the barracks, in the jolly light. It was the roll-call arena. Every morning Rosa had to conceal Magda under the shawl against a wall of the barracks and go out and stand in the arena with Stella and hundreds of others, sometimes for hours, and Magda, deserted, was quiet under the shawl, sucking on her corner. Every day Magda was silent, and so she did not die. Rosa saw that today Magda was going to die, and at the same time a fearful joy ran in Rosa's two palms, her fingers were on fire, she was astonished, febrile: Magda, in the sunlight, swaying on her pencil legs was howling. Ever since the drying up of Rosa's nipples, ever since Magda's last scream on the road, Magda had been devoid of any syllable; Magda was a mute. Rosa believed that something had gone wrong with her vocal cords, with her windpipe, with the cave of her larynx; Magda was defective, without a voice; perhaps she was deaf; there might be something amiss with her intelligence; Magda was dumb. Even the laugh that came when the ash-stippled wind made a clown out of Magda's shawl was only the air-blown showing of her teeth. Even when the lice, head lice and body lice, crazed her so that she became as wild as one of the big rats that plundered the

mute *silent.*

faltered *hesitated.*

febrile *agitated.*

devoid of any syllable *silent.*

larynx *voice box.*

ash-stippled *as if the wind had been touched with grey paint.*

183

barracks at daybreak looking for carrion, she rubbed and scratched and kicked and bit and rolled without a whimper. But now Magda's mouth was spilling a long viscous rope of clamor.

"Maaa —"

It was the first noise Magda had ever sent out from her throat since the drying up of Rosa's nipples.

"Maaaa . . . aaa!"

Again! Magda was wavering in the perilous sunlight of the arena, scrabbling on such pitiful little bent shins. Rosa saw. She saw that Magda was grieving for the loss of her shawl, she saw that Magda was going to die. A tide of commands hammered in Rosa's nipples: "Fetch, get, bring!" But she did not know which to go after first, Magda or the shawl. If she jumped out into the arena to snatch Magda up, the howling would not stop, because Magda would still not have the shawl; but if she ran back into the barracks to find the shawl, and if she found it, and if she came after Magda holding it and shaking it, then she would get Magda back, Magda would put the shawl in her mouth and turn dumb again.

Rosa entered the dark. It was easy to discover the shawl. Stella was heaped under it, asleep in her thin bones. Rosa tore the shawl free and flew — she could fly, she was only air — into the arena. The sunheat murmured of another life, of butterflies in summer. The light was placid, mellow. On the other side of the steel fence, far away, there were green meadows speckled with dandelions and deep-coloured violets; beyond them, even farther, innocent tiger lilies, tall, lifting their orange bonnets. In the barracks they spoke of 'flowers', of 'rain': excrement, thick turd-braids, and the slow stinking maroon waterfall that slunk down from the upper bunks, the stink mixed with a bitter fatty floating smoke that greased Rosa's skin. She stood for an instant at the margin of the arena. Sometimes the electricity inside the fence would seem to hum; even Stella said it was only an imagining, but Rosa heard real sounds in the wire: grainy sad voices. The farther she was from the fence, the more clearly the voices crowded at her. The lamenting voices strummed so convincingly, so passionately, it was impossible to suspect them of being phantoms. The voices told her to hold up the shawl, high; the voices told her to shake it, to whip with it, to unfurl it like a flag. Rosa lifted, shook, whipped, unfurled. Far off, very far, Magda leaned across her air-fed belly, reaching out with the rods of her arms. She was high up, elevated, riding someone's shoulder. But the shoulder that carried Magda was not coming toward Rosa and the shawl, it was drifting away, the speck of Magda was moving more and more into the smoky distance. Above the shoulder, a helmet glinted. The light tapped the helmet and sparkled it into a goblet. Below the helmet a black body like a domino and a pair of black boots hurled themselves in the direction of the electrified fence. The electric voices began to chatter wildy. "Maamaa, maaamaaa," they all hummed together. How far Magda was from Rosa now, across the whole square, past a dozen barracks, all the way on the other

carrion *dead flesh.*

viscous rope of clamor *monotonous cry of unhappiness.*

perilous *dangerous.*

scrabbling *uncertain on her feet.*

placid *peaceful.*

mellow *kind.*

margin *edge.*

goblet *wineglass.*

side! She was no bigger than a moth.

All at once Magda was swimming through the air. The whole of Magda travelled through loftiness. She looked like a butterfly touching a silver vine. And the moment Magda's feathered round head and her pencil legs and balloonish belly and zigzag arms splashed against the fence, the steel voices went mad in their growling, urging Rosa to run and run to the spot where Magda had fallen from her flight against the electrified fence; but of course Rosa did not obey them. She only stood, because if she ran they would shoot, and if she tried to pick up the sticks of Magda's body they would shoot, and if she let the wolf's screech ascending now through the ladder of her skeleton break out, they would shoot; so she took Magda's shawl and filled her own mouth with it, stuffed it in and stuffed it in, until she was swallowing up the wolf's screech and tasting the cinnamon and almond depth of Magda's saliva; and Rosa drank Magda's shawl until it dried.

Talking/Thinking Points

▷ 'They were in a place without pity . . .'
Which details in the first two paragraphs give you this impression?

▷ How do you picture Stella?
Are you able to understand her feelings?

▷ Pick out half a dozen details from the text which suggest a much more beautiful world than Magda has known.
What is the effect of including those details in the story?

▷ 'A tide of commands hammered in Rosa's nipples: "Fetch, get, bring!" But she did not know which to go after first, Magda or the shawl.'
See if you can explain in your own way the confused feelings Rosa has at this point in the story.

▷ What happened to Magda?

▷ Which details give you the strongest impression (a) of the camp and (b) of the guard who took Magda?

▷ See if you can describe the effect reading this story has had on you.
Which of the following feelings did you find the story stirred in you?: fear; excitement; pleasure; anger; a sense of powerlessness; a sense of power; frustration; anxiety; hatred; love; amusement; indifference; shock; disbelief; confusion . . .
Add some words of your own to those you select.
Do you think *The Shawl* should be read by people of your age?
Give your reasons.

Assignments

English

○ *Stella's Version*

'They were in a place without pity . . . all pity was annihilated in Rosa, she looked at Stella's bones without pity. She was sure that Stella was waiting for Magda to die so she could put her teeth into the little thighs.'

Do you think Rosa was correct here? What do you think was passing through Stella's mind?

Write a piece as if it is the private thoughts of Stella as they march along the road. Use details from the story, but add lots of your own ideas – things Stella was remembering, noticing as they tramped along, feeling about her mother and sister, wondering about what lay ahead.

You may like to begin your piece like this:

> I was cold, so cold. It was the coldness of hell. We trudged through strange villages, across dead fields which seemed to stretch to the ends of the earth . . .

English Literature

○ Essay: 'The trouble with stories which describe human cruelty is that they are as likely to appeal to the worst as to the kindest feelings of human beings. Instead of making people more compassionate, they may actually make them more insensitive.' Do you agree? Discuss the effect reading *The Shawl* has had on you (refer to half a dozen particular details in the story).

Do you think such stories should be published? How can an editor decide whether a story is pornographic rather than likely to make the readers more compassionate?

Some further reading

Cynthia Ozick   *Rosa* (a sequel to *The Shawl*)
Anthony Hecht   *More Light! More Light!*
Primo Levi   *If This Is a Man*
Bruno Bettleheim *The Informed Heart*

For further study

You may like to consider the issues discussed here in relation to a harrowing collection of concentration camp stories written by a survivor of Auschwitz and Belsen, Tadeus Borowski: *This Way to the Gas, Ladies and Gentlemen.*

★

THE GREEN
BEHIND THE GLASS

Assignment

English Literature: Unseen Criticism

○ Look at the following story. Imagine that other readers have looked at it and reached a variety of conclusions about whether they like it or not.

You have been asked to write a detailed, carefully considered study of the story, and to decide on your opinion for a prize. In preparing your report, pick out a dozen or so brief quotations from the story to illustrate the points you wish to make.

The Green Behind the Glass

1916 November

The telegram was addressed to Enid. Sarah put it carefully on the table in the hall. The white envelope turned red in the light that fell through the coloured squares of glass above the front door. She had no desire to open it. She knew that Philip was dead. The possibility that he might be wounded, missing, captured, never occurred to her. It was death she had been expecting, after all. These were only the official words setting it out in writing. For a moment, Sarah wondered about the people whose work it was every day to compose such messages. Perhaps they grew used to it. The telegraph boy, though, couldn't meet her eyes.

"Telegram for Miss Enid Hurst," he'd said.
"I'll take it. I'm her sister. They're all out."
"Much obliged, I'm sure." He had thrust the envelope into her hand and run towards the gate without looking back, his boots clattering on the pavement. The envelope had fluttered suddenly in a rush of wind.

Sarah sat on the oak settle in the hall and wondered whether to take the message to Enid in the shop. "To them," she thought, "to the writers of this telegram, Philip is Enid's young man. He was. Was. Haven't we been embroidering and stitching and preparing for the wedding since before the War! Enid will enjoy mourning," thought Sarah. "It will become her. She will look elegant in black, and she'll cry delicately so as not to mar the whiteness of her skin, and dab her nose with a lace-edged handkerchief, and wear Mother's jet brooch, and all the customers will sigh and say how sad it is, and young men will want to comfort and console her, and they will, oh yes, because she didn't really love him."

oak settle *wooden bench with back and arms.*

mourning *wearing black in memory of somebody who has died.*
become *suit, flatter.*
mar *spoil.*
jet *a black semi-precious stone.*
console *lessen her grief.*

187

"She didn't really love him," Sarah shouted aloud in the empty house, and blushed as if there were a part of Enid lurking somewhere that could overhear her. "Not really," she whispered. "Not like I did."

"I know," she thought, "because she told me."

Enid is sewing, I ask her: "Do you really love him, Enid? Does your heart beat so loudly sometimes that you feel the whole world can hear it? Can you bear it, the thought of him going away? Do you see him in your dreams?"

"Silly goose, you're just a child." She smiles at me. She is grown-up. Her face is calm. Pale. "And you've been reading too many novels. I respect him. I admire him. I am very fond of him. He is a steady young man. And besides, ladies in real life don't feel those things, you know. It wouldn't be right."

"But I felt them," thought Sarah. "And other feelings, too, which made me blush. I turned away, I remember, so that Enid should not see my face, and thought of his arms holding me, and his hands in my hair and his mouth . . . oh, such a melting, a melting in my stomach. I loved him. I can never say anything. I shall only be able to weep for him at night, after Enid has fallen asleep. And I shall have to look at that photograph that isn't him at all, just a soldier in uniform, sepia, like all soldiers. Enid will keep it there between our beds. Perhaps she will put it in a black frame, but after a while, I shall be the only one who really sees it."

sepia *a pale brown colour.*

Sarah tried to cry and no tears would come. It seemed to her that her heart had been crushed in metal hands, icy cold and shining. How could she bear the tight pain of those hands? But soon, yes, she would have to take the telegram and walk to the shop and watch Enid fainting and Mother rustling out from behind the counter. Mrs Feathers would be there. She was always there, and she would tell, as she had told so often before, the remarkable story of her Jimmy, who'd been posted as dead last December and who, six months later, had simply walked into the house, bold as you please, and asked for a cup of tea.

"You're mine now," Sarah said aloud to the telegram, and giggled. "Maybe I'm going mad," she thought. "Isn't talking to yourself the first sign? I don't care. I don't care if I am mad. I shall go and change into my blue dress, just for a little while. Later, I shall have to wear dark colours, Philip, even though I promised you I wouldn't. Mother will make me wear them. What will the neighbours say, otherwise!"

"Philip is like a son to me," Mother used to say, long before he proposed to Enid, "One of the family."

"Perhaps that is why he proposed. Or perhaps Mother arranged the whole thing. She is so good at arranging. Enid is piqued, sometimes, by the attention Philip pays to me. I am scarcely more

piqued *upset, put out.*

189

than a child. Mother says: 'But of course, he loves Sarah, too. Isn't she like a little sister to him?' When she says this, I clench my fists until the nails cut into my palms. I don't want that kind of love, no, not that kind at all."

Sarah laid the blue dress on the bed, and began to take off her pinafore. The sun shone steadily outside, but the leaves had gone. Swiftly, she pulled the hat box from under the bed, and lifted out her straw hat with the red satin ribbons. It was a hat for long days of blue sky, green trees and roses. "I can't wear it in November," she thought. It had been wrapped in tissue paper, like a treasure. Sarah had looked at it often, remembering the afternoon in Kew Gardens, so long ago, a whole three months. She had thought of it as the happiest day of her life, a day with only a small shadow upon it, an insignificant wisp of fear, nothing to disturb the joy. But now Philip was dead, and that short-lived moment of terror spread through her beautiful memories like ink stirred into clear water.

Enid's sewing-basket was on the chest of drawers. Sarah was seized suddenly with rage at Philip for dying, for leaving her behind in the world. She took the dress-making scissors out of the basket, and cut and cut into the brim of the hat until it hung in strips, like a fringe. The ribbons she laid beside her on the bed and she crushed the crown in her hands until the sharp pieces of broken straw pricked her, hurt her. Then she snipped the long, long strips of satin into tiny squares. They glittered on her counterpane like drops of blood. When she had finished, her whole body throbbed, ached, was raw, as if she had been cutting up small pieces of herself. She lay back on the bed, breathless. "I must go to the shop," she told herself. "In a little while. If I close my eyes, I can see him, I can hear his voice. And Enid's voice. Her voice was so bossy, that day."

counterpane *bedspread.*

"You can't wear that hat," Enid says. "It's too grown-up."

"I am grown up." I dance around the kitchen table, twirling the hat on my hand, so that the ribbons fly out behind it. "I shall be seventeen at Christmas, and it's just the hat for Kew."

"I don't know why you're coming, anyway," says Enid.

"She's coming because it's a lovely day, and because I invited her," Philip says.

He is leaning against the door, smiling at me.

"Thank you, kind sir." I sweep him a curtsey.

"A pleasure, fair lady," he answers, and bows gracefully.

"When will you two stop clowning?" Enid is vexed. "You spoil her all the time. I've had my hat on for fully five minutes."

vexed *cross.*

"Then let us go," he says, and offers an arm to Enid and an arm to me.

In the street, Enid frowns: "It's not proper. Walking along arm-in-arm . . . like costermongers."

"Stuff and nonsense," says Philip. "It's very jolly. Why else do you suppose we have two arms?" I laugh. Enid wrinkles her nose.

"August is a silly time to come here." There is complaint in

costermongers *street traders.*

Enid's voice. She is sitting on a bench between me and Philip. "The camellias are long since over, and I love them so much. Even the roses are past their best." She shudders. "I do dislike them when all the petals turn brown and flap about in that untidy way."

camellias *elegant spring flowers.*

"Let's go into the Glass House." I jump up and stand in front of them. Enid pretends to droop.

"Philip," she sighs, "you take her. I don't think I could bear to stand in that stifling place ever again, among the drips and smells."

Philip rises reluctantly, touches Enid's shoulder.

"What about you, though," he says. "What will you do?"

"I shall sit here until you return." Enid spreads her skirts a little. "I shall look at all the ladies and enjoy the sunshine."

"We'll be back soon," I say, trying to keep my voice from betraying my excitement. Have I ever before been alone with him? Will I ever be alone with him again? "Please, please, please," I say to myself, "let the time be slow, don't let it go too quickly."

betraying *giving away.*

Philip and I walk in silence. I am afraid to talk, afraid to open my mouth in case all the dammed-up love words that I am feeling flood out of it.

We stand outside the Glass House for a moment, looking in at the dense green leaves pressing against the panes. A cloud passes over the sun, darkens the sky, and we are both reflected in the green. Philip's face and mine, together. In the dark mirror we turn towards each other. I stare at his reflection, because I dare not look at him, and for an instant his face disappears, and the image is of a death's head grinning at me, a white skull: bones with no flesh, black sockets with no eyes. I can feel myself trembling. Quickly, I look at the real Philip. He is there. His skin is brown, he is alive.

"What is it, Sarah? Why are you shaking?"

I try to laugh, and a squeak comes from my lips. How to explain? "I saw something reflected in the glass," I say.

"There's only you and me."

"It was you and me, but you . . . you had turned into a skeleton."

The sun is shining again. Philip's face is sad, shadows are in his eyes as he turns to look. I look too, and the skull has vanished. I let out a breath of relief.

"It's only me, after all," he says.

"But it *was* there. I saw it so clearly. Philip, please don't die."

"I shan't," he says seriously, carefully, "I shan't die. Don't be frightened. It was only a trick of the light."

I believe him because I want to believe him. He takes my hand. "Let's go in," he says.

Inside the Glass House, heat surrounds us like wet felt. Thickly about our heads a velvety, glossy, spiky, tangled jungle sucks moisture from the air. Leaves, fronds, ferns and creepers glisten, wet and hot, and the earth that covers their roots is black, warm.

Drops of water trickle down the panes of glass. The smell of growing is everywhere, filling our nostrils with a kind of mist. We walk between the towering plants. There is no one else there at all. A long staircase, wrought-iron painted white, spirals upwards, hides itself in green as it winds into the glass roof. Philip is still holding my hand, and I say nothing. I want him to hold it forever. I want his hand to grow into mine. Why doesn't he speak to me? We always laugh and joke and talk so much that Enid hushes us perpetually, and now he has nothing to say. I think: "Perhaps he is angry. He wants to sit with Enid in the cool air. He is cross at having come here when his time with Enid is so short. He is leaving tomorrow, and I have parted them with my selfishness and my love." Tears cloud my eyes. I stumble, nearly falling. My hat drops to the ground. Philip's hand catches me round the waist. I clutch at his arm, and he holds me, and does not let me go when I am upright. We stand, locked together. "Sarah . . ." It is a whisper. "Sarah, I must speak." The hand about my waist pulls me closer. I can feel the fingers spread out now, stroking me. Philip looks away. "I can't marry Enid," he says. "It wouldn't be right."

perpetually *all the time.*

"Why?" There are other words, but they will not come.

"I can't tell her," he mutters. "I've tried, I can't." He looks at me. "I shall write to her. Soon. It's a cowardly thing to do, but I cannot bear to face her . . . not yet. Not now. Sarah?"

"Yes?" I force myself to look up.

"Sarah, do you know," his voice fades, disappears, " . . . my feelings? For you?"

"Me?" My heart is choking me, beating in my throat.

"I . . . I don't know how to say it." He looks over my head, cannot meet my eyes. He says, roughly: "I've thought it and thought it, and I don't know how to say it." He draws me closer, close to him. I can feel his buttons through my dress. I am going to faint. I am dissolving in the heat, turning into water. His arms are around me, enfolding me. His mouth is on my hair, moving in my hair. Blindly, like a plant in search of light, I turn my face up and his lips are there, on my lips, and my senses and my nerve ends and my heart and my body, every part of me, all my love, everything is drawn into the sweetness of his mouth.

Later, we stand together, dazed, quivering. I can feel his kiss still, pouring through me.

"Philip, Philip," I bury my head in his jacket. "I love you. I've always loved you." Half hoping he will not hear me. He lifts my face in his fingers.

"And I love you, Sarah. Lovely Sarah, I love you. I don't know how I never said it before. How did I make such a mistake?"

I laugh. Everything is golden now. What has happened, what will happen. Enid, the rest of the world, nothing is important.

"I'm only a child," I say smiling, teasing.

"Oh no," he says, "no longer. Not a child." He kisses me again, softly. His fingers are in my hair, on my neck, touching and touching me. I have imagined it a thousand times and it was not like this. Wildly, I think of us growing here in this hothouse forever, like two plants curled and twined into one another, stems interlocked, leaves brushing . . . I move away from him.

"We must go back," I say.

"Yes." He takes my hat from the ground and puts it on my head. "You must promise me," he says, "never to wear mourning."

"Mourning?" What has mourning to do with such happiness?

"If I die . . ."

"You won't die, Philip." I am myself again now. "You said you wouldn't. I love you too much. You'll come back, and we'll love one another forever, and live happily ever after, just like a prince and princess in a fairy tale."

He laughs. "Yes, yes we will. We will be happy."

Walking back together to Enid's bench, we make plans. He will write to me. He will send the letters to Emily, my friend. I shall tell her everything. He will write to Enid. Not at once but quite soon. We can see Enid now. She is waving at us. We wave back.

"Remember that I love you," Philip whispers when we are nearly oh nearly there. I cannot answer. Enid is too close. I sit on the bench beside her, dizzy with loving him.

"You've been away for ages," she says. "I was quite worried."

His voice is light, full of laughter. "There's such a lot to look at. A splendid place. You really should have come."

I am amazed at him. I dare not open my mouth, here in the fresh air, I cannot look at Enid. The dreadfulness of what I am doing to her, what I am going to do to her makes me feel ill. But how can I live with my love pushed down inside me forever? Will she forgive us? Will we have to elope? Emigrate? There will be time enough to worry when she finds out, when Philip tells her. Now, my happiness curls through me like a vine. We set off again along the gravel paths. I have to stop myself from skipping. I remember, briefly, the skeleton I saw reflected in the glass, and I laugh out loud at my childish fear. It was only a trick of the light, just as Philip had said. A trick of the light.

There are stone urns near the Temperate House, and curved stone flowers set about their bases. A lady is sitting on a bench in the sunshine under a black silk parasol. The light makes jagged pools of colour in the inky taffeta of her skirts, and her hat is massed with ostrich feathers like funeral plumes. She turns to look at us as we go by, and I see that her face is old: small pink lips lost in a network of wrinkles, eyes still blue, still young under a pale, lined brow. She wears black gloves to cover her hands and I imagine them veined and stiff under the fabric. She smiles at me and I feel a sudden shock, a tremor of fear.

Enid says: "Forty years out of date at least. Do you think she realises how out of place she looks?"

"Poor old thing," says Philip. "Rather like a pressed flower, all

elope *run away to get married.*

urns *huge ornamental flowerpots.*

parasol *sunshade.*

taffeta *silky fabric.*

tremor *trembling.*

alone in the world." He whistles the tune 'Mademoiselle from Armentières.' "How would you like it?"

"I hope," says Enid, "that if I ever wear mourning, I shall not be so showy. Ostrich feathers, indeed! Mutton dressed as lamb."

I look back at the old woman, marvelling at Enid and Philip for finding her interesting enough to talk about. I feel pity for her, and a faint amusement, but she does not hold my attention. She is as remote from me, as strange, as if she belonged to another time. I start to run across the grass, as fast as I can. They are chasing me, yes, even Enid, dignity forgotten, is running and running. We stop under a tree, all of us breathless. Philip puts his hands on my waist and twirls me round. I glance fearfully at Enid, but she is smiling at us like an indulgent mother.

indulgent *kind, generous.*

We walk home in the dusk. I must leave him alone with Enid at the gate. He kisses me goodbye on the cheek, like a brother, and I go indoors quickly. I am burning in the places where he touched me.

Sarah sat up. Slowly, like a sleepwalker, she gathered up the torn, bruised straw and the scraps of ribbon from the bed and the floor, and put them in the hatbox. "When there is time," she thought, "I shall burn them in the kitchen fire." She struggled into the blue dress and looked at herself in the mirror. What she saw was the face of a stranger who resembled her: mouth pulled out of shape, skin white, hair without colour. She fastened, carefully, the buttons on her cuffs. Her skin, all the soft surfaces of her body, felt raw, scraped, wounded. "I am wounded all over," she thought, and went slowly downstairs. She put the telegram in her pocket, and left the house.

1917 May

"I think James will come to call this afternoon." Enid's fingers made pleats in the lilac skirt she was wearing.

Sarah said: "Do you like him?"

Enid considered the question. The sisters were walking in Kew Gardens. Enid wanted to see the camellias. "Yes," she said at last, "he is a fine man." Sarah thought of James's solid body and long teeth, his black hair and the small brush of his moustache. Over the months, scars had slowly covered the sore places in her mind but sometimes, especially at Kew, the pain took her breath away. She should not, she knew, walk there so often, but she did. She should have avoided the Glass House, but she went there at every opportunity, and stood beside the streaming panes with her eyes closed, willing herself to capture something. Her feelings on that day had been so overpowering, had filled her with such sharp pleasure that always she hoped that their ghosts must still be lingering among the leaves.

194

Now, she looked at Enid. "I think," she said, "that he will suit you very well."

"He hasn't proposed to me yet," Enid said placidly. "Although I don't think it will be too long. In any case, I shall have to wait at least until November . . ." Her voice trailed away, losing itself among the branches.

placidly calmly.

"Philip," Sarah said (and the word felt strange in her mouth, an unfamiliar taste, like forgotten fruit), "Philip would be pleased to think you were happy."

"Do you think so, really?" Enid looked relieved. "Of course, I was heartbroken, heartbroken at his death. You remember? I fainted, there and then on the floor of the shop. I shall never forget it."

"Neither shall I," said Sarah.

Enid comes out from behind the counter. She says: "What's the matter, Sarah? Are you ill? You look so white. Why are you wearing that thin dress?"

Mother is talking to Mrs Feathers. It is absorbing talk. I do not think they have seen me.

I say nothing, I give the envelope to Enid. She tears it open: a ragged fumbling of her hands, not like her at all.

"It's Philip," she says. "Philip is dead."

I watch, mesmerized, as she falls in a liquid movement to the ground.

Mother loosen's Enid's collar, her waistband, brings out smelling salts. She is weeping noisily. Mrs Feather says. "I'll put the kettle on for a cup of tea. Plenty of sugar, that's the thing for shock."

I envy my mother every tear she is shedding. I want to cry, and I cannot. The iron grip tightens round my heart.

Thinking/Talking Points

Did the story hold your attention? Is this a story you would read again and/or recommend to others?

Do you find the situation believable, interesting? Is this rivalry between sisters likely? Which moments would you quote to support your points?

What do you think of the way in which the main characters are described? Which particular details helped you to imagine each of them? Did you find all the characters equally life-like?

Do you think the writer has made the various settings convincing? Which details did you most/least like? Why?

How did you respond to the supernatural elements in the story?

What do you think of the way the story is told, its structure? Do you think using different tenses to distinguish different times is effective?

Finally, would you recommend the story for a prize?

When you have made your judgement, you may like to compare it with what others in the class have written about the story.

Further reading

This is an exercise you could repeat with a selection of stories taken from anthologies and magazines, and from stories produced in school. If they are all word-processed in a similar way, is it still possible to tell which have been bought by publishers and why?

Acknowledgements

The authors and publisher would like to thank the following for permission to reproduce from copyright material:

'Bus Queue' copyright © 1987 Agnes Owens. 'Breakfast' from *The Long Valley* by John Steinbeck. Copyright 1938 renewed © 1966 by John Steinbeck. Reproduced by permission of Curtis Brown Ltd, London, on behalf of the Author's Estate. 'After the Fair' by Dylan Thomas reprinted from *The Collected Stories of Dylan Thomas* (Dent) by permission of David Higham Associates Limited. 'Rapunzel, Let Down Your Hair' copyright © 1980 Chris Hawes. 'New Girl' copyright © 1980 Catherine Storr, reprinted by permission of the Peters Fraser & Dunlop Group Ltd. 'Seeing Me' copyright Rahila Kahn. 'The Night Out' copyright © Robert Westall 1980. 'Computers Don't Argue' by Gordon R Dickson copyright © Science Fiction Writers of America. 'Fathers' Day' copyright © Nathaniel Benchley. 'Superman and Paula Brown's New Snowsuit' copyright © Ted Hughes 1977, reprinted from *Johnny Panic and the Bible of Dreams* (Harper & Row) by permission of Olwyn Hughes. 'A Cap for Steve' copyright © 1952/1980 Morley Callaghan. 'Missing' by Yuko Tsushima, translated from the Japanese by Geraldine Harcourt, reprinted from *The Shooting Gallery* by permission of the author and the translator. 'Absent' by Tui de Hann, reprinted by permission of the author and Michael Marland, North Westminster Community School. 'A Red-Letter Day' copyright © 1948 Elizabeth Taylor. 'Mine on Thursdays' reprinted from *8 + 1 Stories* by Robert Cormier by permission of Collins Publishers. 'The Rain Horse' reprinted by permission of Faber and Faber Ltd from *Wodwo* by Ted Hughes. 'The Hawk in the Rain' reprinted by permission of Faber and Faber Ltd from *The Hawk in the Rain* by Ted Hughes. 'The Shawl' copyright © Cynthia Ozick/agents Raines and Raines. 'The Green Behind the Glass' copyright © Adèle Geras.

Every effort has been made to reach copyright holders; the publishers would be glad to hear from anyone whose rights they have unknowingly infringed.

Thanks are due to the following for permission to reproduce photographs:
pp. 2–3 © Estate of H. M. Bateman (1983). p. 8 Sally and Richard Greenhill. p. 18 Texas Department of Commerce. p. 23 © Claude Germeri, p. 29 Sally and Richard Greenhill. p. 35 Ann Golzen. p. 54 Sally and Richard Greenhill. p. 100 Nancy Durrell McKenna/The Hutchinson Library. p. 108 *The Fall of Icarus* (1975), Musée National d'Art Moderne, Centre Georges Pompidou, Paris. p. 115 © David Trainer. p. 128 Geoff Howard. p. 144 Charley Toorop: *Zelfportret met hoed* (1938); Stedelijk Museum, Amsterdam. p. 160 Henry Koerner: *Mirror of Life* (1946). Oil composition board. 36 × 42 inches (91.4 × 106.7cm). Purchase. Collection of Whitney Museum of American Art. 48.2. p. 168 John Henry Fuseli: *The Nightmare*; Freies Deutsches Hochstift – Frankfurt am Main. p. 180 © Sebastiao Salgado/Magnum. p. 188 Nigel Luckhurst.